4.80 א/2   אח

D0857670

Political
and
Social
Thought
in America
1870-1970

READINGS IN POLITICS AND SOCIETY

GENERAL EDITOR: Bernard Crick
*Professor of Political Theory and Institutions,
University of Sheffield*

ALREADY PUBLISHED

W. L. Guttsman, *The English Ruling Class*
A. J. Beattie, *English Party Politics (in two volumes)*
Frank W. Bealey, *The Social and Political Thought of the British Labour Party*

Forthcoming volumes
J. P. Macintosh, *The Growth of the Cabinet System*
J. K. Kumar, *Revolution*
William Thornhill, *The Growth and Reform of Local Government*
N. D. Deakin, *Race in British Politics*
Maurice Bruce, *The Rise of the Welfare State*

Previously published in this series by Routledge & Kegan Paul

David Nicolls, *Church and State in Britain Since 1820*

Political and Social Thought in America 1870-1970

Edited and introduced by
EDMUND IONS

WEIDENFELD AND NICOLSON
5 Winsley Street London W1

Burgess
HN
57
.I65

SBN 297 00136 1

Printed in Great Britain by
Cox & Wyman Ltd, London, Fakenham and Reading

Contents

General Editor's Preface

The purpose of this series is to introduce students of society to a number of important problems through the study of sources and contemporary documents. It should be part of every student's education to have some contact with the materials from which the judgements of authors of secondary works are reached, or the grounds of social action determined. Students may actually find this more interesting than relying exclusively on the pre-digested diet of textbooks. The readings will be drawn from as great a variety of documents as is possible within each book: Royal Commission reports, Parliamentary debates, letters to the Press, newspaper editorials, letters and diaries both published and unpublished, sermons and literary sources, et cetera, will all be drawn upon. For the aim is both to introduce the student to carefully selected extracts from the principal contemporary books and documents (the things he always hears about but never reads), and to show him a great range of subsidiary and representative source materials available (the memorials of actors in the actual events).

The prejudice of this series is that the social sciences need to be taught and developed in an historical context. Those of us who wish to be relevant and topical (and this no bad wish) sometimes need reminding that the most usual explanation of why a thing is as it is, is that things happened in the past to make it so. These things might not have happened. They might have happened differently. And nothing in the present is, strictly speaking, *determined* from the past; but everything is limited by what went before.

Every present problem, whether of understanding or of action, will always have a variety of relevant antecedent factors, all of which must be understood before it is sensible to commit ourselves to an explanatory theory or to some course of practical action. No present problem is completely novel and there is never any single cause for it, but always a variety of conditioning factors, arising through time, whose relative importance is a matter of critical judgement as well as of objective knowledge.

The aim of this series is, then, to give the student the opportunity to examine with care an avowedly selective body of source materials. The topics have been chosen both because they are of contemporary importance and because they cut across established pedagogic boundaries between the various disciplines and between courses of professional instruction. We hope that these books will supplement, not replace, other forms of introductory reading; so both the length and the character of the Introductions will vary according to whether the particular editor has already written on the subject or not. Some Introductions will summarize what is already to be found elsewhere at greater length, but some will be original contributions to knowledge or even, on occasions, reasoned advocacies. Above all, however, I hope that this series will help to develop a method of introductory teaching that can show how and from where we come to reach the judgements that are to be found in secondary accounts and textbooks.

University of Sheffield   *BERNARD CRICK*

Foreword

The American debate on politics and society during the period covered by these readings has been richly diverse. To do it full justice would require more than one volume, but I have sought to include the essential elements here. In selecting the extracts my chief criterion has been that the writer or speaker presented an argument, not merely an utterance. Each reading has thus a specific concern and argues a case.

I have also wished to identify distinctive streams in the debate rather than place the readings in a random or even a purely chronological sequence. To that end I have divided the book into six parts, each containing a separate theme. Anyone familiar with American democracy will appreciate that the parts are by no means mutually exclusive; nor are they meant to be. My purpose is to clarify the exposition in order to assist those who are less familiar with the political and intellectual history of the United States.

I am most grateful to Bernard Crick for valuable suggestions for improving the manuscript, and to Mrs Gillian Hughes for so patiently seeing the book through the press.

York, July 1970   EDMUND IONS

Acknowledgements

The author and the publisher would like to thank the following for permission to quote from copyright sources:

Harcourt, Brace and World, Inc., for *Main Currents in American Thought* by Vernon L. Parrington; the Herbert Hoover Foundation for *American Individualism* by Herbert Hoover; Constable and Co. Ltd., for *Democracy and Leadership* by Irving Babbitt; Harvard University Press for *The Holmes-Laski Letters: the Correspondence of Mr Justice Holmes and Harold J. Laski* edited by Mark de Wolfe Howe; Little, Brown and Co., for *An Inquiry into the Principles of the Good Society* by Walter Lippmann; Victor Publishing Co. Inc., for *The Conscience of a Conservative* by Barry Goldwater; Yale University Press for *Modern Democracy* by Carl Becker; the Western Political Quarterly for 'The Pragmatic Course of Liberalism' by Alan P. Grimes; Laurence Pollinger Ltd., for *America as a Civilization* by Max Lerner and *Stride Towards Freedom* by Martin Luther King; the Rockerfeller Fund for *The Power of the Democratic Idea*; Alfred A. Knopf Inc., for *Notes on Democracy* by H. L. Mencken; The Macmillan Company for *After the New Deal, What?* by Norman Thomas and *The End of Ideology: On the Exhaustion of Political Ideas in the Fifties* by Daniel Bell; the American Academy of Political and Social Science for 'Fascism for America' by Lawrence Dennis; Marshall Jones Company for *The End of Democracy* by Ralph Adams Cram; Victor Gollancz Ltd., for *Marx and America* by Earl Browder; Humanities Press Inc., for *The Era of McCarthyism* by Herbert Aptheker; I. F. Stone for 'People Without a Country'; Michael Joseph Ltd., for *The Fire Next Time* by James Baldwin; Joan Daves for *Why We Can't Wait* by Martin Luther King; Jonathan Cape Ltd., for *Black Power: the Politics of Liberation in America* by Stokely Carmichael and Charles Hamilton; the American Political Science Association for a report by Arnold B. Hall; G. P. Putnam's Sons for *Philosophy and Civilization* by John Dewey; the Southwestern Social Science Quarterly and Alpheus T. Mason for 'Politics, Art or Science?' by Alpheus T. Mason.

Introduction

The American political tradition, like American society and culture, is richly varied. A number of paradoxical, even contradictory strands run side by side in American thought. Piety and the things of the spirit co-exist with a devotion to material wealth and the things of the flesh. Self-reliance and independent effort are alloyed with a remarkable sense of community and common endeavour. An almost mystical belief in the virtues of competition and free enterprise is wedded to a distrust of those monopolistic powers which are merely the final fruits of unrelieved competition between industrialists. The profiteer who hoards his wealth for private pleasure is reviled, yet socialist doctrines for redistributing wealth are regarded as the work of the devil.

A nation with so many contradictory elements in its political and social values deserves careful study. Perhaps our first task should be to disentangle the apparently conflicting strands in American thought, reducing them to two or three at most, and then indicate how they may be reconciled with each other. I will suggest that there are three main elements in American political thought, each going back to the very foundations of the American Republic, each replenished and sustained by the subsequent history of America, and all still entrenched in American thinking today.

The first may be called the providential tradition in American political thought. The Pilgrim Fathers who founded and built the early American settlements devoutly believed that their 'new found land' enjoyed a special dispensation from Heaven. If the first, crude settlements on the eastern seaboard of a strange continent were not flowing with milk and honey, these blessings would surely come through time, with the help of faith and hard work under Divine guidance. The Pilgrims of New England never doubted that they enjoyed a special blessing from the Almighty they worshipped. Even though disease reduced their numbers catastrophically in the first year of settlement (1620–1) they nevertheless dedicated to God their first Thanksgiving feast in November 1621.

'God's Own Country' was an idiom which crept into American discourse rather later, but it reflects a view deeply and sincerely held by the first settlers. Such a faith or belief was certainly necessary in order to face the terrifying prospect of the voyage in the *Mayflower*, as well as the threat of Indian tribes known to inhabit the distant continent; and when the settlements spread along the eastern seaboard of America, hard work – always sustained by a devout faith – brought material blessings and increased bounty, confirming the settlers' belief that a special providence guarded them.

This view of America as the promised land across the ocean was also held by the Quakers and Presbyterians who followed those already settled in 'Earth's only Paradise', as the Virginia settlers often called their new domains. And when, after more than a century of settlement, the colonists determined to sever the 'political bands' which connected them to the mother country, their Declaration of Independence once more invoked 'the protection of Divine Providence' to sustain them through the troubled times they knew would follow.

The providential strain in American thought runs deep, therefore. It was present at the very foundation of the American settlements; it was reaffirmed by the Declaration of Independence; and it sustained those who fought and won the Revolutionary War which transformed America into a Republic. In a secularized form it also beckoned the successive waves of immigrants who left Europe throughout the nineteenth century to seek a better life in America. Long before the words were carved on the base of the Statue of Liberty in New York harbour, America was metaphorically bidding the nations of Europe to

> Give me your tired, your poor,
> Your huddled masses yearning to breathe free. . . .

Of course, the nineteenth century brought new elements to the immigrant stream, representing different religions and different sects within the same religion, so that fewer and fewer shared the austere faith of the original Founding Fathers. By then the Christian belief in America as the promised land was further secularized and America was seen as 'the land of the free and the home of the brave'. The words are from Francis Scott Key's poem, composed originally in 1814, and used more than a century later to provide the words for the national anthem 'The Star Spangled Banner'.

The immigrants of the nineteenth century left Europe for a variety of reasons. Many fled political or religious persecution; some fled both. Others were driven by deprivation and want, or came to 'better themselves', as the immigrants themselves put it. The Irish peasants, for instance, and later the Italian poor, the Greeks, Russians, Poles and Scandinavians – all looked for and expected a better life in the New World. The idea, then, of a special beneficence and providence in America accompanied the hopes of every poor immigrant, just as it had attended the more pious aspirations of those who sailed in the *Mayflower*. Nothing less could sustain the Pilgrims of 1620 or the nineteenth-century immigrants sailing with their few chattels.

Yet something more than high hopes and expectations was required of those who departed from family and friends, from hearth and home, from the country where they were born. There was also a strong element of self-justification in the immense step they were taking. A second main strand written into the American tradition, therefore, may be called the justificatory one. It emerges throughout American history, whether we consider the early sermons of the Puritans or the later conviction of every immigrant that he could 'make good' in America. It emerges strongly in the revealing, almost self-conscious phrasing of the Declaration of Independence in 1776: 'When, in the course of human events, it becomes necessary for one people to dissolve the political bands which have connected them with another . . . a decent respect to the opinions of mankind requires that they should declare the causes which impel them. . . .'

This 'decent respect to the opinions of mankind' is as characteristic of American thinking as it is unique. From one point of view it may be regarded as a search for legitimacy; from another, as a sense of conviction, even of rectitude, of the readiness *and* the ability to justify the action taken by those who signed the Declaration of Independence.

Again, therefore, whether we are considering the Pilgrims who sailed in 1620, or the men who signed the Declaration in 1776, or the immigrants who left Europe behind in the nineteenth and twentieth centuries, this element of self-justification is always present. To seek religious freedom abroad on a strange continent in the seventeenth century, or to defy kingly power in the late eighteenth century were hazardous steps, and those undertaking them needed to justify their actions not only to their friends and their families, not only to the authority set over them by Church and State, but also, and more fundamentally, to themselves.

'What then is the American, this new man?' The question was posed by the Frenchman Hector St John de Crèvecoeur in 1782, and though he sought an environmental answer as he travelled and finally settled in America, the question has always lain on the table of history in a philosophical sense. Historically, de Crèvecoeur's question has been unavoidable, for America was the 'First New Nation', as the title of a recent work reminds us.* There is thus a self-consciousness written into American history by the very nature of its foundations: Americans have been inescapably involved in the felt need to justify their nationhood and the nature of their society, both in its egalitarian aspects or, nearer our own time, as an attempt to create a truly multi-racial society. To be an American has always been a special and conscious commitment of one sort or another – political, social or religious, and often enough all three: no other nation has required such a commitment from its citizens.

Given the historical circumstances which forged the American nation, therefore, we should not be surprised at the continuance of a justificatory element in American thought. The documents and readings in this book demonstrate this underlying attitude often enough. Occasionally we see both the providential and the justificatory strains in American thought combined in one utterance. In the American political tradition, reformers commonly include in their speeches or writings a portrait of an America falling from grace; of a nation failing to match the hopes or intentions of the Founding Fathers. Equally, arguments for reform are invariably appeals to

* Seymour M. Lipset, *The First New Nation*, London, 1964.

restore institutions and ideals which are uniquely 'American' but which are at the time threatened by political circumstances. Whether the reformer is radical and progressive, or covertly attempting to preserve the *status quo*, the rhetoric is often couched in terms of defining what is American and what is un-American. It is impossible to imagine the equivalent of the 'Un-American Activities' committee of the United States Congress in any European political system. 'Americanism' has always been a commitment and a philosophy as well as a way of life.

The belief in a special dispensation, together with the justificatory element in the American mind, lie chiefly in the realm of the abstraction, of course, though it is often noted that the American temperament does not lend itself too readily to abstract ideas. The paradox may be resolved by considering a third main strand in the American tradition. One may call it the practical or, to give it a more refined name, the pragmatic strain in American history.

There has always been of necessity a high regard for practical enterprise in America. Whether we speak of the early colonists struggling to clear virgin forest or of later immigrants seeking to establish themselves in a strange society, individual enterprise and self-help were always the touchstones of public esteem. Men who build a new nation are essentially practical men. Men who fight a revolutionary war – and win it – are also severely practical. The settlers and colonists of the seventeenth century owed little to their patrimony and nothing to charity. Hard work and self-help were the shortest roads to survival. As the American frontier expanded westwards, men relied on themselves first and on their religious faith second. No rule of law protected the frontiersmen; no public militia protected them whilst they slept. Religion and prayer were common virtues, but from a purely practical point of view they buttered no parsnips. Even on the urban frontiers of east-coast America, self-reliance and self-help were the main props of immigrant life. Egalitarianism itself ensured that men would strive and compete one against the other, for they started from a common base. The European institutions of class and caste – a cushion for some, a barrier for others – were absent in a society dedicated to the 'self-evident truth' that all men are created equal.

This ethic of practicality and self-help was also bolstered by one of the most remarkable accidents of history – the tremendous natural and mineral wealth of the American land mass. As the frontier pushed westwards and vast natural resources were tapped, the steel towns of Pennsylvania, the copper mines of Montana, the silver mines of Colorado and Californian gold all seemed to declare that America's natural wealth was boundless. But the exploitation of this wealth required human effort – whatever the division of the spoils thereafter. The ideal American was thus the hard-working American who could tap these vast resources of the earth. The engineer was more important than the philosopher; the doer more urgently needed than the thinker. As steel railroads were flung across the continent, straddling it from east to west and from north to south, Americans could indulge the belief in an Eldorado as well as a promised land, rich in promise because it was so rich in resources.

The age of invention reinforced this belief. In the second half of the nineteenth century America first began to astound the world by its accomplishments in the fields of applied science and engineering. Huge steel bridges, taller and taller buildings, and endless railroads seemed to confirm that there were no limits to American resourcefulness. The swift exploitation of electricity, of the telephone and of wireless telegraphy confirmed the willingness to experiment, the readiness to exploit. As the American economy expanded, far outstripping the economies of Europe, it was natural that Americans should feel more and more convinced that the applied sciences were more useful than philosophical abstractions and speculative thinking. The visible, tangible rewards of the American approach showed themselves on all sides. From this, it was but a short step to the conviction that skill comes with performance; one learns best by doing, rather than by thinking about it. It was at this point that pragmatism itself became an orthodoxy ingrained in the American temperament.

Pragmatism asserted that ideas must be judged by their observable, practical effects on human activity. Abstract thought was useful only in so far as it resulted in purposive action. Theories which could not be applied, or which did not stand up to the test of practice, were merely idle, and probably useless speculation. Clearly, this American attitude owed a good deal to the charge laid upon all Americans to make the nation prosper; to show by deeds and not simply by words that the individual was prepared to contribute to the common weal. The inventor and the entrepreneur were much nearer to the American ideal than the mere theorist. Intellectualism for its own sake was highly suspect.*

The three main strands in the American tradition outlined above can be detected at many points in the documents and readings given in this book. The year 1870 is an appropriate starting point for understanding modern American thought. The Civil War of 1861–5 forced upon Americans a mood of self-questioning, of national doubt, even of pessimism. The debate on slavery had challenged the very basis on which the American Republic was founded, and the victory of the North at Appomattox in 1865 did not end the debate; indeed, it merely inaugurated a debate which continues to this day in the Civil Rights movement.

Another profound shock to American beliefs arrived in the early 1870s with the challenge of Darwinism. Europe also felt it, and though the full implications of Darwinism were not immediately recognized when *The Descent of Man* was published in 1871, thoughtful Americans soon realized the fundamental threat to religious orthodoxy entailed in Darwin's thesis. By the mid-1880s agnostic science had found hospitable quarters in North America, and only the novel doctrines of Christian Scientists could reconcile the old religion with the new cult of science.

One further reason for selecting 1870 as a starting point is that by then America's agrarian economy was being transformed into an industrial one. This change brought new cleavages to American society. The city, not the farm, held the clue to the future. The 1870s were thus years of flux and change, and few writers have better captured the sense of restlessness this brought than Vernon Parrington, himself imbued with the spirit of agrarian romanticism.† In the first extract given in the readings here, Parrington remarks of the challenge which agrarian America in 1870 encountered from the city: 'The one was a decaying order, the other a rising one, and between them would be friction till one or the other had become master.'

Romantics usually regard cities as the breeding grounds of vice, corruption and spiritual degeneracy. America has always harboured

---

* Cf. Richard Hofstadter, *Anti-Intellectualism in American Life,* New York, 1962, pp. 233–52.

† See Vernon L. Parrington, *Main Currents in American Thought,* 3 Vols., New York, 1927–30, Vol. 3.

such suspicions, if only because of men like Thomas Jefferson, one of the hallowed names in the American tradition. Jefferson's vision was of America as a rural retreat peopled by honest husbandmen, but this vision dissolved in the burgeoning cities of the mid-nineteenth century.

> Ill fares the land, to hast'ning ills a prey,
> Where wealth accumulates and men decay.

Like the deserted village in Goldsmith's poem, agrarian America was eventually forced to concede that the city, with its temptations, its allure, its wealth, brought an end to the arcadian Jeffersonian dream.

Yet the agrarian West did not capitulate to the urban East without a protracted struggle. As we might expect in a society dedicated to freedom of speech and the right of assembly, the debate between town and country, businessman and farmer, was often bitter, at times savage. In the section of readings devoted to reformers in America, there are purple passages, homespun oratory, and forlorn hopes, The debate represents a sectional conflict, and not simply an economic one, between the agrarian Midwest and the more populous urban East.

There was another bitter debate which the cities themselves spawned within their own boundaries, for America was not lacking in cold-eyed men who saw opportunities for quick profits in the overcrowded cities where labour was cheap. As the population of the cities multiplied explosively with the immigrant tides, speculators were very willing to use their knowledge – or their friends – in order to corrupt voters and politicians alike. In the 1870s President Ulysses Grant demonstrated that not even the Executive Mansion was entirely free from peculation, corruption and that unholy alliance between business and politics which was the chief characteristic of American politics during those years.

Some saw the explanation for a growing corruption in the godless materialism brought by industrial capitalism. Others blamed unrestricted immigration and the dilution of the supposedly 'pure' Anglo-Saxon strain of New England settlers with more exotic ethnic strains from the shores of the Mediterranean and eastern Europe. The debate became confused as wealth accumulated for the rich, free land became scarce in the American West, and the immigrant tides continued to arrive at the eastern seaboard, repeating the conditions of urban squalor which the industrial revolution had already brought to the main cities of Europe.

It is not an entirely simple task to detach and distinguish the various dialogues in the political sphere during the century following the Civil War. It seems advisable, therefore, to divide up the several lines of discussion into separate – though not mutually exclusive – sections for the purpose of exposition. Such a separation, like the labels attached to the section, should not be regarded as a hard and fast guide to the documents contained within. Thus although one section is devoted to 'Reformers' and another to 'Dissenters', a reformer is clearly a dissenter of a sort, just as a dissenter is one who usually – but not always – puts forward positive alternatives to right the wrongs which move his conscience.

It seems fitting to begin with a section devoted to those reformers who wrote in passionate protest against the conditions brought about by industrialism and monopoly capitalism in the decades following the Civil War. The condition of the poor deeply affected men like Henry George and Henry Demarest Lloyd, and though they proposed different solutions for the social evils they observed, they started from a common feeling of humanitarian conscience. Henry George, in his book *Progress and Poverty* (1879), argued that scarcity of land produced unearned profits for land holders. He urged a tax on these gains in order to discourage speculation as well as to redistribute this wealth to the poor, who alone supplied the profits of the land speculator. Henry George's proposal was not an original one – the idea and the reasoning behind it had already been aired by the Mills in England, by Marx, and in the eighteenth century by the Physiocrats. But we find in Henry George's statement a compassion for the poor, a concern for justice, a self-identification with the oppressed which give his writings a force and simplicity often lacking in those of the European intellectuals who wrote on similar themes.

The same can be said of Henry Demarest Lloyd, another writer acutely affected by the condition of the poor in American cities. His book *Wealth Against Commonwealth* (1894) opens with a declaration reminiscent of Rousseau's *Contrat Social*: 'Nature is rich, but everywhere man ... is poor.' Lloyd specifically attacked the large-scale corporations which were stifling genuine competition and arranging the market to suit their own monopolistic

9

interests. Like Henry George, Lloyd was convinced that America was falling from grace and failing to live up to the principles of the Founding Fathers of the Republic.

In a letter written some years before *Progress and Poverty*, Henry George observed: 'How I long for the Golden Age, for the promised Millennium, when each one will be free to follow his best and noblest impulses, unfettered by the restrictions and necessities which our present state of society imposes upon him. . . .'* The belief in a golden age, when man's noblest instincts could find free expression, uncorrupted by wealth or material possessions, affected many novelists in the 1880s and 1890s. The utopian novel was thus a popular genre at this time, and Edward Bellamy's *Looking Backward: 2000–1887* is a good example. Another novel which enjoyed immense popularity was Ignatius Donnelly's *Caesar's Column: A Story of the Twentieth Century*, which appeared in 1891, and equally reflected the wish to escape from the ugly horizons presented by capitalism and urban growth.

The utopian tradition in American thought did not, of course, originate in the 1880s. Before the Civil War there were attempts to found utopian communities, such as Brook Farm in Massachusetts, an experiment in utopian socialism which attracted Nathaniel Hawthorne and Ralph Waldo Emerson from the world of letters. But the utopian novel, like the utopian community, is a flight from reality and rarely lasts. Before long the real world intrudes, and the experiment fails as it encounters the reefs and shoals of human nature, and the harsh practical problems of politics.

As monopoly capitalism increased its power, practical-minded men like Samuel Gompers saw the need to organize their fellow workers into trade unions to challenge the power of corporate wealth. Others formed socialist parties and nominated candidates at national conventions to take their case to the American voters. Others again sought for reform within the structure of the existing party machinery. One such was William Jennings Bryan, the fiery Democrat who scourged the gold speculators of eastern America with his speech to the Democratic Convention of 1896. It was Bryan who brought the Democrats to their feet with his shrill ultimatum to the money changers of eastern America: 'You shall

* See G. R. Geiger, *The Philosophy of Henry George,* New York 1933, p. 33.

not press down upon the brow of labor this crown of thorns, you shall not crucify mankind on a cross of gold.'

Bryan was a politician, of course, and a very ambitious one at that. His speech at Chicago in 1896 was an attempt to capture the Democratic Party, at that time divided against itself. As with many speeches to political conventions, truth was partly a hostage to rhetoric. Bryan was nominated by the Democratic Party in 1896, and the Republican Party claimed the Presidency for the next three administrations. But the agrarian and urban problems which divided the nation did not vanish. Indeed, in the cities conditions grew worse, and it required the caustic pen of Lincoln Steffens and the 'Muckraker' journalists in the first few years of the new century to bring home to Americans the low level to which politics as a trade had sunk, especially in the cities, as the alliance between politicians and businessmen flourished.

The era of progressivism, roughly spanning the first decade of the twentieth century, brought further attacks upon the worst evils of monopoly capitalism and corporate wealth. The reform impulse was now assisted by the power of the Presidential office under Theodore Roosevelt, whose vigorous attacks upon the Trusts helped to break up some, though by no means all of the biggest monopolies. But the momentum of reform was diluted by sectionalism as the economy expanded and diversified. Moreover, the reformers themselves were often divided in their aims and programmes, as Herbert Croly pointed out in a notable work, *The Promise of American Life* (1909).

There were other obstacles to fundamental reform of the American system, however, and whilst it may seem tempting to discuss these obstacles under the label of conservatism, the term can be very misleading in the American context. A nation born by an act of rebellion, deeply opposed to aristocratic principles, and nurtured on egalitarianism cannot have a strong tradition of conservatism, even though it may contain conservative elements. The American message has been one of equal opportunity. Those who work prosper. Advantages conferred by inheritance run counter to this ethic. 'No title of nobility shall be granted by the United States,' the Constitution declares. Americans infinitely prefer the title 'Mr President' to 'Your Royal Highness'. A hereditary aristocracy would seem as ludicrous to the average American as an established church would seem offensive and out of place. If we are to discover the spirit or essence of conservatism in the United States, therefore, we must look for it in regions well removed from privilege or pomp. It must somehow fit – or at least seem to fit – the cult of the common man.

One central belief which identifies and unites the conservative tradition in American thought is that of individualism. It is not difficult to see that this is sustained by the basic American belief in liberty for the individual, in the virtue of independence and self-help, and beyond this is a conviction that the Republic prospers by free competition between individuals and groups, rather than by government regulation and interference. In the section of readings on individualism, these sentiments can be detected in statements whose subject and content may otherwise seem to differ widely. 'The public be damned,' declares the millionaire railroad owner William Vanderbilt in 1882. 'A free man in a democracy has no duty whatever toward other men of the same rank and standing,' writes Charles Graham Sumner in a different context only one year later. Theodore Roosevelt himself was to preach 'rugged individualism' to the American people from the White House, whilst his successor Herbert Hoover wrote a book on the virtues of individualism. In our own time, the unrepentant conservative Senator Barry Goldwater writes in his *Conscience of a Conservative* : 'Every man, for his individual good and for the good of his society, is responsible for his *own* development.'

If there is a central theme to the conservative tradition in American thought, it is this accent on individualism. Collectivism is viewed as a threat to personal liberty, whether it comes from mass parties or the growing power of government to interfere with the lives of ordinary citizens. Some thinkers grew pessimistic about the effects of universal suffrage and unrestricted egalitarianism. E. L. Godkin's 'Doubts on Equality' is a good example of this in the essay included here. Others, like the Reverend Josiah Strong, saw the main threat to American life in unrestricted immigration to the United States. The ultimate effects of this, he felt, would be a dilution of what he deemed to be the unique qualities of the Anglo-Saxon race.

Yet Godkin's pessimism and Josiah Strong's phobias are untypical of the American tradition. In ideas and institutions the American message has been one of open-minded optimism. Individualism has been one source of strength; progressivism has been another. Once again the term resists specific definition or easy categorization. The progressive temperament is forward-looking, confident, but not over-confident; opposed to narrow scepticism, receptive to new opportunities and possibilities. In the section of readings devoted to the progressive spirit in American thought, these qualities can be found in good measure.

In most political systems, one would not turn to the courts of law for examples of the progressive temperament. By their nature and their calling, judges are rarely disposed to blaze new trails. Yet when the jurist Oliver Wendell Holmes declared, in his book on the Common Law in 1881, 'the life of the law has not been logic, it has been experience,' he opened the door to sociological jurisprudence and invited judges to be social engineers rather than guardians of legal precedent.

In the decades that followed, the Justices of the Supreme Court showed a new willingness to enter those difficult and often controversial areas where social and political behaviour are subjects of disagreement and dispute. This is not to say that the Supreme Court has been a forward-looking, liberalizing institution throughout the past hundred years. It clearly has not been – as President Franklin Roosevelt discovered when his New Deal proposals were rejected by the Court. But the Court has repeatedly acknowledged that it has a part to play in helping to shape American society and it has made important contributions to the political dialogue. If the student of political ideas wishes to trace the main elements of the discourse throughout the period, he could do worse than to examine the arguments contained in both the majority and the dissenting opinions delivered by the Supreme Court Justices in the more important cases coming before the Court.

The progressive spirit in American thinking has been highly pragmatic and never doctrinaire. This raises one of the most intriguing questions in American political thought – the repeated failure of doctrinaire theories of politics to gather any widespread support or even acceptance. Neither socialism nor communism captured the public mind, even though the United States has not lacked individual proselytizers. The explanations for this resistance to political doctrine are numerous and complex. Clearly, the belief in and commitment to 'Americanism' reduces the appeal of any alternative doctrine, unless 'Americanism' can be subsumed within it. And if the essence of Americanism is individual liberty, coupled with basically egalitarian assumptions *and* a high rate of social mobility in the society (whether or not the myth fits the facts at any one time or for any one individual), then doctrines of the extreme left are pre-empted at the outset: the most they can feed on are sectional animosities or local inequities, and these cannot capture a nation.

There was a brief moment in the early 1930s when communism might have taken hold in the minds of the workers, in the city and on the farm, when the American economic system suffered its most disastrous collapse. But the success of Franklin Roosevelt's New Deal in restoring the monetary system, organizing public works programmes, and gradually reducing unemployment, all brought successive and cumulative setbacks to communist and socialist doctrines. Since then, the Marxist prediction of an inevitable head-on clash between the forces of capital and organized labour has seemed less and less likely to be proved correct. For as more and more ordinary Americans, from taxi-drivers to farm workers, invest in stocks and shares, the 'vested interests' of classical Marxist theory are translated into the immediate economic interests of the majority of ordinary Americans. Classical Marxist theory becomes less and less suited to the contemporary facts. Despite this, however, the United States has not lacked able scholars and men of ideas who have put the Marxist case to their contemporaries, and three of them – I. F. Stone, Earl Browder, and Herbert Aptheker – are included in these readings.

These writers take their place in the section of readings devoted to the 'Dissenters' in the American political tradition. It has been a vigorous and impressive tradition, whether we consider the caustic writings of Thorstein Veblen or the appeal of the anarchist Emma Goldman, or again the commentaries of two modern American Marxists, Earl Browder and Herbert Aptheker. For more than thirty years another dissenter, Norman Thomas, continually put forward the case for socialism, and if the candidate of the American Socialist Party never created a wide following at election times, the explanation lies chiefly in the fact that both the major parties in America are already coalitions of very divergent views and interests.

Dissent, then, has not been absent from the political dialogue in the century following the Civil War, though there have been times, particularly during the two World Wars and again in the 1950s during the Cold War and the McCarthy era, when the government has been less tolerant than a truly liberal climate of opinion would have allowed. As Herbert Aptheker argues in the piece included in these readings, American scholars in the past seemed much more willing to acknowledge Marx's contribution to political thinking than were many of Aptheker's contemporaries in the 1950s.

The struggle of the American Negro during the last hundred years deserves a separate section in these readings, for it represents not simply an attitude of dissent but much more one of anguish, and often despair. For the Negro, the American Dream has not come true. The problem is simple to state, yet infinitely difficult to resolve. Buried within it are the white man's feelings of guilt, the Negro's search for identity, feelings of bitterness, hate, distrust and fear.

The dimensions of the problem were not fully grasped until Gunnar Myrdal completed his monumental work on the American Negro.* Since then, a considerable literature has been added, and no one would deny that it presents the most fundamental challenge to American society since the foundation of the Republic. The method of Negro protest has itself undergone many changes during the last half century, and in the documents included here we may contrast the mild, almost supplicatory tone of a writer like Booker T. Washington writing in 1900 with that of the younger generation of leaders in the 1960s gathered together under demands for Black Power. From the viewpoint of the present, the late Martin Luther King can be seen as an interim figure, reaching back to the pacific policies advocated by Booker T. Washington on the one hand, yet moving, just before his tragic assassination in 1968, to a position of greater militancy in pressing the demand for Negro civil rights.

The militancy of the leaders of the Black Power movement has coincided with a widespread resort to violence on the part of other protesting groups in American politics, and one may question whether violence has not fed upon the worldwide pattern of violence which has dominated international relations during the 1960s. There is little doubt that American participation in the Viet-Nam War helped to sharpen the mood of militant protest

* Gunnar Myrdal, *An American Dilemma*: Vol. 1, *The Negro in a White Nation*; Vol. 2, *The Negro Social Structure*, 1944.

among the idealists and radicals who together form what is loosely termed the New Left in American politics. For some, the protest is intended to convey a total rejection of the American system. They sincerely believe that only a complete restructuring of the American political and economic system can produce the fundamental changes they seek. What those fundamental changes will be, and what will be the shape of society which follows them, has not so far been set out: the radicals of the New Left are clearer on what they wish to destroy than on what they intend to create.

A principal target is the 'consumer society' – that is, a society which puts its main emphasis, economically but also spiritually, on material possessions and consumer goods. This emphasis reduces all human relationships to a cash nexus, leading to all the evils associated with capitalist society – money grubbing, conspicuous waste, poverty for the many, vast wealth for a privileged few, and ultimately spiritual bankruptcy for all. Nothing short of a revolution will bring about the root and branch structural changes needed to transform the present relationships, the argument runs. Yet every revolution needs a vanguard, and for many the American university has seemed the natural choice for providing both the intellectual *élite* and the shock troops to lead the masses to the barricades, once students and workers have achieved solidarity.

It is part of the credo of the New Left that 'bourgeois' institutions are maintained by the 'concealed violence' of capitalist society which allows dissent only within certain limits: that when a fundamental challenge is made, the system uses violence – in the form of police power – to defend its institutions. Of course this is a feature of any political system, and not merely 'bourgeois' society, and it might be argued that the police powers, and even para-military police powers, are self-evidently the mark of totalitarian systems rather than of liberal-democratic systems. Nevertheless, the thesis of 'concealed violence' and 'repressive tolerance' has been put forward by Herbert Marcuse, and accepted by his disciples in the student protest movements.

In the late 1960s, the New Left has itself developed fissiparous tendencies. The relationship between the Negro civil rights movement and movements of radical protest such as the Progressive Labor Movement are uneasy at best and mutually suspicious at worst. Nor have the revolutionary groups on the left been able so far to find solidarity with American trade unions and workers.

These difficulties have tended to split the radicals into different factions, though there are occasional attempts to unite or discover common ground. The March 1969 resolution passed by the Students for a Democratic Society, included in these documents, shows one such attempt.

Whatever the shortcomings of the new radicals in terms of political analysis, and despite their tendency to confuse slogans with arguments, they have nevertheless enlivened the American political debate during the 1960s and helped to rescue it from the dead hand of consensus politics. Writing in 1960, the sociologist Daniel Bell gave to his book *The End of Ideology* the subtitle *On the Exhaustion of Political Ideas in the Fifties*. It is extremely unlikely that an American author would select such a subtitle as a suitable summary of the 1960s. If a complaint could be made, perhaps it would be that too *many* ideas – unformulated, naïve, utopian, at times incoherent – are now issuing from too many quarters. Too many groups and organizations are now claiming to speak for – and even to salve – the political conscience of the nation.*

There have been students of politics in America during the last century who have pursued other lines of inquiry, well removed from the rhetoric of the dissenters, and it would be a serious omission if we did not examine in these readings, however briefly, the search for a science of politics. The reasons for and the history of that search is a complex one, and it cannot be treated in any detail here, but the documents selected may serve as signposts to the present.†

In 1877 Theodore Woolsey, a professor of law at Yale University, published a two-volume work *Political Science : or the State Theoretically and Practically Considered*. In that work, the emphasis was on the practical rather than the theoretical. Woolsey indulged in a form of social engineering in which the State was regarded not as an abstract idea, as Hegel had portrayed it, but more as a mechanical contrivance similar to a locomotive, with the specific task of transporting the body politic to brighter pastures.

---

* In *The New Radicals* (1966) Paul Jacobs and Saul Landau provide a preliminary list of twenty-five 'radical action' groups in American politics today, not including the militant Negro organizations.

† The reader who is interested in exploring the development of political science in the United States should consult Bernard Crick's book, *The American Science of Politics*, London, 1959.

At the same time, the study of sociology with its promise of a science of society was taking root in America. The writings of Herbert Spencer, an Englishman who came to sociology by way of engineering, enjoyed a great vogue. Spencer's 'synthetic sociology' seemed to promise the elusive millennium, a society that could be constructed scientifically, and free of the social and political ills which had plagued mankind down the centuries.

The concurrent appeal of pragmatism, with its emphasis on action rather than abstraction, strengthened the call for a science of politics as part of a science of society, so that politics came to be regarded as a set of observable skills rather than mysterious qualities or some subtle art. That which could be observed could be classified and compared, in the manner of the natural scientists; deduction could replace induction; perhaps scientific prediction could one day replace the subjective hunch or inspired guesswork.

In 1908 Professor Arthur Bentley of the University of Chicago issued his book *The Process of Government*, a panegyric for the measurement and classification of political phenomena. 'Measure conquers chaos', the professor succinctly observed. 'There is no political process that is not a balancing of quantity against quantity.' The understanding of political phenomena, Bentley continued, meant simply the measurement of the elements that had gone into them.*

Such a view of political processes from an established professor was a seductive doctrine for younger students struggling to understand the complexities of the subject. It promised rigour and order in place of the more opaque realms of inquiry traditionally explored. Political theory was the first casualty of the new orthodoxy, for by its nature it was not susceptible to measurement.

The doctrine 'Measure conquers chaos' invited the view that everything that could be measured should be measured. At the National Conference on the Science of Politics held at Chicago in 1924 the chairman remarked: 'The need of placing political science upon a really scientific basis will be obvious to everyone. There is scarcely a phase of the subject that does not offer the most alluring and virgin opportunities.' The discussion which followed the chairman's remarks produced a working paper in which the methods to be adopted in the search for a rigorous political science were set out.

* Arthur Bentley, *The Process of Government*, 1935 edn., pp. 200, 202.

Thereafter the pursuit of a political science by quantitative methods spread to other universities in America, though not everyone accepted the new doctrine. Some felt that the new political science was inadequate on many counts, and that its claims to scientism were grandiose. But the apologists for the new 'science' argued that they were chiefly concerned to systematize the discipline; to free it from old-fashioned – and often untested – hypotheses or assumptions. They sought, and are seeking, greater certainty. Nor is the quest a purely academic one. Modern political scientists are searching for what is common to the various political systems in the world today, and what are the explanations for the differences between systems. Only by adopting a dispassionate and scientific approach, they feel, can the process of detailed comparison go forward. Today, the apparatus of modern technology, especially computers, assists the political scientists in their work. In this as in so many other respects, the American mind has shown its readiness to adopt new ideas and new approaches to ancient disciplines.

The essays and documents gathered in this book will perhaps convey how varied have been the contributions to the debate on politics and society in America during the past century. In different sections of the readings, occasionally within the same section, proposals and arguments will seem contradictory, even mutually exclusive. This healthy discord is the best possible testimony to that freedom of opinion – both spoken and written – which the American Republic fosters and preserves.

Prologue: America in 1870

The 1870s were years of change and restlessness in America. The Civil War was still fresh in most men's minds, and reconstruction did little to heal the nation's wounds. From Europe fresh waves of immigrants arrived, willing to accept – for a time – the poverty and insecurity which is the common lot of the newcomer in an alien land. The frontier expanded in the West, but the worst fruits of industrialism now disfigured the urban areas of the East. Politics was at a low ebb in the public esteem and in the larger cities great wealth existed alongside abysmal poverty.

THE GILDED AGE

The mood of America in 1870 is vividly captured in the following extract from Vernon L. Parrington's Main Currents in American Thought (3 vols., 1927–30). *The passage appears at the beginning of volume three, pp. 7–9.*

The pot was boiling briskly in America in the tumultous post-war years. The country had definitely entered upon its freedom and was settling its disordered household to suit its democratic taste. Everywhere new ways were feverishly at work transforming the countryside. In the South another order was rising uncertainly on the ruins of the plantation system; in the East an expanding factory economy was weaving a different pattern of industrial life; in the

Middle Border a recrudescent agriculture was arising from the application of the machine to the rich prairie soil. All over the land a spider web of iron rails was being spun that was to draw the remotest outposts into the common whole and bind the nation together with steel bands. Nevertheless two diverse worlds lay on the map of continental America. Facing in opposite directions and holding different faiths, they would not travel together easily or take comfort from the yoke that joined them. Agricultural America, behind which lay two and a half centuries of experience, was a decentralized world, democratic, individualistic, suspicious; industrial America, behind which lay only half a dozen decades of bustling experiment, was a centralizing world, capitalistic, feudal, ambitious. The one was a decaying order, the other a rising, and between them would be friction till one or the other had become master.

Continental America was still half frontier and half settled country. A thin line of homesteads had been thrust westward till the outposts reached well into the Middle Border – an uncertain thread running through eastern Minnesota, Nebraska, Kansas, overleaping the Indian Territory and then running west into Texas – approximately halfway between the Atlantic and the Pacific. Behind these outposts was still much unoccupied land, and beyond stretched the unfenced prairies till they merged in the sagebrush plains, grey and waste, that stretched to the foothills of the Rocky Mountains. Beyond the mountains were other stretches of plains and deserts, vast and forbidding in their alkali blight, to the wooded coast ranges and the Pacific Ocean. In all this immense territory were only scattered settlements – at Denver, Salt Lake City, Sacramento, San Francisco, Portland, Seattle, and elsewhere – tiny outposts in the wilderness, with scattered hamlets, mining camps, and isolated homesteads lost in the great expanse. On the prairies from Mexico to Canada – across which rumbled great herds of buffalo – roved powerful tribes of hostile Indians who fretted against the forward thrust of settlement and disputed the right of possession. The urgent business of the times was the subduing of this wild region, wresting it from Indians and buffalo and wilderness; and the forty years that lay between the California Gold Rush of '49 and the Oklahoma Land Rush of '89 saw the greatest wave of pioneer expansion – the swiftest and most reckless – in all our pioneer experience. Expansion on so vast a scale necessitated building, and the seventies became the railway age, bonding the future to break down present barriers of isolation, and opening new territories for later exploitation. The reflux of the great movement swept back upon the Atlantic coast and gave to life there a fresh note of spontaneous vigour, of which the Gilded Age was the inevitable expression.

It was this energetic East, with its accumulations of liquid capital awaiting investment and its factories turning out the materials needed to push the settlements westward, that profited most from the conquest of the far West. The impulsion from the frontier did much to drive forward the industrial revolution. The war that brought devastation to the South had been more friendly to northern interests. In gathering the scattered rills of capital into central reservoirs at Philadelphia and New York, and in expanding the factory system to supply the needs of the armies, it had opened to capitalism its first clear view of the Promised Land. The bankers had come into control of the liquid wealth of the nation, and the industrialists had learned to use the machine for production; the time was ripe for exploitation on a scale undreamed-of a generation before. Up till then the potential resource of the continent had not even been surveyed. Earlier pioneers had only scratched the surface – felling trees, making crops, building pygmy watermills, smelting a little iron. Mineral wealth had been scarcely touched. Tools had been lacking to develop it, capital had been lacking, transportation lacking, technical methods lacking, markets lacking.

In the years following the war, exploitation for the first time was provided with adequate resources and a competent technique, and busy prospectors were daily uncovering new sources of wealth. The coal and oil of Pennsylvania and Ohio, the copper and iron ore of upper Michigan, the gold and silver, lumber and fisheries, of the Pacific Coast, provided limitless raw materials for the rising industrialism. The Bessemer process quickly turned an age of iron into an age of steel and created the great rolling mills of Pittsburgh from which issued the rails for expanding railways. The reaper and binder, the sulky plow and the threshing machine, created a large-scale agriculture on the fertile prairies. Wild grasslands provided grazing for immense herds of cattle and sheep; the development of the corn-belt enormously increased the supply of hogs; and with railways at hand the Middle Border poured into

Omaha and Kansas City and Chicago an endless stream of produce. As the line of the frontier pushed westward new towns were built, thousands of homesteads were filed on, and the speculator and promoter hovered over the prairies like buzzards seeking their carrion. With rising land-values money was to be made out of unearned increment, and the creation of booms was a profitable industry. The times were stirring and it was a shiftless fellow who did not make his pile. If he had been too late to file on desirable acres he had only to find a careless homesteader who had failed in some legal technicality and 'jump his claim'. Good bottom land could be had even by latecomers if they were sharp at the game.

This bustling America of 1870 accounted itself a democratic world. A free people had put away all aristocratic privileges and conscious of its power went forth to possess the last frontier. Its social philosophy, which it found adequate to its needs, was summed up in three words—preëmption, exploitation, progress. Its immediate and pressing business was to dispossess the government of its rich holdings. Lands in the possession of the government were so much idle waste, untaxed and profitless; in private hands they would be developed. They would provide work, pay taxes, support schools, enrich the community. Preëmption meant exploitation and exploitation meant progress. It was a simple philosophy and it suited the simple individualism of the times. The Gilded Age knew nothing of the Enlightenment; it recognized only the acquisitive instinct. That much at least the frontier had taught the great American democracy; and in applying to the resources of a continent the lesson it had been so well taught the Gilded Age wrote a profoundly characteristic chapter of American history.

I *Reformers*

1.1. THE BASIS OF ARISTOCRACY

From Book VII of Henry George's Progress and Poverty, *1938 ed., pp. 350–3.*

Henry George (1839–97) was born in Philadelphia of English stock. He left school at fourteen to go to sea, but disliked the life and returned to become a printer, then a journalist. On a visit to New York City he was deeply shocked by the contrast he noticed between 'monstrous wealth and debasing want'. Henry George devoted the rest of his life to attacking what he held to be the root cause of these conditions.

The principal cause, he argued, was the unearned increment received by land owners wherever land was scarce. In his most famous work, *Progress and Poverty* (1879) Henry George proposed a tax on this unearned increment wherever it existed.

When the idea of individual ownership, which so justly and naturally attaches to things of human production is extended to land, all the rest is a mere matter of development. The strongest and most cunning easily acquire a superior share in this species of property, which is to be had, not by production, but by appropriation, and in becoming lords of the land they become necessarily lords of their fellow-men. The ownership of land is the basis of aristocracy. It was not nobility that gave land, but the possession of land that gave nobility. All the enormous privileges of the nobility of medieval Europe flowed from their position as the owners of the soil. The simple principle of the ownership of the soil produced on the one side, the lord, on the other, the vassal – the one having all rights, the other none. The right of the lord to the soil acknowledged and maintained, those who lived upon it could do so only upon his terms. The manners and conditions of the times made those terms include services and servitudes, as well as rents in produce or money, but the essential thing that compelled them was the ownership of land. This power exists wherever the ownership of land exists, and can be brought out wherever the competition for the use of land is great enough to enable the landlord to make his own terms. The English landowner of today has, in the law which recognizes his exclusive right to the land, essentially all the power which his predecessor the feudal baron had. He might command rent in services or servitudes. He might compel his tenants to dress themselves in a particular way, to profess a particular religion, to send their children to a particular school, to submit their differences to his decision, to fall upon their knees when he spoke to them, to follow him around dressed in his livery, or to sacrifice to him female honour, if they would prefer these things to being driven off his land. He could demand, in short, any terms on which men would still consent to live on his land, and the law could not prevent him so long as it did not qualify his ownership, for compliance with them would assume the form of a free contract or voluntary act. And English landlords do exercise such of these powers as in the manners of the times they care to. Having shaken off the obligation of providing for the defence of the country, they no longer need the military service of their tenants, and the possession of wealth and power being now shown in other ways than by long trains of attendants, they no longer care for personal service. But they habitually control the votes of their tenants, and dictate to them in many little ways. That 'right reverend father in God', Bishop Lord Plunkett, evicted a number of his poor Irish tenants because they would not send their children to Protestant Sunday-schools; and to that Earl of Leitrim for whom Nemesis tarried so long before she sped the bullet of an assassin, even darker crimes are imputed; while, at the cold promptings of greed, cottage after cottage has been pulled down and family after family forced into the roads. The principle that permits this is the same principle that in ruder times and a simpler social state enthralled the great

25

masses of the common people and placed such a wide gulf between noble and peasant. Where the peasant was made a serf, it was simply by forbidding him to leave the estate on which he was born, thus artificially producing the condition we supposed on the island. In sparsely settled countries this is necessary to produce absolute slavery, but where land is fully occupied, competition may produce substantially the same conditions. Between the condition of the rack-rented Irish peasant and the Russian serf, the advantage was in many things on the side of the serf. The serf did not starve.

Now, as I think I have conclusively proved, it is the same cause which has in every age degraded and enslaved the labouring masses that is working in the civilized world today. Personal liberty – that is to say, the liberty to move about – is everywhere conceded, while of political and legal inequality there are in the United States no vestiges, and in the most backward civilized countries but few. But the great cause of inequality remains, and is manifesting itself in the unequal distribution of wealth. The essence of slavery is that it takes from the labourer all he produces save enough to support an animal existence, and to this minimum the wages of free labour, under existing conditions, unmistakably tend. Whatever be the increase of productive power, rent steadily tends to swallow up the gain, and more than the gain.

Thus the condition of the masses in every civilized country is, or is tending to become, that of virtual slavery under the forms of freedom. And it is probable that of all kinds of slavery this is the most cruel and relentless. For the labourer is robbed of the produce of his labour and compelled to toil for a mere subsistence; but his taskmasters, instead of human beings, assume the forms of imperious necessities. Those to whom his labour is rendered and from whom his wages are received are often driven in their turn – contact between the labourers and the ultimate beneficiaries of their labour is sundered, and individuality is lost. The direct responsibility of master to slave, a responsibility which exercises a softening influence upon the great majority of men, does not arise; it is not one human being who seems to drive another to unremitting and ill-requited toil, but 'the inevitable laws of supply and demand,' for which no one in particular is responsible. The maxims of Cato the Censor – maxims which were regarded with abhorrence even in an age of cruelty and universal slaveholding – that after as much work as possible is obtained from a slave he should be turned out to die, become the common rule; and even the selfish interest which prompts the master to look after the comfort and well-being of the slave is lost. Labour has become a commodity, and the labourer a machine. There are no masters and slaves, no owners and owned, but only buyers and sellers. The higgling of the market takes the place of every other sentiment.

1.2 UTOPIAN FICTION

The political novel often provides valuable insights to the temper of a decade or era. In the 1880s and 1890s the American novel was frequently the vehicle of social conscience and sometimes of socialist rhetoric. There was also a vogue in the utopian novel, in which socialist theories were wedded to a projected view of some golden age. Two examples are given in the extracts which follow. In both cases the author projects his narrative into the twentieth century and discourses on the golden age which followed the destruction of the capitalist system.

1.2.1 *From Edward Bellamy,* Looking Backward: 2000–1887, *1st ed. 1888, Chapter V, pp. 53–8.*

[Dr Leete, one of the central characters in the novel, is recalling the breakdown of the old order from his utopian vantage-point.]

'The records of the period show that the outcry against the concentration of capital was furious. Men believed that it threatened society with a form of tyranny more abhorrent than it had ever endured. They believed that the great corporations were preparing for them the yoke of a baser servitude than had ever been imposed on the race, servitude not to men but to soulless machines incapable of any motive but insatiable greed. Looking back, we cannot wonder at their desperation, for certainly humanity was never confronted with a fate more sordid and hideous than would have been the era of corporate tyranny which they anticipated.

'Meanwhile, without being in the smallest degree checked by the clamour against it, the absorption of business by ever larger monopolies continued. In the United States there was not, after the beginning of the last quarter of the century, any opportunity whatever for individual enterprise in any important field of industry, unless backed by a great capital. During the last decade of the century, such small businesses as still remained were fast-failing survivals of a past epoch, or mere parasites on the great corporations, or else existed in fields too small to attract the great capitalists. Small businesses, as far as they still remained, were reduced to the condition of rats and mice, living in holes and corners, and counting on evading notice for the enjoyment of existence. The railroads had gone on combining till a few great syndicates controlled every rail in the land. In manufactories, every important staple was controlled by a syndicate. These syndicates, pools, trusts, or whatever their name, fixed prices and crushed all competition except when combinations as vast as themselves arose. Then a struggle, resulting in a still greater consolidation, ensued. The great city bazaar crushed its country rivals with branch stores, and in the city itself absorbed its smaller rivals till the business of a whole quarter was concentrated under one roof, with a hundred former proprietors of shops serving as clerks. Having no business of his own to put his money in, the small capitalist, at the same time that he took service under the corporation, found no other investment for his money [and] buys its stocks and bonds, thus becoming doubly dependent upon it.

'The fact that the desperate popular opposition to the consolidation of business in a few powerful hands had no effect to check it proves that there must have been a strong economical reason for it. The small capitalists, with their innumerable petty concerns, had in fact yielded the field to the great aggregations of capital, because they belonged to a day of small things and were totally incompetent to the demands of an age of steam and telegraphs and the gigantic scale of its enterprises. To restore the former order of things, even if possible, would have involved returning to the day of stage-coaches. Oppressive and intolerable as was the régime of the great consolidations of capital, even its victims, while they cursed it, were forced to admit the prodigious increase of efficiency which had been imparted to the national industries, the vast economies effected by concentration of management and unity of organization, and to confess that since the new system had taken the place of the old the wealth of the world had increased at a rate before undreamed of. To be sure this vast increase had gone chiefly to make the rich richer, increasing the gap between them and the poor; but the fact remained that, as a means merely of producing wealth, capital had been proved efficient in proportion to its consolidation. The restoration of the old system with the subdivision of capital, if it were possible, might indeed bring back a greater equality of conditions, with more individual dignity and freedom, but it would be at the price of general poverty and the arrest of material progress.

'Was there, then, no way of commanding the services of the mighty wealth-producing principle of consolidated capital without bowing down to a plutocracy like that of Carthage? As soon as men began to ask themselves these questions, they found the answer ready for them. The movement towards the conduct of business by larger and larger aggregations of capital, the tendency towards monopolies, which had been so desperately and vainly resisted, was recognized at last, in its true significance, as a process which only needed to complete its logical evolution to open a golden future to humanity.

'Early in the last century the evolution was completed by the final consolidation of the entire capital of the nation. The industry and commerce of the country, ceasing to be conducted by a set of irresponsible corporations and syndicates of private persons at their caprice and for their profits, were entrusted to a single syndicate representing the people, to be conducted in the common interest for the common profit. The nation, that is to say, organized as the one great business corporation in which all other corporations were absorbed; it became the one capitalist in the place of all other capitalists, the sole employer, the final monopoly in which all previous and lesser monopolies were swallowed up, a monopoly in the profits and economies of which all citizens shared. The epoch of trusts had ended in The Great Trust. In a word, the people of the United States concluded to assume the conduct of their own business, just as one hundred-odd years before they had assumed the conduct of their own government, organizing now for industrial purposes on precisely the same grounds that they had then organized for political purposes. At last, strangely late in the world's history, the obvious fact was perceived that no business is so essentially the public business as the industry and commerce on which the people's livelihood depends, and that to entrust it to private persons to be managed for private profit is a folly similar in kind, though vastly greater in magnitude, to that of surrendering the functions of political government to kings and nobles to be conducted for their personal glorification.'

'Such a stupendous change as you describe,' said I, 'did not, of course, take place without great bloodshed and terrible convulsions.'

'On the contrary,' replied Dr Leete, 'there was absolutely no violence. The change had been long foreseen. Public opinion had become fully ripe for it, and the whole mass of the people was behind it. There was no more possibility of opposing it by force than by argument. On the other hand the popular sentiment towards the great corporations and those identified with them had ceased to be one of bitterness, as they came to realize their necessity as a link, a transition phase, in the evolution of the true industrial system. The most violent foes of the great private monopolies were now forced to recognize how invaluable and indispensable had been their office in educating the people up to the point of assuming control of their own business. Fifty years before, the consolidation of the industries of the country under national control would have seemed a very daring experiment to the most sanguine. But by a series of object lessons, seen and studied by all men, the great corporations had taught the people an entirely new set of ideas on this subject. They had seen for many years syndicates handling revenues greater than those of states, and directing the labours of hundreds of thousands of men with an efficiency and economy unattainable in smaller operations. It had come to be recognized as an axiom that the larger the business the simpler the principles that can be applied to it; that, as the machine is truer than the hand, so the system, which in a great concern does the work of the master's eye in a small business, turns out more accurate results. Thus it came about that, thanks to the corporations themselves, when it was proposed that the nation should assume their functions, the suggestion implied nothing which seemed impracticable even to the timid. To be sure it was a step beyond any yet taken, a broader generalization, but the very fact that the nation would be the sole corporation in the field would, it was seen, relieve the undertaking of many difficulties with which the partial monopolies had contended.'

1.2.2 *From Ignatius Donnelly,* Caesar's Column: A Story of the Twentieth Century, *1st ed. 1891, pp. 308–11.*

[The writer is once more securely lodged in utopia.]

We decreed, next, universal and compulsory education. No one can vote who cannot read and write. We believe that one man's ignorance should not countervail the just influence of another man's intelligence. Ignorance is not only ruinous to the individual, but destructive to society. It is an epidemic which scatters death everywhere.

We abolish all private schools, except the higher institutions and colleges. We believe it to be essential to the peace and safety of the commonwealth that the children of all the people, rich and poor, should, during the period of growth, associate together. In this way, race, sectarian and caste prejudices are obliterated, and the whole community grow up together as brethren. Otherwise, in a generation or two, we shall have the people split up into hostile factions, fenced in by doctrinal bigotries, suspicious of one another, and antagonizing one another in politics, business and everything else.

But, as we believe that it is not right to cultivate the heads of the young to the exclusion of their hearts, we mingle with abstract knowledge a cult of morality and religion, to be agreed upon by the different churches; for there are a hundred points wherein they agree to one wherein they differ. And, as to the points peculiar to each creed, we require the children to attend school but five days in the week, thus leaving one day for the parents or pastors to take charge of their religious training in addition to the care given them on Sunday.

We abolish all interest on money, and punish with imprisonment the man who receives it.

The state owns all roads, streets, telegraph or telephone lines, railroads and mines, and takes exclusive control of the mails and express matter.

As these departments will in time furnish employment for a

great many officials, who might be massed together by the party in power, and wielded for political purposes, we decree that any man who accepts office relinquishes, for the time being, his right of suffrage. The servants of the people have no right to help rule them; and he who thinks more of his right to vote than of an office is at liberty to refuse an appointment.

As we have not an hereditary nobility, as in England, or great geographical subdivisions, as in America, we are constrained, in forming our Congress or Parliament, to fall back upon a new device.

Our governing body, called The People, is divided into three branches. The first is elected exclusively by the producers, to wit: the workmen in the towns and the farmers and mechanics in the country; and those they elect must belong to their own class. As these constitute the great bulk of the people, the body that represents them stands for the House of Representatives in America. The second branch is elected exclusively by and from the merchants and manufacturers, and all who are engaged in trade, or as employers of labour. The third branch, which is the smallest of the three, is selected by the authors, newspaper writers, artists, scientists, philosophers and literary people generally. This branch is expected to hold the balance of power, where the other two bodies cannot agree. It may be expected that they will be distinguished by broad and philanthropic views and new and generous conceptions. Where a question arises as to which of these three groups or subdivisions a voter belongs to, the matter is to be decided by the president of the Republic.

No law can be passed, in the first instance, unless it receives a majority vote in each of the three branches, or a two-thirds vote in two of them. Where a difference of opinion arises upon any point of legislation, the three branches are to assemble together and discuss the matter at issue, and try to reach an agreement. As, however, the experience of the world has shown that there is more danger of the upper classes combining to oppress the producers than there is of the producers conspiring to govern them – except in the last desperate extremity, as shown recently – it is therefore decreed that if the Commons, by a three-fourths vote, pass any measure, it becomes a law, notwithstanding the veto of the other two branches.

The executive is elected by the Congress for a period of four years, and is not eligible for re-election. He has no veto and no control of any patronage. In the election of president, a two-thirds vote of each branch is necessary.

Whenever it can be shown, in the future, that in any foreign country the wages of labour and the prosperity of the people are as high as in our own, then free trade with that people is decreed. But, whenever the people of another country are in greater poverty, or working at a lower rate of wages than our own, then all commercial intercourse with them shall be totally interdicted. For, impoverished labour on one side of a line, unless walled out, must inevitably drag down labour on the other side of the line to a like condition. Neither is the device of a tariff sufficient; for, although it is better than free trade, while it tends to keep up the price of goods, it lets in the products of foreign labour; this diminishes the wages of our own labourers by decreasing the demand for their productions to the extent of the goods imported; and thus, while the price of commodities is held up for the benefit of the manufacturers, the price of labour falls. There can be no equitable commerce between two peoples representing two different stages of civilization and both engaged in producing the same commodities. Thus the freest nations are constantly pulled down to ruin by the most oppressed. What would happen to heaven if you took down the fence between it and hell? We are resolved that our republic shall be of itself, by itself – in a great pool, a swans' nest.

As a corollary to these propositions, we decree that our Congress shall have the right to fix the compensation for all forms of labour, so that wages shall never fall below a rate that will afford the labourer a comfortable living, with a margin that will enable him to provide for his old age. It is simply a question of the adjustment of values. This experiment has been tried before by different countries, but was always tried in the interest of the employers; the labourers had no voice in the matter; and it was the interest of the upper classes to cheapen labour; and hence Muscle became a drug and Cunning invaluable and masterful; and the process was continued indefinitely until the catastrophe came. Now labour has its own branch of our Congress, and can defend its rights and explain its necessities.

In the comparison of views between the three classes, some reasonable ground of compromise will generally be found; and if error is committed we prefer that it should enure to the benefit of the many, instead of, as heretofore, to the benefit of the few.

We declare in the preamble of our constitution that 'this government is intended to be merely a plain and simple instrument, to insure to every industrious citizen not only liberty, but an educated mind, a comfortable home, an abundant supply of food and clothing, and a pleasant, happy life.'

Are not these the highest objects for which governments can exist? And, if government, on the old lines, did not yield these results, should it not have been so reformed as to do so?

1.3 TRADE UNIONS DEFENDED

From, Relations Between Labor and Capital, *Report and Testimony of the Senate Committee on Education and Labor, 48th Congress, 1885, I, 373–5.*

The name Samuel Gompers is the most illustrious in the history of American trade unionism. Born in London in 1850, Gompers was brought to America as a boy and joined the Cigarmakers' Union at the age of fourteen. By 1877 he was President of his union and helped to found the American Federation of Labor in 1886. Gompers was President of the American Federation of Labor from its foundation until his death in 1924 (with the exception of the year 1895).

Trade unionism was initially resented and attacked by employers and officials in the USA, just as it was in Europe. In 1883 Gompers was summoned to a Senate Committee inquiring into the activities of trade unions. The following is a portion of his testimony. As we might expect, it is lacking in ornament, but there can be no doubting its sincerity and directness.

. . . [The] organizations of labour are the conservators of the public peace; for when strikes occur among men who are unorganized, often acting upon ill-considered plans, hastily adopted, acting upon passion, and sometimes not knowing what they have gone on strike for, except possibly some fancied grievance, and hardly knowing by what means they can or may remedy their grievances, each acts upon his own account without the restraint of organization, and feels that he serves the cause of the strike best when he does something that just occurs to him; while the man who belongs to a trades union that is of some years' standing is, by the very fact of his membership of the organization and his experience there, taught to abide by the decision of the majority. Therefore when anything of that kind I have mentioned occurs or is heard of in the organizations that are of long standing, it is condemned in the most strenuous terms and action is taken to prevent the accomplishment of any such purpose, or if it is accomplished to prevent the recurrence of it. The members of our organization are made to well understand that such a mode of warfare in strikes is not tolerated in any well-regulated or well-organized trades union. . . .

When we strike as organized workingmen, we generally win, and that is the reason of the trouble that our employers go to when they try to show that strikes are failures, but you will notice that they generally or always point to unorganized workers. That is one reason also why when the employers know that the workingmen are organized and have got a good treasury strikes are very frequently avoided. There are fewer strikes among organized workingmen, but when they do strike they are able to hold out much longer than the others, and they generally win. The trades unions are not what too many men have been led to believe they are, importations from Europe: if they are imported, then, as has been said, they were landed at Plymouth Rock from the *Mayflower*. Modern industry evolves these organizations out of the existing conditions where there are two classes in society, one incessantly striving to obtain the labour of the other class for as little as possible, and to obtain the largest amount or number of hours of labour; and the members of the other class being, as individuals, utterly helpless in a contest with their employers, naturally resort to combinations to improve their condition, and, in fact, they are forced by the conditions which surround them to organize for self-protection. Hence trades unions. Trades unions are not barbarous, nor are they the outgrowth of barbarism. On the contrary they are only possible where civilization exists. Trades unions cannot exist in China; they cannot exist in Russia; and in all those semi-barbarous countries they can hardly exist, if indeed they can exist at all. But they have been formed successfully in this country, in Germany, in England, and they are gradually gaining strength in France. In Great Britain they are very strong; they have been forming there for fifty years, and they are still forming, and I think there is a great future for them yet in America. Wherever trades unions have organized and are most firmly organized, there are the right[s] of the people most respected. A people may be educated, but to me it appears that the greatest amount of intelligence exists in that country or that State where the people are best able to defend their rights, and their liberties as against those who are desirous of undermining them. Trades unions are organizations that instill into men a higher motive-power and give them a higher goal to look to. The hope that is too frequently deadened in their breasts when unorganized is awakened by the trades unions as it can be by nothing else. . . .

Q. The outside public, I think, very largely confound the conditions out of which the trades union grows or is formed, with the, to the general public mind, somewhat revolutionary ideas that are embraced under the names of socialism and communism. Before you get through, won't you let us understand to what extent the trades union is an outgrowth or an evolution of those ideas, and to what extent it stands apart from them and is based on different principles?

A. The trades unions are by no means an outgrowth of socialistic or communistic ideas or principles, but the socialistic and communistic notions are evolved from some of the trades unions' movements. As to the question of the principles of communism or socialism prevailing in trades unions, there are a number of men who connect themselves as workingmen with the trades unions who may have socialistic convictions, yet who never gave them currency; who say, 'Whatever ideas we may have as to the future state of society, regardless of what the end of the labour movement as a movement between classes may be, they must remain in the background, and we must subordinate our convictions, and our views and our acts to the general good that the trades-union movement brings to the labourer.' A large number of them think and act in that way. On the other hand, there are men – not so numerous now as they have been in the past – who are endeavouring to conquer the trades-union movement and subordinate it to those doctrines, and in a measure, in a few such organizations that condition of things exists, but by no means does it exist in the largest, most powerful, and best organized trades unions. There the view of which I spoke just now, the desire to improve the condition of the workingmen by and through the efforts of the trades union, is fully lived up to. I do not know whether I have covered the entire ground of the question. . . .

Q. You state, then, that the trades unions generally are not propagandists of socialistic views?

A. They are not. On the contrary, the endeavours of which I have spoken, made by certain persons to conquer the trades unions in certain cases, are resisted by the trades unionists; in the first place for the trades unions' sake, and even persons who have these convictions perhaps equally as strong as the others will yet subordinate them entirely to the good to be received directly through the trades unions. These last help those who have not such convictions to resist those who seek to use the trades unions to propagate their socialistic ideas.

Q. Do you think the trades unions have impeded or advanced the spread of socialistic views?

A. I believe that the existence of the trades union movement, more especially where the unionists are better organized, has evoked a spirit and a demand for reform, but has held in check the more radical elements in society. . . .

1.4 'RUIN OR REFORM?'

The following extract is from Wealth Against Commonwealth (*1898 edition*), *Chapter XXV, 'The New Self-Interest', by Henry Demarest Lloyd.*

Henry Demarest Lloyd (1847–1903) trained for the New York Bar but turned to journalism in 1872. He too was deeply shocked by the social and economic conditions in the big cities of the eastern United States. Lloyd felt that an unholy alliance was developing between monopoly power and government institutions. This argument dominates his book *Wealth Against Commonwealth* (1894). The work begins with Lloyd's declamatory phrase 'Nature is rich; but everywhere man, the heir of nature, is poor'. Here, as elsewhere, Lloyd's style and expression bring to mind the romanticism of Rousseau.

We have given the prize of power to the strong, the cunning, the arithmetical, and we must expect nothing else but that they will use it cunningly and arithmetically. For what else can they suppose we gave it to them? If the power really flows from the people, and should be used for them; if its best administration can be got, as in government, only by the participation in it of men of all views and interests; if in the collision of all these, as in democracy, the better policy is progressively preponderant; if this is a policy which, with whatever defects, is better than that which can be evolved by narrower or more selfish or less multitudinous influences of persons or classes, then this power should be taken up by the people. 'The mere conflict of private interests will never produce a well-ordered commonwealth of labour,' says the author of the article on political economy in the *Encyclopaedia Britannica*. The failure of monarchy and feudalism and the visibly impending failure of our business system all reveal a law of nature. The harmony of things insists that that which is the source of power, wealth, and delight shall also be the ruler of it. That which is must also seem. It is the people from whom come the forces with which kings and millionaires ride the world, and until the people take their proper place in the seat of sovereignty, these pseudo owners – mere claimants and usurpers – will, by the very falsity and iniquity of their position, be pushed into deceit, tyranny, and cruelty, ending in downfall.

Thousands of years' experience has proved that government must begin where it ends – with the people; that the general welfare demands that they who exercise the powers and they upon whom these are exercised must be the same, and that higher political ideals can be realized only through higher political forms. Myriads of experiments to get the substance of liberty out of the forms of tyranny, to believe in princes, to trust good men to do good as kings, have taught the inexorable truth that, in the economy of nature, form and substance must move together, and are as inextricably interdependent as are, within our experience, what we call matter and spirit. Identical is the lesson we are learning with regard to industrial power and property. We are calling upon their owners, as mankind called upon kings in their day, to be good and kind, wise and sweet, and we are calling in vain. We are asking them not to be what we have made them to be. We put power into their hands and ask them not to use it as power. If the spirit of power is to change, institutions must change as much. Liberty recast the old forms of government into the Republic, and it must remould our institutions of wealth into the Commonwealth.

The question is not whether monopoly is to continue. The sun sets every night on a greater majority against it. We are face to face with the practical issue: Is it to go through ruin or reform? Can we forestall ruin by reform? If we wait to be forced by events we shall be astounded to find how much more radical they are than our utopias. Louis XVI waited until 1793, and gave his head and all his investitures to the people who in 1789 asked only to sit at his feet and speak their mind. Unless we reform of our own free will, nature will reform us by force, as nature does. Our evil courses have already gone too far in producing misery, plagues, hatreds, national enervation. Already the leader is unable to lead, and has begun to drive with judges armed with bayonets and Gatling guns. History is the serial obituary of the men who thought they could drive men.

Reform is the science and conscience with which mankind in its manhood overcomes temptations and escapes consequences by killing the germs. Ruin is already hard at work among us. Our libraries are full of the official inquiries and scientific interpretations which show how our master-motive is working decay in all our parts. The family crumbles into a competition between the father and the children whom he breeds to take his place in the factory, to unfit themselves to be fathers in their turn. A thorough stalwart resimplification, a life governed by simple needs and loves, is the imperative want of the world. It will be accomplished: either self-conscious volition does it, or the slow wreck and decay of superfluous and unwholesome men and matters. The latter is the method of brutes and brute civilizations. The other is the method of man, so far as he is divine. Has not man, who has in personal reform risen above the brute method, come to the height at which he can achieve social reform in masses and by nations? We must learn; we can learn by reason. Why wait for the crueller teacher?

We have a people like which none has ever existed before. We have millions capable of conscious co-operation. The time must come in social evolution when the people can organize the free will to choose salvation which the individual has been cultivating for 1,900 years, and can adopt a policy more dignified and more effective than leaving themselves to be kicked along the path of reform by the recoil of their own vices. We must bring the size of our morality up to the size of our cities, corporations, and combinations, or these will be brought down to fit our half-grown virtue. . . .

The break-down of all other civilizations has been a slow decay. It took the Northerners hundreds of years to march to the Tiber. They grew their way through the old society as the tree planting itself on a grave is found to have sent its roots along every fibre and muscle of the dead. Our world is not the simple thing theirs was, of little groups sufficient to themselves, if need be. New York would begin to die tomorrow if it were not for Illinois and Dakota. We cannot afford a revulsion in the hearts by whose union locomotives run, mills grind, factories make. Practical men are speculating today on the possibility that our civilization may some afternoon be flashed away by the tick of a telegraph. All these co-operations can be scattered by a word of hate too many, and be left, with no one who knows how to make a plough or a match, a civilization cut off as by the Roman curse from food and fire. Less sensitive civilizations than ours have burst apart.

Liberty and monopoly cannot live together. What chance have we against the persistent coming and the easy coalescence of the confederated cliques, which aspire to say of all business, 'This belongs to us', and whose members, though moving among us as brothers, are using against us, through the corporate forms we have given them, powers of invisibility, of entail and accumulation, unprecedented because impersonal and immortal, and, most peculiar of all, power to act as persons, as in the commission of crimes, with exemption from punishment as persons? Two classes study and practise politics and government: place hunters and privilege hunters. In a world of relativities like ours, size of area has a great deal to do with the truth of principles. America has grown so big – and the [election] tickets to be voted, and the powers of government, and the duties of citizens, and the profits of personal use of public functions have all grown so big – that the average citizen has broken down. No man can half understand or half operate the fullness of this big citizenship, except by giving his whole time to it. This the place hunter can do, and the privilege hunter. Government, therefore – municipal, State, national – is passing into the hands of these two classes, especialized for the functions of power by their appetite for the fruits of power. The power of citizenship is relinquished by those who do not and cannot know how to exercise it to those who can and do – by those who have a livelihood to make to those who make politics their livelihood.

These specialists of the ward club, the primary, the campaign, the election, and office unite, by a law as irresistible as that of the sexes, with those who want all the goods of government – charters, contracts, rulings, permits. From this marriage it is easy to imagine that among some other people than ourselves, and in some other century than this, the offspring might be the most formidable, elusive, unrestrained, impersonal, and cruel tyranny the world has yet seen. There might come a time when the policeman and the railroad president would equally show that they cared nothing for the citizen, individually or collectively, because aware that they and not he were the government. Certainly such an attempt to corner 'the dear people' and the earth and the fullness thereof will break down. It is for us to decide whether we will let it go on till it breaks down of itself, dragging down to die, as a savage dies of his vice, the civilization it has gripped with its hundred hands; or whether, while we are still young, still virtuous, we will break it down, self-consciously, as the civilized man, reforming, crushes down the evil. If we cannot find a remedy, all that we love in the word America must die. It will be an awful price to pay if this attempt at government of the people, by the people, for the people must perish from off the face of the earth to prove to mankind that political brotherhood cannot survive where industrial brotherhood is denied. But the demonstration is worth even that.

Aristotle's lost books of the Republics told the story of two hundred and fifty attempts at free government, and these were but some of the many that had to be melted down in the crucible of fate to teach Hamilton and Jefferson what they knew. Perhaps we must be melted by the same fierce flames to be a light to the feet of those who come after us. For as true as that a house divided against itself cannot stand, and that a nation half slave and half free cannot permanently endure, is it true that a people who are slaves to market-tyrants will surely come to be their slaves in all else, that all liberty begins to be lost when one liberty is lost, that a people half democratic and half plutocratic cannot permanently endure.

1.5 THE GOLD 'CONSPIRACY'

Extracts from key portions of William Jennings Bryan's speech given before the Democratic Convention at Chicago, *8 July 1896.*

At the 1896 Convention William Jennings Bryan made one of the most famous speeches in American history, known thereafter as the 'Cross of Gold' speech. In it Bryan routed the Gold Democrats with the Biblical fervour of a fundamentalist preacher. William Jennings Bryan (1860–1925) was born and raised in the American Mid West. In the 1880s he was active in Nebraska politics and was elected to the United States Congress in 1890 and 1892 as a Democrat. At the party convention in 1896, held at Chicago, in the heart of the Mid West, a bitterly divisive issue came to a head. The issue was bimetallism, and two blocks of delegates met in open conflict for control of the convention. The Silver delegates were for the free coinage of silver, whilst the Gold delegates demanded a single currency, tied to a gold standard. The quarrel was in fact a sectional one, with the agrarian West and South (for bimetallism) opposed by the industrial and commercial North and East (for gold).

... Never before in the history of American politics has a great issue been fought out as this issue has been, by the voters of a great party. On 4 March 1895 a few Democrats, most of them members of Congress, issued an address to the Democrats of the nation, asserting that the money question was the paramount issue of the hour; declaring that a majority of the Democratic party had the right to control the action of the party on this paramount issue; and concluding with the request that the believers in the free coinage of silver in the Democratic party should organize, take charge of, and control the policy of the Democratic party. Three months later, at Memphis, an organization was perfected, and the silver Democrats went forth openly and courageously proclaiming their belief, and declaring that, if successful, they would crystallize into a platform the declaration which they had made. Then began the conflict. With a zeal approaching the zeal which inspired the crusaders who followed Peter the Hermit, our silver Democrats went forth from victory unto victory until they are now assembled, not to discuss, not to debate, but to enter up the judgement already rendered by the plain people of this country. In this contest brother has been arrayed against brother, father against son. The warmest ties of love, acquaintance and association have been disregarded; old leaders have been cast aside when they have refused to give expression to the sentiments of those whom they would lead, and new leaders have sprung up to give direction to this cause of truth. Thus has the contest been waged, and we have assembled here under as binding and solemn instructions as were ever imposed upon representatives of the people. . . . When you [turning to the gold delegates] come before us and tell us that we are about to disturb your business interests, we reply that you have disturbed our business interests by your course.

We say to you that you have made the definition of a business man too limited in its application. The man who is employed for wages is as much a business man as his employer; the attorney in a country town is as much a business man as the corporation counsel in a great metropolis; the merchant at the crossroads store is as much a business man as the merchant of New York; the farmer who goes forth in the morning and toils all day – who begins in the spring and toils all summer – and who by the application of brain and muscle to the natural resources of the country creates wealth, is as much a business man as the man who goes upon the board of trade and bets upon the price of grain; the miners who go down a thousand feet into the earth, or climb two thousand feet upon the cliffs, and bring forth from their hiding places the precious metals to be poured into the channels of trade are as much business men as the few financial magnates who, in a back room, corner the money of the world. We come to speak for this broader class of business men.

Ah, my friends, we say not one word against those who live upon the Atlantic coast, but the hardy pioneers who have braved all the dangers of the wilderness, who have made the desert to blossom as the rose – the pioneers away out there [pointing to the West], who rear their children near to Nature's heart, where they can mingle their voices with the voices of the birds – out there where they have erected schoolhouses for the education of their young, churches where they praise their Creator, and cemeteries where rest the ashes of their dead – these people, we say, are as deserving of the consideration of our party as any people in this country. It is for these that we speak. We do not come as aggressors. Our war is not a war of conquest; we are fighting in the defence of our homes, our families, and posterity. We have petitioned, and our petitions have been scorned; we have entreated, and our entreaties have been disregarded; we have begged, and they have mocked when our calamity came. We beg no longer; we entreat no more; we petition no more. We defy them. . . .

We go forth confident that we shall win. Why? Because upon the paramount issue of this campaign there is not a spot of ground upon which the enemy will dare to challenge battle. If they tell us that the gold standard is a good thing, we shall point to their platform and tell them that their platform pledges the party to get rid of the gold standard and substitute bimetallism. If the gold standard is a good thing, why try to get rid of it? I call your attention to the fact that some of the very people who are in this convention today and who tell us that we ought to declare in favour of international bimetallism – thereby declaring that the gold standard is wrong and that the principle of bimetallism is better – these very people four months ago were open and avowed advocates of the gold standard, and were then telling us that we could not legislate two metals together, even with the aid of all the world. If the gold standard is a good thing, we ought to declare in favour of its retention and not in favour of abandoning it; and if the gold standard is a bad thing why should we wait until other nations are willing to help us to let go? Here is the line of battle, and we care not upon which issue they force the fight; we are prepared to meet them on either issue or on both. If they tell us that the gold standard is the standard of civilization, we reply to them that this, the most enlightened of all the nations of the earth, has never declared for a gold standard and that both the great parties this year are declaring against it. If the gold standard is the standard of civilization, why, my friends, should we not have it? If they come to meet us on that issue we can present the history of our nation. More than that; we can tell them that they will search the pages of history in vain to find a single instance where the common people of any land have ever declared themselves in favour of the gold standard. They can find where the holders of fixed investments have declared for a gold standard, but not where the masses have.

Mr Carlisle* said in 1878 that this was a struggle between 'the idle holders of idle capital' and 'the struggling masses, who produce the wealth and pay the taxes of the country'; and, my friends, the question we are to decide is: Upon which side will the Democratic party fight; upon the side of 'the idle holders of idle capital' or upon the side of 'the struggling masses'? That is the question which the party must answer first, and then it must be answered by each individual hereafter. The sympathies of the Democratic party, as shown by the platform, are on the side of the struggling masses who have ever been the foundation of the Democratic party. There are those who believe that, if you will only legislate to make the well-to-do prosperous, their prosperity will leak through on those below. The Democratic idea, however, has been that if you legislate to make the masses prosperous, their prosperity will find its way up through every class which rests upon them.

You come to us and tell us that the great cities are in favour of the gold standard; we reply that the great cities rest upon our broad and fertile prairies. Burn down your cities and leave our farms, and your cities will spring up again as if by magic; but destroy our farms and the grass will grow in the streets of every city in the country.

My friends, we declare that this nation is able to legislate for its own people on every question, without waiting for the aid or consent of any other nation on earth; and upon that issue we expect to carry every State in the Union. I shall not slander the inhabitants of the fair State of Massachusetts nor the inhabitants of the State of New York by saying that, when they are confronted with the proposition, they will declare that this nation is not able to attend to its own business. It is the issue of 1776 over again. Our ancestors, when but three millions in number, had the courage to declare their political independence of every other nation; shall we, their descendants, when we have grown to seventy millions, declare that we are less independent than our forefathers? No, my friends, that will never be the verdict of our people. Therefore, we care not upon what lines the battle is fought. If they say bimetallism is good, but that we cannot have it until other nations help us, we reply that,

* John G. Carlisle (1835–1910), Democratic Congressman (1877–90), Speaker of the House of Representatives (1883–90) and Secretary of the Treasury (1893–6). Active in tariff reform and a strong supporter of 'sound money' policies.

instead of having a gold standard because England has, we will restore bimetallism, and then let England have bimetallism because the United States has it. If they dare to come out in the open field and defend the gold standard as a good thing, we will fight them to the uttermost. Having behind us the producing masses of this nation and the world, supported by the commercial interests, the labouring interests, and the toilers everywhere, we will answer their demand for a gold standard by saying to them: You shall not press down upon the brow of labour this crown of thorns, you shall not crucify mankind upon a cross of gold.

1.6 SOCIALIST PLATFORM

The following is an extract from the 1912 platform of the Socialist Party of America.

The Socialist Labor platform was no less militant in the same year. The notion that there is no socialist tradition in the United States is a mistaken one. A number of socialist parties were organized in the late nineteenth century, at the local and at the national level. The Socialist Labor Party (formed 1874), the Socialist Workers' Party, and the Socialist Party (founded 1901) have each survived to the present. Their rhetoric has always been extremely militant.

The Socialist party declares that the capitalist system has outgrown its historical function, and has become utterly incapable of meeting the problems now confronting society. We denounce this outgrown system as incompetent and corrupt and the source of unspeakable misery and suffering to the whole working class.

Under this system the industrial equipment of the nation has passed into the absolute control of a plutocracy which exacts an annual tribute of hundreds of millions of dollars from the producers. Unafraid of any organized resistance, it stretches out its greedy hands over the still undeveloped resources of the nation – the land, the mines, the forests and the water-powers of every State in the Union.

In spite of the multiplication of labour-saving machines and improved methods in industry which cheapen the cost of production, the share of the producers grows ever less, and the prices of all the necessities of life steadily increase. The boasted prosperity of this nation is for the owning class alone. To the rest it means only greater hardship and misery. The high cost of living is felt in every home. Millions of wage-workers have seen the purchasing power of their wages decrease until life has become a desperate battle for mere existence.

Multitudes of unemployed walk the streets of our cities or trudge from State to State awaiting the will of the masters to move the wheels of industry.

The farmers in every state are plundered by the increasing prices exacted for tools and machinery and by extortionate rents, freight rates and storage charges.

Capitalist concentration is mercilessly crushing the class of small business men and driving its members into the ranks of property-less wage-workers. The overwhelming majority of the people of America are being forced under a yoke of bondage by this soulless industrial despotism.

It is this capitalist system that is responsible for the increasing burden of armaments, the poverty, slums, child labour, most of the insanity, crime and prostitution, and much of the disease that afflicts mankind.

Under this system the working class is exposed to poisonous conditions, to frightful and needless perils to life and limb, is walled around with court decisions, injunctions and unjust laws, and is preyed upon incessantly for the benefit of the controlling oligarchy of wealth. Under it also, the children of the working class are doomed to ignorance, drudging toil and darkened lives. . . .

We declare, therefore, that the longer sufferance of these conditions is impossible, and we propose to end them all. We declare them to be the product of the present system in which industry is carried on for private greed, instead of for the welfare of society. We declare, furthermore, that for these evils there will be and can be no remedy and no substantial relief except through Socialism under which industry will be carried on for the common good and every worker receive the full social value of the wealth he creates.

Society is divided into warring groups and classes, based upon material interests. Fundamentally, this struggle is a conflict between the two main classes, one of which, the capitalist class, owns the means of production, and the other, the working class, must use these means of production on terms dictated by the owners.

The capitalist class, though few in numbers, absolutely controls the government – legislative, executive and judicial. This class owns the machinery of gathering and disseminating news through its organized press. It subsidizes seats of learning – the colleges and schools – and even religious and moral agencies. It has also the added prestige which established customs give to any order of society, right or wrong.

The working class, which includes all those who are forced to work for a living, whether by hand or brain, in shop, mine or on the soil, vastly outnumbers the capitalist class. Lacking effective organization and class solidarity, this class is unable to enforce its will. Given such a class solidarity and effective organization, the workers will have the power to make all laws and control all industry in their own interest.

All political parties are the expression of economic class interests. All other parties than the Socialist party represent one or another group of the ruling capitalist class. Their political conflicts reflect merely superficial rivalries between competing capitalist groups. However they result, these conflicts have no issue of real value to the workers. Whether the Democrats or Republicans win politically, it is the capitalist class that is victorious economically.

The Socialist party is the political expression of the economic interests of the workers. Its defeats have been their defeats and its victories their victories. It is a party founded on the science and laws of social development. It proposes that, since all social necessities today are socially produced, the means of their production and distribution shall be socially owned and democratically controlled.

In the face of the economic and political aggressions of the capitalist class the only reliance left the workers is that of their economic organizations and their political power. By the intelligent and class-conscious use of these, they may resist successfully the capitalist class, break the fetters of wage-slavery, and fit themselves for the future society, which is to displace the capitalist system. The Socialist party appreciates the full significance of class organization and urges the wage-earners, the working farmers and all other useful workers to organize for economic and political action, and we pledge ourselves to support the toilers of the fields as well as those in the shops, factories and mines of the nation in their struggles for economic justice.

In the defeat or victory of the working class party in this new struggle for freedom lies the defeat or triumph of the common people of all economic groups, as well as the failure or triumph of popular government. Thus the Socialist party is the party of the present-day revolution which marks the transition from economic individualism to socialism, from wage slavery to free co-operation, from capitalist oligarchy to industrial democracy.

WORKING PROGRAM

As measures calculated to strengthen the working class in its fight for the realization of its ultimate aim, the co-operative commonwealth, and to increase its power of resistance against capitalist oppression, we advocate and pledge ourselves and our elected officers to the following programme:

Collective Ownership

1. The collective ownership and democratic management of railroads, wire and wireless telegraphs and telephones, express service, steamboat lines, and all other social means of transportation and communication and of all large-scale industries.

2. The immediate acquirement by the municipalities, the states or the federal government of all grain elevators, stock yards, storage warehouses, and other distributing agencies, in order to reduce the present extortionate cost of living.

3. The extension of the public domain to include mines, quarries, oil wells, forests and water power.

4. The further conservation and development of natural resources for the use and benefit of all the people:

(a) By scientific forestation and timber protection.

(b) By the reclamation of arid and swamp tracts.

(c) By the storage of flood waters and the utilization of water power.

(d) By the stoppage of the present extravagant waste of the soil and of the products of mines and oil wells.

(e) By the development of highway and waterway systems.

5. The collective ownership of land wherever practicable, and in cases where such ownership is impracticable, the appropriation by taxation of the annual rental value of all land held for speculation or exploitation.

6. The collective ownership and democratic management of the banking and currency system.

Unemployment

The immediate government relief of the unemployed by the extension of all useful public works. All persons employed on such works to be engaged directly by the government under a work day of not more than eight hours and at not less than the prevailing union wages. The government also to establish employment bureaus; to lend money to states and municipalities without interest for the purpose of carrying on public works, and to take such other measures within its power as will lessen the widespread misery of the workers caused by the misrule of the capitalist class.

Industrial Demands

The conservation of human resources, particularly of the lives and well-being of the workers and their families:

1. By shortening the work day in keeping with the increased productiveness of machinery.

2. By securing to every worker a rest period of not less than a day and a half in each week.

3. By securing a more effective inspection of workshops, factories and mines.

4. By forbidding the employment of children under sixteen years of age.

5. By the co-operative organization of the industries in the federal penitentiaries for the benefit of the convicts and their dependents.

6. By forbidding the interstate transportation of the products of child labour, of convict labour and of all uninspected factories and mines.

7. By abolishing the profit system in government work and substituting either the direct hire of labour or the awarding of contracts to co-operative groups of workers.

8. By establishing minimum wage scales.

9. By abolishing official charity and substituting a non-contributory system of old age pensions, a general system of insurance by the State of all its members against unemployment and invalidism and a system of compulsory insurance by employers of their workers, without cost to the latter, against industrial diseases, accidents and death.

Political Demands

1. The absolute freedom of press, speech and assemblage.

2. The adoption of a graduated income-tax, the increase of the rates of the present corporation tax and the extension of inheritance taxes, graduated in proportion to the value of the estate and to nearness of kin – the proceeds of these taxes to be employed in the socialization of industry.

3. The abolition of the monopoly ownership of patents and the substitution of collective ownership, with direct rewards to inventors by premiums or royalties.

4. Unrestricted and equal suffrage for men and women.*

5. The adoption of the initiative, referendum and recall and of proportional representation, nationally as well as locally.†

6. The abolition of the Senate and of the veto power of the President.‡

7. The election of the President and Vice-President by direct vote of the people.

8. The abolition of the power usurped by the Supreme Court of the United States to pass upon the constitutionality of the legislation enacted by Congress. National laws to be repealed only by act of Congress or by a referendum vote of the whole people.

9. Abolition of the present restrictions upon the amendment of the constitution, so that instrument may be made amendable by a majority of the voters in a majority of the States.§

10. The granting of the right of suffrage in the District of Columbia with representation in Congress and a democratic form of municipal government for purely local affairs. ‖

11. The extension of democratic government to all United States territory.

12. The enactment of further measures for general education

* Women's suffrage was granted under the 19th Amendment to the US Constitution, ratified 26 August 1920.

† The 'Initiative'. An electoral device by which citizens may propose legislation when supported by a specified number of signatures. A number of States have adopted, and retain the device, but it has never existed at the Federal level. The 'Recall'. A device whereby public officials may be removed from office by means of a citizens' petition, followed by a public vote.

‡ In 1912 the Senate was elected indirectly by State legislatures, deeply conservative. The 17th Amendment (1913) brought election by popular vote.

§ For the amendment procedure see Article V of the Constitution.

‖ The right of suffrage for citizens of the District of Columbia was granted by the 23rd Amendment to the Constitution, ratified 29 March 1961.

and particularly for vocational education in useful pursuits. The Bureau of Education to be made a Department.

13. The enactment of further measures for the conservation of health. The creation of an independent bureau of health, with such restrictions as will secure full liberty to all schools of practice.

14. The separation of the present Bureau of Labor from the Department of Commerce and Labor and its elevation to the rank of a department.

15. Abolition of all federal district courts and the United States circuit courts of appeals. State courts to have jurisdiction in all cases arising between citizens of the several states and foreign corporations. The election of all judges for short terms.

16. The immediate curbing of the power of the courts to issue injunctions.

17. The free administration of the law.

18. The calling of a convention for the revision of the constitution of the United States.

Such measures of relief as we may be able to force from capitalism are but a preparation of the workers to seize the whole powers of government, in order that they may thereby lay hold of the whole system of socialized industry and thus come to their rightful inheritance.

1.7 CHIEF MUCKRAKER

An extract from the Introduction to Lincoln Steffens's The Shame of Cities, *1904.*

Lincoln Steffens (1866–1936) introduced a form of political commentary which came to be known as 'Muckraking'. Theodore Roosevelt coined the phrase as a description of the rhetorical, alarmist style Steffens used in order to arouse Americans to the political corruption entrenched in their cities. Steffens's articles first appeared in *McClure's Magazine* (New York), but he collected them under the title *The Shame of the Cities* (1904). He could certainly claim to have aroused, if not alarmed, American citizens to the state of their cities, and the reform administrations which came into being thereafter owed something to the caustic journalism of Lincoln Steffens.

When I set out on my travels, an honest New Yorker told me honestly that I would find that the Irish, the Catholic Irish, were at the bottom of it all everywhere. The first city I went to was St Louis, a German city. The next was Minneapolis, a Scandinavian city, with a leadership of New Englanders. Then came Pittsburg, Scotch Presbyterian, and that was what my New York friend was. 'Ah, but they are all foreign populations,' I heard. The next city was Philadelphia, the purest American community of all, and the most hopeless. And after that came Chicago and New York, both mongrel-bred, but the one a triumph of reform, the other the best example of good government that I had seen. The 'foreign element' excuse is one of the hypocritical lies that save us from the clear sight of ourselves.

Another such conceit of our egotism is that which deplores our politics and lauds our business. This is the wail of the typical American citizen. Now, the typical American citizen is the business man. The typical business man is a bad citizen; he is busy. If he is a 'big business man' and very busy, he does not neglect, he is busy with politics, oh, very busy and very businesslike. I found him buying boodlers in St Louis, defending grafters in Minneapolis, originating corruption in Pittsburg, sharing with bosses in Philadelphia, deploring reform in Chicago, and beating good government with corruption funds in New York. He is a self-righteous fraud, this big business man. He is the chief source of corruption, and it were a boon if he would neglect politics. But he is not the business man that neglects politics; that worthy is the good citizen, the typical business man. He too is busy, he is the one that has no use and therefore no time for politics. When his neglect has permitted bad government to go so far that he can be stirred to action, he is unhappy, and he looks around for a cure that shall be quick, so that he may hurry back to the shop. Naturally, too, when he talks politics, he talks shop. His patent remedy is quack; it is business.

'Give us a business man,' he says ('like me,' he means). 'Let him introduce business methods into politics and government; then I shall be left alone to attend to my business.'

There is hardly an office from United States Senator down to

53

Alderman in any part of the country to which the business man has not been elected; yet politics remains corrupt, government pretty bad, and the selfish citizen has to hold himself in readiness like the old volunteer firemen to rush forth at any hour, in any weather, to prevent the fire; and he goes out sometimes and he puts out the fire (after the damage is done) and he goes back to the shop sighing for the business man in politics. The business man has failed in politics as he has in citizenship. Why?

Because politics is business. That's what's the matter with it. That's what's the matter with everything – art, literature, religion, journalism, law, medicine – they're all business, and all – as you see them. Make politics a sport, as they do in England, or a profession, as they do in Germany, and we'll have – well, something else than we have now – if we want it, which is another question. But don't try to reform politics with the banker, the lawyer, and the dry-goods merchant, for these are business men and there are two great hindrances to their achievement of reform: one is that they are different from, but no better than, the politicians; the other is that politics is not 'their line'. There are exceptions both ways. Many politicians have gone out into business and done well (Tammany ex-mayors, and nearly all the old bosses of Philadelphia are prominent financiers in their cities), and business men have gone into politics and done well (Mark Hanna, for example). They haven't reformed their adopted trades, however, though they have sometimes sharpened them most pointedly. The politican is a business man with a specialty. When a business man of some other line learns the business of politics, he is a politician, and there is not much reform left in him. Consider the United States Senate, and believe me.

The commercial spirit is the spirit of profit, not patriotism; of credit, not honour; of individual gain, not national prosperity; of trade and dickering, not principle. 'My business is sacred,' says the business man in his heart. 'Whatever prospers my business, is good; it must be. Whatever hinders it, is wrong; it must be. A bribe is bad, that is, it is a bad thing to take; but it is not so bad to give one, not if it is necessary to my business.' 'Business is business' is not a political sentiment, but our politician has caught it. He takes essentially the same view of the bribe, only he saves his self-respect by piling all his contempt upon the bribe-giver, and he has the great advantage of candour. 'It is wrong, maybe,' he says, 'but if a rich merchant can afford to do business with me for the sake of a convenience or to increase his already great wealth, I can afford, for the sake of a living, to meet him half-way. I make no pretensions to virtue, not even on Sunday.' And as for giving bad government or good, how about the merchant who gives bad goods or good goods, according to the demand?

But there is hope, not alone despair, in the commercialism of our politics. If our political leaders are to be always a lot of political merchants, they will supply any demand we may create. All we have to do is to establish a steady demand for good government. The bosses have us split up into parties. To him parties are nothing but means to his corrupt ends. He 'bolts' his party, but we must not; the bribe-giver changes his party, from one election to another, from one county to another, from one city to another, but the honest voter must not. Why? Because if the honest voter cared no more for his party than the politician and the grafter, then the honest vote would govern, and that would be bad – for graft. It is idiotic, this devotion to a machine that is used to take our sove-reignty from us. If we would leave parties to the politicians, and would vote not for the party, not even for men, but for the city, and the State, and the nation, we should rule parties, and cities, and States, and nation. If we would vote in mass on the more promising ticket, or, if the two are equally bad, would throw out the party that is in, and wait till the next election and then throw out the other party that is in – then, I say, the commercial politician would feel a demand for good government and he would supply it. That process would take a generation or more to complete, for the politicians now really do not know what good government is. But it has taken as long to develop bad government, and the politicians know what that is. If it would not 'go', they would offer something else, and, if the demand were steady, they, being so commercial, would 'deliver the goods'.

But do the people want good government? Tammany says they don't.* Are the people honest? Are the people better than Tammany? Are they better than the merchant and the politician? Isn't our corrupt government, after all, representative?

President Roosevelt has been sneered at for going about the

* Tammany – i.e. Tammany Hall in New York City, which housed one of the most famous, or infamous, political machines in the history of American politics.

country preaching, as a cure for our American evils, good conduct in the individual, simple honesty, courage, and efficiency. 'Platitudes!' the sophisticated say. Platitudes? If my observations have been true, the literal adoption of Mr Roosevelt's reform scheme would result in a revolution, more radical and terrible to existing institutions, from the Congress to the Church, from the bank to the ward organization, than socialism or even than anarchy.

1.8 REFORMERS DIVIDED

From Herbert Croly, The Promise of American Life, *1909, pp. 145–7.*

Herbert Croly (1869–1930) was a vigorous journalist who helped to found the *New Republic* in 1914. This weekly often took up the cause of reform for many aspects of American life, but in a book which attracted wide attention, *The Promise of American Life* (1909) Croly reminded his readers that reformers by themselves could achieve little.

Reformers have always tended to believe that their agitation ought to be and essentially was non-partisan. They considered it inconceivable either that patriotic American citizens should hesitate about restoring the purity and vigour of American institutions, or such an object should not appeal to every disinterested man, irrespective of party. It was a fight between the law and its violators, between the Faithful and the Heretic, between the Good and the Wicked. In such a fight there was, of course, only one side to take. It was not to be doubted that the honest men, who constitute, of course, an enormous majority of the 'plain people', would rally to the banners of reform. The rascals would be turned out; the people would regain their economic opportunities and political rights; and the American democracy would pursue undefiled its triumphant career of legalized prosperity.

These hopes have never been realized. Reform has rarely been non-partisan – except in the minds of its more innocent advocates. Now and then an agitation for municipal reform in a particular city will suffer a spasm of non-partisanship; but the reformers soon develop such lively differences among themselves, that they separate into special groups or else resume their regular party ties. Their common conception of reform as fundamentally a moral awakening, which seeks to restore the American political and economic system to its early purity and vigour, does not help them to unity of action or to unity in the framing of a remedial policy. Different reformers really mean something very different by the traditional system, from which American practice has departed and which they propose to restore. Some of them mean thereby a condition of spiritual excellence, which will be restored by a sort of politico-moral revivalism and which will somehow make the results of divine and popular election coincide. Others mean nothing more than the rigid enforcement of existing laws. Still others mean a new legal expression of the traditional democratic principle, framed to meet the new political and social conditions; but the reformers who agree upon this last conception of reform disagree radically as to what the new legal expression should be. The traditional system, which they seek to restore, assumes almost as many shapes as there are leading reformers; and as the reforming movement develops, the disagreements among the reformers become more instead of less definite and acute.

The inability of the reformers to co-operate in action or to agree as to the application of their principles is in part merely a natural result of their essential work. Reformers are primarily protestants; and protestants are naturally insubordinate. They have been protesting against the established order in American business and politics. Their protest implies a certain degree of moral and intellectual independence, which makes them dislike to surrender or subordinate their own personal opinions and manner of action. Such independence is a new and refreshing thing, which has suddenly made American politics much more interesting and significant than it has been at any time since the Civil War. It has a high value wholly apart from its immediate political results. It means that the American people are beginning a new phase of their political experience – a phase in which there will be room for a much freer play of individual ability and character. Inevitably the sudden realization by certain exceptional politicians that they have a right to be individuals, and that they can take a strong line of their own in politics without being disqualified for practical political association with their fellow-countrymen – such a new light could hardly break without tempting the performers to over-play the part. The fact that they have over-played their parts, and have wasted time and energy over meaningless and unnecessary disagreements is not in itself a matter of much importance. The great majority of them are disinterested and patriotic men, who will not allow in the long run either personal ambition or political crotchets to prevent them from co-operating for the good of the cause.

Unfortunately, however, neither public spirit nor patriotism will be sufficient to bring them effectively together – any more than genuine excellence of intention and real public spirit enabled patriotic Americans to co-operate upon a remedial policy during the years immediately preceding the Civil War. The plain fact is that the traditional American political system, which so many good reformers wish to restore by some sort of reforming revivalism, is just as much responsible for the existing political and economic abuses as the Constitution was responsible for the evil of slavery. As long, consequently, as reform is considered to be a species of higher conservatism, the existing abuses can no more be frankly faced and fully understood than the Whig leaders were able to face and understand the full meaning and consequences of any attempt on the part of a democracy to keep house with slavery. The first condition of a better understanding and a more efficient co-operation among the reforming leaders is a better understanding of the meaning of reform and the function of reformers. They will never be united on the basis of allegiance to the traditional American political creed, because that creed itself is overflowing with inconsistencies and ambiguities, which afford a footing for almost every extreme of radicalism and conservatism; and in case they persist in the attempt to reform political and economic abuses merely by a restoration of earlier conditions and methods, they will be compromising much that is good in the present economic and political organization without recovering that which was good in the past.

2 *Individualists*

2.1 'THE PUBLIC BE DAMNED'

The following extract, which begins with the reporter's questions to
Vanderbilt, appeared in The Chicago Daily News, *9 October 1882*

William H. Vanderbilt was one of several railroad proprietors who
made huge fortunes in the second half of the nineteenth century, as
America expanded westwards. His celebrated remark 'The public
be damned' was delivered during an interview with a newspaper
reporter in 1882. Although Vanderbilt's *obiter dictum* made
headlines, it was entirely in keeping with the spirit of commercial
enterprise operating in America at that time.

'Do you think that there is any probability of a lower rate being
charged between the east and west for passenger traffic?'

'No, I do not. The passenger traffic is only a small part of the
business of the railroads. No lower rates could be made to pay
between New York and Chicago. Why, sir, do you know that not
over 150 passengers are sent from Chicago to New York per day
over all the east-bound roads? Of course, if any one road could
have all this business, it could afford to carry them for $15 a head.'

'Does your limited express pay?'

'No; not a bit of it. We only run it because we are forced to do so
by the action of the Pennsylvania road. It doesn't pay expenses. We
would abandon it if it was not for our competitor keeping its train
on.'

'But don't you run it for the public benefit?'

'The public be d——d. What does the public care for the railroads except to get as much out of them for as small a consideration as possible? I don't take any stock in this silly nonsense about working for anybody's good but our own, because we are not. When we make a move we do it because it is our interest to do so, not because we expect to do somebody else some good. Of course we like to do everything possible for the benefit of humanity in general, but when we do, we first see that we are benefiting ourselves. Railroads are not run on sentiment, but on business principles, and to pay, and I don't mean to be egotistic when I say that the roads which I have had anything to do with have generally paid pretty well.'

'Referring to wages paid your employees,' said the reporter, 'do you consider that they are generally what they should be?'

'Yes, I do. There is always a lot of shiftless fellows who spend their money in drink and riotous living, who are ready to complain of anything; but, now take the employees on the New York Central & Hudson River railroads. Among them we have between six and seven hundred engineers who earn from $4 to $5 a day. These men are the best which we have in our employ, and are almost all of them members of the Brotherhood of Engineers, which I consider to be an excellent organization. When any differences of opinion occur between our company and employees, we are always ready to hear them and consider their requests, and when they are reasonable we grant them. When we are making 12 shillings we are always willing to pay our men 10 shillings, but when we make only 12 we don't pay 14. Our men know this, and they are generally satisfied, and we have little difficulty with them.'

'What do you think of this anti-monopoly movement?'

'It is a movement inspired by a set of fools and blackmailers. To be sure, there are some men interested in it whose motives are good, if their sense is not. When I want to buy up any politician I always find the anti-monopolists the most purchasable – they don't come so high. . . .'

2.2 THE IMPACT OF DARWIN

The publication of Charles Darwin's *Origin of Species* (1859) and *The Descent of Man* (1871) profoundly affected the intellectual climate of the United States. Darwin's theories on natural selection and the survival of the fittest were welcomed – and usually misrepresented – by many Americans who had particular axes to grind. These included racialists, anxious to establish that Negroes were a separate (and lower) category of being; industrialists and monopolists seeking to prove that in human society, as in animal society, the race is to the strong and the weak must be vanquished; and Americans of Anglo-Saxon parentage anxious to limit, or even prohibit, a further influx of immigrant peoples from southern or eastern Europe.

Darwinism produced some curious and exotic blooms in the era of imperialism and expansionism in America. Richard Hofstadter gives a detailed treatment of one major species – Social Darwinism – in his important book *Social Darwinism in American Thought* (1st ed. 1944). In the following pages, two examples of misapplied Darwinism are given from the many tracts which erupted in the United States in the 1880s and 1890s.

2.2.1 SOCIAL DARWINISM

Extracts from William Graham Sumner, What Social Classes Owe to Each Other, *1883, Chapters 1, 2 and concluding chapter.*

William Graham Sumner (1840–1910) was an ardent supporter of *laissez-faire*. As a Social Darwinist, he argued that men should be free to compete against each other so that the strong should thrive and the race improve with each succeeding generation. Different groups in society could not be said to owe anything to each other beyond normal human respect and good will. Sumner argued this at length in *What Social Classes Owe to Each Other* (1883).

[Chapter 1]
It is commonly asserted that there are in the United States no

classes, and any allusion to classes is resented. On the other hand, we constantly read and hear discussions of social topics in which the existence of social classes is assumed as a simple fact. 'The poor', 'the weak', 'the labourers', are expressions which are used as if they had exact and well-understood definition. Discussions are made to bear upon the assumed rights, wrongs, and misfortunes of certain social classes; and all public speaking and writing consists, in a large measure, of the discussion of general plans for meeting the wishes of classes of people who have not been able to satisfy their own desires. These classes are sometimes discontented, and sometimes not. Sometimes they do not know that anything is amiss with them until the 'friends of humanity' come to them with offers of aid. Sometimes they are discontented and envious. They do not take their achievements as a fair measure of their rights. They do not blame themselves or their parents for their lot, as compared with that of other people. Sometimes they claim that they have a right to everything of which they feel the need for their happiness on earth. To make such a claim against God or Nature would, of course, be only to say that we claim a right to live on earth if we can. But God and Nature have ordained the chances and conditions of life on earth once for all. The case cannot be re-opened. We cannot get a revision of the laws of human life. We are absolutely shut up to the need and duty, if we would learn how to live happily, of investigating the laws of Nature, and deducing the rules of right living in the world as it is. These are very wearisome and commonplace tasks. They consist in labour and self-denial repeated over and over again in learning and doing. When the people whose claims we are considering are told to apply themselves to these tasks they become irritated and feel almost insulted. They formulate their claims as rights against society – that is, against some other men. In their view they have a right, not only to pursue happiness, but to *get* it; and if they fail to get it, they think they have a claim to the aid of other men – that is, to the labour and self-denial of other men – to get it for them. They find orators and poets who tell them that they have grievances, so long as they have unsatisfied desires. . . .

Certain ills belong to the hardship of human life. They are natural. They are part of the struggle with Nature for existence. We cannot blame our fellow-men for our share of these. My neighbour and I are both struggling to free ourselves from these ills. The fact that my neighbour has succeeded in this struggle better than I constitutes no grievance for me. Certain other ills are due to the malice of men, and to the imperfections or errors of civil institutions. These ills are an object of agitation, and a subject of discussion. The former class of ills is to be met only by manly effort and energy; the latter may be corrected by associated effort. The former class of ills is constantly grouped and generalized, and made the object of social schemes. We shall see, as we go on, what that means. The second class of ills may fall on certain social classes, and reform will take the form of interference by other classes in favour of that one. The last fact is, no doubt, the reason why people have been led, not noticing distinctions, to believe that the same method was applicable to the other class of ills. The distinction here made between the ills which belong to the struggle for existence and those which are due to the faults of human institutions is of prime importance.

It will also be important, in order to clear up our ideas about the notions which are in fashion, to note the relation of the economic to the political significance of assumed duties of one class to another. That is to say, we may discuss the question whether one class owes duties to another by reference to the economic effects which will be produced on the classes and society; or we may discuss the political expediency of formulating and enforcing rights and duties respectively between the parties. In the former case we might assume that the givers of aid were willing to give it, and we might discuss the benefit or mischief of their activity. In the other case we must assume that some at least of those who were forced to give aid did so unwillingly. Here, then, there would be a question of rights. The question whether voluntary charity is mischievous or not is one thing; the question whether legislation which forces one man to aid another is right and wise, as well as economically beneficial, is quite another question. Great confusion and consequent error is produced by allowing these two questions to become entangled in the discussion. Especially we shall need to notice the attempts to apply legislative methods of reform to the ills which belong to the order of Nature.

There is no possible definition of 'a poor man'. A pauper is a person who cannot earn his living; whose producing powers have fallen positively below his necessary consumption; who cannot, therefore, pay his way. A human society needs the active co-operation and productive energy of every person in it. A man who is present as a consumer, yet who does not contribute either by land, labour, or capital to the work of society, is a burden. On no sound political theory ought such a person to share in the political power of the State. He drops out of the ranks of workers and producers. Society must support him. It accepts the burden, but he must be cancelled from the ranks of the rulers likewise. So much for the pauper. About him no more need be said. But he is not the 'poor man'. The 'poor man' is an elastic term, under which any number of social fallacies may be hidden.

Neither is there any possible definition of 'the weak'. Some are weak in one way, and some in another; and those who are weak in one sense are strong in another. In general, however, it may be said that those whom humanitarians and philanthropists call the weak are the ones through whom the productive and conservative forces of society are wasted. They constantly neutralize and destroy the finest efforts of the wise and industrious, and are a dead-weight on the society in all its struggles to realize any better things. Whether the people who mean no harm, but are weak in the essential powers necessary to the performance of one's duties in life, or those who are malicious and vicious, do the more mischief, is a question not easy to answer.

Under the names of the poor and the weak, the negligent, shiftless, inefficient, silly, and imprudent are fastened upon the industrious and prudent as a responsibility and a duty. On the one side, the terms are extended to cover the idle, intemperate, and vicious, who, by the combination, gain credit which they do not deserve, and which they could not get if they stood alone. On the other hand, the terms are extended to include wagereceivers of the humblest rank, who are degraded by the combination. The reader who desires to guard himself against fallacies should always scrutinize the terms 'poor' and 'weak' as used, so as to see which or how many of these classes they are made to cover.

The humanitarians, philanthropists, and reformers, looking at the facts of life as they present themselves, find enough which is sad and unpromising in the condition of many members of society. They see wealth and poverty side by side. They note great inequality of social position and social chances. They eagerly set about the attempt to account for what they see, and to devise schemes for remedying what they do not like. In their eagerness to recommend the less fortunate classes to pity and consideration they forget all about the rights of other classes; they gloss over all the faults of the classes in question, and they exaggerate their misfortunes and their virtues. They invent new theories of property, distorting rights and perpetrating injustice, as anyone is sure to do who sets about the readjustment of social relations with the interests of one group distinctly before his mind, and the interests of all other groups thrown into the background. When I have read certain of these discussions I have thought that it must be quite disreputable to be respectable, quite dishonest to own property, quite unjust to go one's own way and earn one's own living, and that the only really admirable person was the good-for-nothing. The man who by his own effort raises himself above poverty appears, in these discussions, to be of no account. The man who has done nothing to raise himself above poverty finds that the social doctors flock about him, bringing the capital which they have collected from the other class, and promising him the aid of the State to give him what the other had to work for. In all these schemes and projects the organized intervention of society through the State is either planned or hoped for, and the State is thus made to become the protector and guardian of certain classes. The agents who are to direct the State action are, of course, the reformers and philanthropists. Their schemes, therefore, may always be reduced to this type – that A and B decide what C shall do for D. It will be interesting to inquire, at a later period of our discussion, who C is, and what the effect is upon him of all these arrangements. In all the discussions attention is concentrated on A and B, the noble social reformers, and on D, the 'poor man'. I call C the Forgotten Man, because I have never seen that any notice was taken of him in any of the discussions. When we have disposed of A, B, and D we can better appreciate the case of C, and I think that we shall find that he deserves our attention, for the worth of his character and the magnitude of his unmerited burdens. Here it may suffice to observe that, on the theories of the social philosophers to whom I have referred, we should get a new maxim of judicious living: Poverty is the best policy. If you get wealth, you will have to support other people; if you do not get wealth, it will be the duty of other people to support you.

No doubt one chief reason for the unclear and contradictory

theories of class relations lies in the fact that our society, largely controlled in all its organization by one set of doctrines, still contains survivals of old social theories which are totally inconsistent with the former. In the Middle Ages men were united by custom and prescription into associations, ranks, guilds, and communities of various kinds. These ties endured as long as life lasted. Consequently society was dependent, throughout all its details, on status, and the tie, or bond, was sentimental. In our modern state, and in the United States more than anywhere else, the social structure is based on contract, and status is of the least importance. Contract, however, is rational – even rationalistic. It is also realistic, cold, and matter-of-fact. A contract relation is based on a sufficient reason, not on custom or prescription. It is not permanent. It endures only so long as the reason for it endures. In a state based on contract sentiment is out of place in any public or common affairs. It is relegated to the sphere of private and personal relations, where it depends not at all on class types, but on personal acquaintance and personal estimates. The sentimentalists among us always seize upon the survivals of the old order. They want to save them and restore them. Much of the loose thinking also which troubles us in our social discussions arises from the fact that men do not distinguish the elements of status and of contract which may be found in our society. . . .

[Chapter 2]
A free man in a free democracy has no duty whatever towards other men of the same rank and standing, except respect, courtesy, and goodwill. We cannot say that there are no classes, when we are speaking politically, and then say that there are classes, when we are telling A what it is his duty to do for B. In a free state every man is held and expected to take care of himself and his family, to make no trouble for his neighbour, and to contribute his full share to public interests and common necessities. If he fails in this he throws burdens on others. He does not thereby acquire rights against the others. On the contrary, he only accumulates obligations towards them; and if he is allowed to make his deficiencies a ground of new claims, he passes over into the position of a privileged or petted person – emancipated from duties, endowed with claims. This is the inevitable result of combining democratic political theories with humanitarian social theories. . . .

[Conclusion]

The men who have not done their duty in this world never can be equal to those who have done their duty more or less well. If words like wise and foolish, thrifty and extravagant, prudent and negligent, have any meaning in language, then it must make some difference how people behave in this world, and the difference will appear in the position they acquire in the body of society, and in relation to the chances of life. They may, then, be classified in reference to these facts. Such classes always will exist; no other social distinctions can endure. If, then, we look to the origin and definition of these classes, we shall find it impossible to deduce any obligations which one of them bears to the other. The class distinctions simply result from the different degrees of success with which men have availed themselves of the chances which were presented to them. Instead of endeavouring to redistribute the acquisitions which have been made between the existing classes, our aim should be to *increase, multiply, and extend the chances.* Such is the work of civilization. Every old error or abuse which is removed opens new chances of development to all the new energy of society. Every improvement in education, science, art, or government expands the chances of man on earth. Such expansion is no guarantee of equality. On the contrary, if there be liberty, some will profit by the chances eagerly and some will neglect them altogether. Therefore, the greater the chances the more unequal will be the fortune of these two sets of men. So it ought to be, in all justice and right reason. The yearning after equality is the offspring of envy and covetousness, and there is no possible plan for satisfying that yearning which can do aught else than rob A to give to B; consequently all such plans nourish some of the meanest vices of human nature, waste capital, and overthrow civilization. But if we can expand the chances we can count on a general and steady growth of civilization and advancement of society by and through its best members. In the prosecution of these chances we all owe to each other goodwill, mutual respect, and mutual guarantees of liberty and security. Beyond this nothing can be affirmed as a duty of one group to another in a free state.

2.2.2 AN ANGLO SAXON MYTH

From Our Country *by the Reverend Josiah Strong, 1885.*

The Reverend Josiah Strong (1847–1916) feared that Protestant America was being engulfed by immigrants drawn from other faiths – Catholics, Jews, Muslims among them – and also by a Godless materialism. Strong seized on portions of Darwin's writings to argue the case for an Anglo-Saxon hegemony in America in order to preserve its traditional values – as the Reverend Strong viewed them. His book *Our Country*, which appeared in 1885, was an immediate success, and sold more than 180,000 copies. As the following extract shows, the Reverend Strong shared at least one characteristic with the overt racialists of his time – a predilection for quoting other writers out of context.

In 1880, the United States was the home of more than one-half of the Anglo-Saxon race; and, if the computations already given are correct, a much larger proportion will be here a hundred years hence. It has been shown that we have room for at least a thousand millions. According to recent figures, there is in France a population of 180·88 to the square mile; in Germany, 216·62; in England and Wales, 428·67; in Belgium, 481·71; in the United States – not including Alaska – 16·88. If our population were as dense as that of France, we should have this side of Alaska, 537,000,000; if as dense as that of Germany, 643,000,000; if as dense as that of England and Wales 1,173,000,000; if as dense as that of Belgium, 1,430,000,000.

But we are to have not only the larger portion of the Anglo-Saxon race for generations to come, we may reasonably expect to develop the highest type of Anglo-Saxon civilization. If human progress follows a law of development, if

> Time's noblest offspring is the last,

our civilization should be the noblest; for we are

> The heirs of all the ages in the foremost files of time,

and not only do we occupy the latitude of power, but *our land is the last to be occupied in that latitude*. There is no other virgin soil in the North Temperate Zone. If the consummation of human progress is not to be looked for here, if there is yet to flower a higher civilization, where is the soil that is to produce it? Whipple says: 'There has never been a great migration that did not result in a new form of national genius.' Our national genius is Anglo-Saxon, but not English, its distinctive type is the result of a finer nervous organization, which is certainly being developed in this country. . . .

Mr Darwin is not only disposed to see, in the superior vigour of our people, an illustration of his favourite theory of natural selection, but even intimates that the world's history thus far has been simply preparatory for our future, and tributary to it. He says: 'There is apparently much truth in the belief that the wonderful progress of the United States, as well as the character of the people, are the results of natural selection; for the more energetic, restless, and courageous men from all parts of Europe have emigrated during the last ten or twelve generations to that great country, and have there succeeded best. Looking at the distant future, I do not think that the Rev. Mr Zincke takes an exaggerated view when he says: "All other series of events – as that which resulted in the culture of mind in Greece, and that which resulted in the Empire of Rome – only appear to have purpose and value when viewed in connection with, or rather as subsidiary to, the great stream of Anglo-Saxon emigration to the West."'

There is abundant reason to believe that the Anglo-Saxon race is to be, is, indeed, already becoming, more effective here than in the mother country. The marked superiority of this race is due, in large measure, to its highly mixed origin. Says Rawlinson: 'It is a general rule, now almost universally admitted by ethnologists, that the mixed races of mankind are superior to the pure ones'; and adds: 'Even the Jews, who are so often cited as an example of a race at once pure and strong, may, with more reason, be adduced on the opposite side of the argument.' The ancient Egyptians, the Greeks, and the Romans, were all mixed races. Among modern races, the most conspicuous example is afforded by the Anglo-Saxons. Mr Green's studies show that Mr Tennyson's poetic line,

Saxon and Norman and Dane are we,

must be supplemented with Celt and Gaul, Welshman and Irishman, Frisian and Flamand, French Huguenot and German Palatine. What took place a thousand years ago and more in England again transpires today in the United States. 'History repeats itself';

69

but, as the wheels of history are the chariot wheels of the Almighty, there is, with every revolution, an onward movement towards the goal of his eternal purposes. There is here a new commingling of races; and, while the largest injections of foreign blood are substantially the same elements that constituted the original Anglo-Saxon admixture, so that we may infer the general type will be preserved, there are strains of other bloods being added, which if Mr Emerson's remark is true, that 'the best nations are those most widely related', may be expected to improve the stock, and aid it to a higher destiny. If the dangers of immigration, which have been pointed out, can be successfully met for the next few years, until it has passed its climax, it may be expected to add value to the amalgam which will constitute the new Anglo-Saxon race of the New World. Concerning our future, Herbert Spencer says: 'One great result is, I think, tolerably clear. From biological truths it is to be inferred that the eventual mixture of the allied varieties of the Aryan race, forming the population, will produce a more powerful type of man than has hitherto existed, and a type of man more plastic, more adaptable, more capable of undergoing the modifications needful for complete social life. I think whatever difficulties they may have to surmount, and whatever tribulations they may have to pass through, the Americans may reasonably look forward to a time when they will have produced a civilization grander than any the world has known.'

It may be easily shown, and is of no small significance, that the two great ideas of which the Anglo-Saxon is the exponent are having a fuller development in the United States than in Great Britain. There the union of Church and State tends strongly to paralyse some of the members of the body of Christ. Here there is no such influence to destroy spiritual life and power. Here, also, has been evolved the form of government consistent with the largest possible civil liberty. Furthermore, it is significant that the marked characteristics of this race are being here emphasized most. Among the most striking features of the Anglo-Saxon is his money-making power – a power of increasing importance in the widening commerce of the world's future. We have seen, in a preceding chapter, that, although England is by far the richest nation of Europe, we have already outstripped her in the race after wealth, and we have only begun the development of our vast resources.

Again, another marked characteristic of the Anglo-Saxon is what may be called an instinct or genius for colonizing. His unequalled energy, his indomitable perseverance, and his personal independence, made him a pioneer. He excels all others in pushing his way into new countries. It was those in whom this tendency was strongest that came to America, and this inherited tendency has been further developed by the westward sweep of successive generations across the continent. So noticeable has this characteristic become that English visitors remark it. Charles Dickens once said that the typical American would hesitate to enter heaven unless assured that he could go further west.

Again, nothing more manifestly distinguishes the Anglo-Saxon than his intense and persistent energy; and he is developing in the United States an energy which, in eager activity and effectiveness, is peculiarly American. This is due partly to the fact that Americans are much better fed than Europeans, and partly to the undeveloped resources of a new country, but more largely to our climate, which acts as a constant stimulus. Ten years after the landing of the Pilgrims, the Rev. Francis Higginson, a good observer, wrote: 'A sup of New England air is better than a whole flagon of English ale.' Thus early had the stimulating effect of our climate been noted. Moreover, our social institutions are stimulating. In Europe the various ranks of society are, like the strata of the earth, fixed and fossilized. There can be no great change without a terrible upheaval, a social earthquake. Here society is like the waters of the sea, mobile; as General Garfield said, and so signally illustrated in his own experience, that which is at the bottom today may one day flash on the crest of the highest wave. Everyone is free to become whatever he can make of himself; free to transform himself from a rail-splitter or a tanner or a canal-boy, into the nation's President. Our aristocracy, unlike that of Europe, is open to all comers. Wealth, position, influence, are prizes offered for energy; and every farmer's boy, every apprentice and clerk, every friendless and penniless immigrant, is free to enter the lists. Thus many causes co-operate to produce here the most forceful and tremendous energy in the world.

What is the significance of such facts? These tendencies infold the future; they are the mighty alphabet with which God writes his prophecies. May we not, by a careful laying together of the letters, spell out something of his meaning? It seems to me that God, with infinite wisdom and skill, is training the Anglo-Saxon race for an

D

hour sure to come in the world's future. Heretofore there has always been in the history of the world a comparatively unoccupied land westward, into which the crowded countries of the East have poured their surplus populations. But the widening waves of migration, which millenniums ago rolled east and west from the valley of the Euphrates, meet today on our Pacific coast. There are no more new worlds. The unoccupied arable lands of the earth are limited, and will soon be taken. The time is coming when the pressure of population on the means of subsistence will be felt here as it is now felt in Europe and Asia. Then will the world enter upon a new stage of its history – *the final competition of races, for which the Anglo-Saxon is being schooled.* Long before the thousand millions are here, the mighty *centrifugal* tendency, inherent in this stock and strengthened in the United States, will assert itself. Then this race of unequalled energy, with all the majesty of numbers and the might of wealth behind it – the representative, let us hope, of the largest liberty, the purest Christianity, the highest civilization – having developed peculiarly aggressive traits calculated to impress its institutions upon mankind, will spread itself over the earth. If I read not amiss, this powerful race will move down upon Mexico, down upon Central and South America, out upon the islands of the sea, over upon Africa and beyond. And can anyone doubt that the result of this competition of races will be the 'survival of the fittest'? . . . 'At the present day,' says Mr Darwin, 'civilized nations are everywhere supplanting barbarous nations, excepting where the climate opposes a deadly barrier; and they succeed mainly, though not exclusively, through their arts, which are the products of the intellect.' Thus the Finns were supplanted by the Aryan races in Europe and Asia, the Tartars by the Russians, and thus the aborigines of North America, Australia and New Zealand are now disappearing before the all-conquering Anglo-Saxons. It would seem as if these inferior tribes were only precursors of a superior race, voices in the wilderness crying: 'Prepare ye the way of the Lord!' The savage is a hunter; by the incoming of civilization the game is driven away and disappears before the hunter becomes a herder or an agriculturist. The savage is ignorant of many diseases of civilization which, when he is exposed to them, attack him before he learns how to treat them. Civilization also has its vices, of which the uninitiated savage is innocent. He proves an apt learner of vice, but dull enough in the school of morals. Every civilization has its destructive and preservative elements. The Anglo-Saxon race would speedily decay but for the salt of Christianity. Bring savages into contact with our civilization, and its destructive forces become operative at once, while years are necessary to render effective the saving influences of Christian instruction. Moreover, the pioneer wave of our civilization carries with it more scum than salt. Where there is one missionary, there are hundreds of miners or traders or adventurers ready to debauch the native. Whether the extinction of inferior races before the advancing Anglo-Saxon seems to the reader sad or otherwise, it certainly appears probable. I know of nothing except climatic conditions to prevent this race from populating Africa as it has peopled North America. And those portions of Africa which are unfavourable to Anglo-Saxon life are less extensive than was once supposed. The Dutch Boers, after two centuries of life there, are as hardy as any race on earth. The Anglo-Saxon has established himself in climates totally diverse – Canada, South Africa, and India – and, through several generations, has preserved his essential race characteristics. He is not, of course, superior to climatic influences; but, even in warm climates, he is likely to retain his aggressive vigour long enough to supplant races already enfeebled. Thus, in what Dr Bushnell calls 'the out-populating power of the Christian stock', may be found God's final and complete solution of the dark problem of heathenism among many inferior peoples.

2.3 DOUBTS ON EQUALITY

From Edwin Lawrence Godkin, Unforeseen Tendencies of Democracy, *1898, an essay on Equality, pp. 31–6, 46–7.*

Edwin Lawrence Godkin (1831–1902) was born in Ireland of middle-class English parents and emigrated to New York in 1856. He helped to found the literary and political journal the *Nation* and later was editor of the influential New York *Evening Post*. Although his editorials usually showed liberal leanings, he was deeply suspicious of socialist theories and rejected strict egalitarian assumptions. In a collection of essays entitled *Unforeseen Tendencies of Democracy* (1898) Godkin showed many of his reservations on democratic theory.

Equality, as everyone acknowledges, is the foundation of democracy. It means democracy when it gets itself embodied in law. When all are equal, there is no reason why all should not rule. But the equality of the French in 1792, when the revolutionary government was established, was something different from the equality of 1789. In 1789 the equality which was asked for was, in the main, simply an equality of rights and burdens between the nobility and the *tiers état*. Equality, as Montesquieu uses the term, means simply love, not of one's order, but of one's country, and as such he made it the equivalent of democracy. Democracy, he says, *is* equality. But the word 'equality' for him evidently had no social signification. It meant rather equality of service to the country: that everyone was held to the same amount of public duty, according to his means, and that everyone was entitled to the same opportunities of taking part in the government. That being born of particular parents made anyone essentially of better quality than anybody else; that if one hundred babies of different conditions were brought up in the same manner, the sons of noblemen or gentlemen among them would show their superiority to the others in their character, was a doctrine which, after the Middle Ages, was probably never fully accepted even by the most ardent believer in heredity. Every generation was witness of the breakdown, if I may use the expression, of the principle of heredity. That is to say, a large number of noble or gentle families in every generation lost their position or property, because the founder did not transmit his qualities of mind or character to his descendants. The folly or extravagance or imprudence which led to this social *déchéance* was generally due to marked departures in intellect or morals from the original type. The believers in heredity were misled by the analogy of the breeding of animals. Horses transmitted speed and bottom, birds peculiar appearance, with extraordinary certainty. Therefore, it was concluded, a man was likely to have his father's wisdom, or foresight, or mental strength. But his descendants rarely inherit from a father more than one or two mental peculiarities, valuable when united with other things, but, standing alone, of little use in the battle of life – a fact which may be verified anywhere by observing the families of distinguished men. A man eminent in politics, or law, or medicine, or commerce, or finance, or war, is seldom succeeded by a son who recalls the *ensemble* of qualites which have secured the father's success, although he may have one or two of his characteristics. Heredity obtained its stronghold in the popular imagination in the Middle Ages, owing to the fact that the son was in possession of the father's power when he died, and that in a rude age, when things were mainly decided by fighting, it offered the readiest means of settling peaceably questions of succession. But as soon as the question of the right of a class to rule in virtue of heredity became a subject of discussion, heredity broke down. It was a custom which was valuable in the time of its origin, but, like most customs, found it impossible to justify itself by any better argument than that, under some circumstances, it had produced good results.

But in America, from the settlement of the colonies, the English doctrine that distinction should serve in place of heredity seems to have held its place in the popular imagination. The founding of colonies, the making of conquests, the growth of trade and commerce, and the early practice of admitting able lawyers to the House of Lords had familiarized Englishmen with the idea of a man's making his fortune by some sort of adventure, no matter what his origin. The peers, too, sapped their own power unconsciously by making legislators of young men of promise no matter of what extraction, and giving them seats in the House of Commons. The result was that the association, in the English mind, of men of mark of some kind with office-holding and the work of government took deep root after the revolution of 1640, and was transferred to America. It was generally leading men of prominence and character who were made governors and judges, and were sent to the legislature and to Washington. The Revolution was carried through, and the Constitution formed and its adoption brought about, by men of this kind. The idea of an obscure man, of a man who was not lifted above the crowd in some way, being fit for the transaction of public affairs was still unfamiliar. All the members of the Constitutional Convention were men of some local note, and so were the earlier administrators of the new government.

This, too, down to that period, had been the strongest tradition of all previous democracies. All democracies, both ancient and modern, had made a practice of electing to office, not always their best men, but their most prominent men. In none of them had a man who was not in some way raised above the mass of his fellow citizens – who had not succeeded in life, in short – much chance of

75

filling a high or an important place. This was eminently true of Greece and Rome and Switzerland. In a small state, where everybody knows everybody well, and where elections and other public affairs are transacted in the market-place, within sound of an orator's voice, this is not difficult. Office-seekers are, in a measure, compelled to be eloquent, or distinguished for something. An obscure man, or a man whose character bears serious blemishes of some kind, will hardly dare to ask the confidence of the citizens in his fitness for great duties. The composition of the Roman Senate, which from the beginning consisted of notables who had in some manner rendered the state marked service, and the selection for which the people for centuries committed to a magistrate, showed better than almost anything else the desire of the ancient democracies to avail themselves of their best talent. What they seem to have insisted on above all things, in the management of the state, was not the right of filling offices with anybody they pleased, but the right of filling them with their most competent men. . . .

The disregard of special fitness, combined with unwillingness to acknowledge that there can be anything special about any man, which is born of equality, constitutes the great defect of modern democracy. That large communities can be successfully administered by inferior men is a doctrine which runs directly counter not only to the experience of the race, but to the order appointed for the advance of civilization, which has been carried forward almost exclusively by the labour of the fittest, despite the resistance or reluctance of the unfit. This order of nature, too, has been recognized fully in private affairs of every description. In all of them competency on the part of administrators is the first thing sought for, and the only thing trusted. But in private affairs the penalty of any disregard of this rule comes quickly; in public affairs the operation of all causes is much slower, and their action is obscure. Nations take centuries to fall, and the catastrophe is preceded by a long period of the process called 'bad government', in which there is much suffering and alarm, but not enough to make the remedy plain. France furnishes the best modern illustration of this rule. The causes of the Revolution undoubtedly began to operate at the majority of Louis xiv, but for over one hundred years their nature and certain results were not perceived, in spite of the great popular suffering which prevailed during the whole period.

The worst of the slowness of this decadence is that it affects national character to a degree which makes recovery more difficult, even after the origin and nature of the disease have become plain. Men soon get accustomed to the evils of their condition, particularly if there is nobody in particular to blame. The inaction or negligence or shortcomings of great numbers assume the appearance of a law of nature, or of repeated failures or attempts at the impossible. The apparent difficulty of reform, except by catastrophe or revolution, begets either despondency or over-cheerfulness.

2.4 PRESIDENT HOOVER'S INDIVIDUALISM

From Herbert Hoover, American Individualism, *1922.*

Herbert Hoover (1874–1964), thirty-first President of the United States, was a vigorous exponent of individualism. After a highly successful career as a mining engineer he turned to politics and became Secretary of Commerce under Presidents Harding and Coolidge (1921–8). In 1928 he was elected to the Presidency, chiefly because his career and character seemed ideally suited to the mood of the Twenties up to that time. Hoover's book *American Individualism* capitalized on the mood of self-indulgence and materialism then prevalent, but also appealed to an older, more deeply implanted strain in the American character. The following extract shows that an essentially conservative appeal may be linked to an apparent concern with corporate welfare.

We in America have had too much experience of life to fool ourselves into pretending that all men are equal in ability, in character, in intelligence, in ambition. That was part of the claptrap of the French Revolution. We have grown to understand that all we can hope to assure to the individual through government is liberty, justice, intellectual welfare, equality of opportunity, and stimulation to service.

It is in maintenance of a society fluid to these human qualities that our individualism departs from the individualism of Europe. There can be no rise for the individual through the frozen strata of classes, or of castes, and no stratification can take place in a mass

77

livened by the free stir of its particles. This guarding of our individualism against stratification insists not only in preserving in the social solution an equal opportunity for the able and ambitious to rise from the bottom; it also insists that the sons of the successful shall not by any mere right of birth or favour continue to occupy their fathers' places of power against the rise of a new generation in process of coming up from the bottom. The pioneers of our American individualism had the good sense not to reward Washington and Jefferson and Hamilton with hereditary dukedoms and fixtures in landed estates, as Great Britain rewarded Marlborough and Nelson. Otherwise our American fields of opportunity would have been clogged with long generations inheriting their fathers' privileges without their fathers' capacity for service.

That our system has avoided the establishment and domination of class has a significant proof in the present Administration in Washington. Of the twelve men comprising the President, Vice-President, and Cabinet, nine have earned their own way in life without economic inheritance, and eight of them started with manual labour.

If we examine the impulses that carry us forward, none is so potent for progress as the yearning for individual self-expression, the desire for creation of something. Perhaps the greatest human happiness flows from personal achievement. Here lies the great urge of the constructive instinct of mankind. But it can only thrive in a society where the individual has liberty and stimulation to achievement. Nor does the community progress except through its participation in these multitudes of achievements.

Furthermore, the maintenance of productivity and the advancement of the things of the spirit depend upon the ever-renewed supply from the mass of those who can rise to leadership. Our social, economic, and intellectual progress is almost solely dependent upon the creative minds of those individuals with imaginative and administrative intelligence who create or who carry discoveries to widespread application. No race possesses more than a small percentage of these minds in a single generation. But little thought has ever been given to our racial dependency upon them. Nor that our progress is in so large a measure due to the fact that with our increased means of communication these rare individuals are today able to spread their influence over so enlarged a number of lesser capable minds as to have increased their potency a millionfold. In truth, the vastly greater productivity of the world with actually less physical labour is due to the wider spread of their influence through the discovery of these facilities. And they can arise solely through the selection that comes from the free-running mills of competition. They must be free to rise from the mass; they must be given the attraction of premiums to effort.

Leadership is a quality of the individual. It is the individual alone who can function in the world of intellect and in the field of leadership. If democracy is to secure its authorities in morals, religion, and statesmanship, it must stimulate leadership from its own mass. Human leadership cannot be replenished by selection like queen bees, by divine right or bureaucracies, but by the free rise of ability, character, and intelligence.

Even so, leadership cannot, no matter how brilliant, carry progress far ahead of the average of the mass of individual units. Progress of the nation is the sum of progress in its individuals. Acts and ideas that lead to progress are born out of the womb of the individual mind, not out of the mind of the crowd. The crowd only feels: it has no mind of its own which can plan. The crowd is credulous, it destroys, it consumes, it hates, and it dreams – but it never builds. It is one of the most profound and important of exact psychological truths that man in the mass does not think but only feels. The mob functions only in a world of emotion. The demagogue feeds on mob emotions and his leadership is the leadership of emotion, not the leadership of intellect and progress. Popular desires are no criteria to the real need; they can be determined only by deliberative consideration, by education, by constructive leadership. . . .

2.5 DOUBTS ON DEMOCRACY

From Irving Babbitt, Democracy and Leadership, *1924, Chapter VII, pp. 240–5.*

Like many New England men of letters Irving Babbitt (1865–1933) disliked the drift of American democracy in the twentieth century. Writing in the 1920s Babbitt wondered whether the United States was not becoming 'a huge mass of standardized mediocrity'. The theme of the extract is 'Democracy and Standards'.

If quantitatively the American achievement is impressive, qualitatively it is somewhat less satisfying. What must one think of a country, asks one of our foreign critics, whose most popular orator is W. J. Bryan, whose favourite actor is Charlie Chaplin, whose most widely read novelist is Harold Bell Wright, whose best-known evangelist is Billy Sunday, and whose representative journalist is William Randolph Hearst? What one must evidently think of such a country, even after allowing liberally for overstatement, is that it lacks standards. Furthermore, America suffers not only from a lack of standards, but also not infrequently from a confusion or an inversion of standards. As an example of the inversion of standards we may take the bricklayer who being able to lay two thousand bricks a day, is reduced by union rules to laying five hundred. There is confusion of standards, again, when we are so impressed by Mr Henry Ford's abilities as organizer and master mechanic that we listen seriously to his views on money; or when, simply because Mr Edison has shown inventive genius along certain lines we receive him as an authority on education. One is reminded of the story of the French butcher who, having need of legal aid, finally, after looking over a number of lawyers, selected the fattest one.

The problem of standards, though not identical with the problem of democracy, touches it at many points and is not therefore the problem of any one country. Europeans, indeed, like to look upon the crudity and chaotic impressionism of people who are no longer guided by standards as something specifically American. 'America,' says the 'Saturday Review', 'is the country of unbalanced minds, of provincial policies and of hysterical utopias.' The deference for standards has, however, been diminished by a certain type of democracy in many other countries besides America. The resulting vulgarity and triviality are more or less visible in all of these countries – for example, if we are to believe Lord Bryce, in New Zealand.* If we in America are perhaps pre-eminent in lack of distinction, it is because of the very completeness of our emancipation from the past. Goethe's warning as to the retarding effect of the commonplace is well known (*Was uns alle bändigt, das Gemeine*). His explanation of what makes for the commonplace is less familiar: 'Enjoyment,' he says, 'makes common.' (*Geniessen*

* See James (Lord) Bryce, *Modern Democracies* (2 vols. 1921) II : 349–51, 360.

macht gemein.) Since every man desires happiness, it is evidently no small matter whether he conceives of happiness in terms of work or of enjoyment. If he works in the full ethical sense that I have attempted to define, he is pulling back and disciplining his temperamental self with reference to some standard. In short, his temperamental self is, in an almost literal sense, undergoing conversion. The whole of life may, indeed, be summed up in the words diversion and conversion. Along which of these two main paths are most of us seeking the happiness to the pursuit of which we are dedicated by our Declaration of Independence? The author of this phrase, Thomas Jefferson, remarks of himself: 'I am an Epicurean.'* It cannot be gainsaid that an increasing number of our young people are, in this respect at least, good Jeffersonians. The phrase that reflects most clearly their philosophy of life is perhaps 'good time'. One might suppose that many of them see this phrase written in great blazing letters on the very face of the firmament. As 'Punch' remarked, the United States is not a country, but a picnic. When the element of conversion with reference to a standard is eliminated from life, what remains is the irresponsible quest of thrills. The utilitarian and industrial side of the modern movement comes into play at this point. Commercialism is laying its greasy paw upon everything (including the irresponsible quest of thrills); so that, whatever democracy may be theoretically, one is sometimes tempted to define it practically as standardized and commercialized melodrama. This definition will be found to fit many aspects of our national life besides the moving-picture industry. The tendency to steep and saturate ourselves in the impression of the moment without reference to any permanent pattern of human experience is even more marked, perhaps, in our newspapers and magazines. It was said of the inhabitants of a certain ancient Greek city that, though they were not fools, they did just the things that fools would do. It is hard to take a glance at one of our news-stands without reflecting that, though we may not be fools, we are reading just the things that fools would read. Our daily press in particular is given over to the most childish sensationalism. 'The Americans are an excellent people,' Matthew Arnold wrote from Boston in 1883, 'but their press seems to me an awful symptom.' This symptom was not so awful then as now; for that was before the day of the scarehead and the comic supplement.

* *Works* (Ford ed.), x, p. 143.

The American reading his Sunday paper in a state of lazy collapse is perhaps the most perfect symbol of the triumph of quantity over quality that the world has yet seen. Whole forests are being ground into pulp daily to minister to our triviality.

One is inclined, indeed, to ask in certain moods, whether the net result of the movement that has been sweeping the Occident for several generations may not be a huge mass of standardized mediocrity; and whether in this country in particular we are not in danger of producing in the name of democracy one of the most trifling brands of the human species that the world has yet seen. To be sure, it may be urged that, though we may suffer loss of distinction as a result of the democratic drift, by way of compensation a great many average people will, in the Jeffersonian sense at least, be made 'happy'. If we are to judge by history, however, what supervenes upon the decline of standards and the disappearance of leaders who embody them is not some equalitarian paradise, but inferior types of leadership. . . .

We are assured, indeed, that the highly heterogeneous elements that enter into our population will, like various instruments in an orchestra, merely result in a richer harmony; they will, one may reply, provided that, like an orchestra, they be properly led. Otherwise the outcome may be an unexampled cacophony. This question of leadership is not primarily biological, but moral. Leaders may vary in quality from the man who is so loyal to sound standards that he inspires right conduct in others by the sheer rightness of his example, to the man who stands for nothing higher than the law of cunning and the law of force, and so is, in the sense I have sought to define, imperialistic. If democracy means simply the attempt to eliminate the qualitative and selective principle in favour of some general will, based in turn on a theory of natural rights, it may prove to be only a form of the vertigo of the abyss. . . .

2.6 HOLMES AND LASKI: CAPITALISM VERSUS COMMUNISM

From Mark deWolfe Howe (ed.), The Holmes-Laski Letters:
The Correspondence of Mr Justice Holmes and Harold J. Laski,
1916–1935, *2 vols, 1953, II, pp. 945–6.*

The published correspondence of scholars, men of letters, statesmen and politicians often contains exchanges of ideas or viewpoints. During the 1920s the significance of the Russian Revolution was often a topic for discussion and disagreement. In the
following exchange the American jurist Oliver Wendell Holmes
Jr is writing to his British friend, the socialist Harold Laski.

Holmes to Laski

Washington D.C., 21 May 1927

My dear Laski:

... Of course I appreciate what you and Keynes say, that the
Russian Communism is a religion and therefore cannot be expected
to be just. But I don't see why sympathetic understanding should
be confined to one side. Capitalism may not be a religion but it
commands a fighting belief on its side and I don't at all agree to
describing its tyrannies with resentment, as coming from bad men
when you gloss those on the other side. I think that most of the
so-called tyrannies of capital express the economic necessities
created by the pressure of population – a pressure for which capitalism is not responsible and for which communism has offered no
remedy. If I praised or blamed (which I don't) either one, I should
blame the communists as consciously and voluntarily contemplat-
ing their despotism whereas on the other side it is largely unconscious and the automatic result of the situation. I may add that
class for class I think the one that communism would abolish is
more valuable – contributes more, a great deal more, than those
whom communism exalts. For as I said the other day, the only
contribution that any man makes that can't be got more cheaply
from the water and the sky is ideas – the immediate or remote
direction of energy which man does not produce, whether it comes
from his muscles or a machine. Ideas come from the despised
bourgeoisie not from labour. ...

Laski to Holmes

Devon Lodge, 29.v.27

My dear Justice:

Your letter was a delight indeed. And even though I see a real disparity between us on intellectual problems, I can't say I greatly mind. For your scepticism drives me back each time on first principle which is an admirable thing for me. A good deal of our difference is, I think, due to our different civilizations. You are living amid a system where the classic principles of capitalism still work successfully, I amid one where the growing inadequacy of that machine is most obvious. In the result you, broadly, are satisfied, I, broadly, dissatisfied with the classic economics. You see a general adequacy which makes you believe in economic liberty; I see a general inadequacy which makes me believe in economic equality. We are looking at different materials and drawing, naturally, different results from their contemplation. I add that I think you have not taken account of an immense new body of experience in economic matters, and that you do not allow enough for necessary modification of economic principle as it meets that new experience. Also, I think, you are over-occupied with pure theory and make quite insufficient allowance for a friction which makes pure theory relatively negligible in its operative influence. However, one day I shall set this all down at length in a short book and then, I hope, I shall drive *you* to revise *your* first principles. . . .

2.7 THE NEW DEAL ATTACKED

From Herbert Hoover, a speech reported in the New York Times, *8 March 1936.*

Franklin Roosevelt's 'New Deal', with its emphasis on the role of the Federal government in regulating employment and economic growth, deeply antagonized American conservatives. They argued that the New Deal struck at the roots of American individualism and the spirit of free enterprise. A typical assault on the New Deal was delivered by former President Herbert Hoover, in a speech reported in the *New York Times*, 8 March 1936.

[A]t the heart of our American system is imbedded a great ideal unique in the world. That is the ideal that there shall be an opportunity in life, an equal opportunity, for every body and girl, every man and woman. It holds that they have the chance to rise to any position to which their character and ability may entitle them. That ideal is limited or ended if this nation is to be goose-stepped from Washington.

About every outstanding advance which has promoted the welfare of mankind in the last century has been born in the countries of free men and women. The steam engine, electricity, radio, free schooling, the great advances in biology, are but part of them. I might include the adding machine, but its present use by the New Deal raises doubts as to its contribution to the welfare of mankind.

On the other hand, almost every one of the world's mistakes has its origin in personal government. Violation of treaties, great wars, persecution of the Jews and other religionists, and so on down to the fantastic laws by a must Congress and the slaughter of pigs.

American young men and women should have the right to plan, to live their own lives with just one limitation – that they shall not injure their neighbours. What they want of government is to keep the channels of opportunity open and equal, not to block them and then charge them for doing it.

They want rewards to the winners in the race. They do not want to be planned down to a pattern. To red-blooded men and women there is a joy of work and joy in the battle of competition. There is the daily joy of doing something worth while, of proving one's worth, of telling every evil person where he can go.

There is the joy of championing justice to the weak and downtrodden. These are the battles that create the national fibre of self-reliance and self-respect. That is what made America. If you concentrate all adventure in the government, it does not leave much constructive joy for the governed.

In economic life there is but one hope of increased security and comfort for the common man, of opportunity for all. That is to adopt every labour-saving device, every discovery, every idea to reduce waste and the cost of producing goods.

We must work our machines heartlessly, but not our men. Thereby goods can be sold cheaper and more people can buy. That is the only road to restored employment. That production of a plenty can spring alone from the initiative and enterprise of free men.

That is no system of robbery. It is action for the common service. That is destroyed at once by the grotesque notion that government shall limit production.

We cannot operate this world of machines and men without leadership. Competent leadership can come only by the rise of men and women in a free society by the impulse of their own ambition, character and abilities. That leadership cannot come by birth, or by wealth, or be nursed like queen bees.

That leadership cannot be chosen by bureaucrats. It comes from the ambition of free men and women against the polishing-wheels of competition.

It comes in a system of rewards. America should not be divided into the 'haves' and the 'have nots', but into the 'doers' and the 'do nots'.

2.8 THE PLANNED SOCIETY

From Walter Lippmann, An Inquiry into the Principles of the Good Society, *1943, pp. 362–7.*

Although Walter Lippmann is usually regarded as a latter-day conservative, his long writing career has featured a consistent sympathy for liberal ideals. In 1936 Lippmann explored the politics of liberalism in his book *An Inquiry into the Principles of the Good Society*. In the following extract Lippmann explores the fallacy of supposing that societies can be totally planned or controlled.

We live in such an immensely diversified civilization that the only intelligible criterion which political thinkers can entertain in regard to it, the only feasible goal which statesmen can set themselves in governing it, is to reconcile the conflicts which spring from this diversity. They cannot hope to comprehend it as a system. For it is not a system. They cannot hope to plan and direct it. For it is not an organization. They can hope only to dispense lawful justice among individuals and associations where their interests conflict, to mitigate the violence of conflict and competition by seeking to make lawful justice more and more equitable.

It requires much virtue to do that well. There must be a strong desire to be just. There must be a growing capacity to be just.

There must be discernment and sympathy in estimating the particular claims of divergent interests. There must be moral standards which discourage the quest of privilege and the exercise of arbitrary power. There must be resolution and valour to resist oppression and tyranny. There must be patience and tolerance and kindness in hearing claims, in argument, in negotiation, and in reconciliation.

But these are human virtues; though they are high, they are within the attainable limits of human nature as we know it. They actually exist. Men do have these virtues, all but the most hopelessly degenerate, in some degree. We know that they can be increased. When we talk about them we are talking about virtues that have affected the course of actual history, about virtues that some men have practised more than other men, and no man sufficiently, but enough men in great enough degree to have given mankind here and there and for varying periods of time the intimations of a Good Society.

But the virtues that are required for the overhead administration of a civilization are superhuman; they are attributes of Providence and not of mortal men. It is true that there have been benevolent despots and that for a little while in a particular place they have made possible a better life than their subjects were able to achieve without the rule of a firm and authoritative guardian. And no doubt it is still true that a community which does not have the essential discipline of liberty can choose only among alternative disciplines by authority. But if a community must have such a guardian, then it must resign itself to living a simple regimented existence, must entertain no hopes of the high and diversified standard of life which the division of labour and modern technology make possible. For despots cannot be found who could plan, organize, and direct a complex economy.

To do that would require a comprehensive understanding of the life and the labour and the purpose of hundreds of millions of persons, the gift of prophesying their behaviour and omnipotence to control it. These faculties no man has ever possessed. When in theorizing we unwittingly postulate such faculties, we are resting our hopes on a conception of human nature which has no warrant whatever in any actual experience. The collectivist planners are not talking about the human race but about some other breed conceived in their dreams. They postulate qualities of intelligence and of virtue so unlike those which men possess that it would be just as intelligible to make plans for a society in which human beings were born equipped to fly like the angels, to feed on the fragrance of the summer breezes, and endowed with all possible knowledge.

Thus while the liberal philosophy is concerned with the reform of the laws in order to adapt them to the changing needs and standards of the dynamic economy, while the agenda of reform are long and varied, no one must look to liberalism for a harmonious scheme of social reconstruction. The Good Society has no architectural design. There are no blueprints. There is no mould in which human life is to be shaped. Indeed, to expect the blueprint of such a mould is a mode of thinking against which the liberal temper is a constant protest.

To design a personal plan for a new society is a pleasant form of madness; it is in imagination to play at being God and Cæsar to the human race. Any such plan must implicitly assume that the visionary or someone else might find the power, or might persuade the masses to give him the power, to shape society to the plan; all such general plans of social reconstruction are merely the rationalization of the will to power. For that reason they are the subjective beginnings of fanaticism and tyranny. In these utopias the best is the enemy of the good, the heart's desire betrays the interests of man. To think in terms of a new scheme for a whole society is to use the idiom of authority, to approach affairs from the underlying premise that they can be shaped and directed by an overhead control, that social relations can be fabricated according to a master plan drawn up by a supreme architect.

The supreme architect, who begins as a visionary, becomes a fanatic, and ends as a despot. For no one can be the supreme architect of society without employing a supreme despot to execute the design. So if men are to seek freedom from the arbitrary dominion of men over men, they must not entertain fantasies of the future in which they play at being the dictators of civilization. It is the bad habit of an undisciplined imagination. The descent from fantasy to fanaticism is easy. Real dictators raised to power by the fanatics who adore them are only too likely to adopt the fantasy to justify their lust for power.

On the other hand, reasonable and civilized people who would like to make the best of the situation before them, but have no ambition for, or expectation of, the power to reshape a whole society, get no help from these architectural designs. The blue-print, be it as grandiose a work of genius as Plato's *Republic*, cannot hope to fit the specific situation. No *a priori* reasoning can antici-pate the precise formula which will reconcile the infinitely varied interests of men. The reconciliation has to be achieved by the treat-ment of specific issues and the solution will appear only after the claims and the evidence have been examined and fairly judged. Thus in Plato's great scheme each man was assigned his station and his duties; any architectural plan is necessarily based on the same presumption. But Plato's scheme worked only in Plato's imagina-tion, never in the real world. No such scheme can ever work in the real world. For the scheme implies that men will remain content in the station which the visionary has assigned to them. To formulate such plans is not to design a society for real men. It is to re-create men to fit the design. For in real life men rest content in their station only if their interests have been successfully reconciled: failing that, they do not fit the design until they have been dosed with castor oil, put in concentration camps, or exiled to Siberia.

That is why the testament of liberty does not contain the project of a new social order. It adumbrates a way of life in which men seek to reconcile their interests by perfecting the rules of justice. No scheme which promises to obliterate the differences of interest can be deduced from it, no architectural design of society in which all human problems have been resolved. There is no plan of the future: there is, on the contrary, the conviction that the future must have the shape that human energies, purged in so far as possible of arbitrariness, will give it. . . .

Thus it is true that the liberal state is not to be conceived as an earthly providence administering civilization. That is the essence of the matter. To the liberal mind the notion that men can authori-tatively plan and impose a good life upon a great society is ignorant, impertinent, and pretentious. It can be entertained only by men who do not realize the infinite variety of human purposes, who do not appreciate the potentialities of human effort, or by men who do not choose to respect them.

2.9 CONSERVATIVE CONSCIENCE

From Barry Goldwater, The Conscience of a Conservative, *1964 ed., Chapter I, pp. 9–14.*

In the years following the New Deal, conservatism in America has usually struck a cautious, often an apologetic note. The Republican Party is regarded as the true home of American conservatism, with the Southern wing of the Democratic Party an aberrant form arising out of the history of the deep South. In the 1960s, Senator Barry Goldwater, a Republican Senator from Arizona, emerged as an unrepentant conservative. He is an intriguing figure, in some ways a latter-day Jefferson in his rooted distrust of big government and bureaucracy. In his book *The Conscience of a Conservative* (1960), Goldwater put forward his credo. The following forms Chapter 1 of that book.

I have been much concerned that so many people today with Conservative instincts feel compelled to apologize for them. Or if not to apologize directly, to qualify their commitment in a way that amounts to breast-beating. 'Republican candidates,' Vice President Nixon has said, 'should be economic conservatives, but conservatives with a heart.' President Eisenhower announced during his first term, 'I am conservative when it comes to economic problems but liberal when it comes to human problems.' Still other Republican leaders have insisted on calling themselves 'progressive' Conservatives.* These formulations are tantamount to an admission that Conservatism is a narrow, mechanistic *economic* theory that may work very well as a book-keeper's guide, but cannot be relied upon as a comprehensive political philosophy.

The same judgement, though in the form of an attack rather than an admission, is advanced by the radical camp. 'We liberals,' they say, 'are interested in *people*. Our concern is with human beings, while you Conservatives are preoccupied with the preservation of economic privilege and status.' Take them a step further, and the Liberals will turn the accusations into a class argument: it is

* This is a strange label indeed: it implies that 'ordinary' Conservatism is opposed to progress. Have we forgotten that America made its greatest progress when Conservative principles were honoured and preserved?

the little people that concern us, not the 'malefactors of great wealth'.

Such statements, from friend and foe alike, do great injustice to the Conservative point of view. Conservatism is *not* an economic theory, though it has economic implications. The shoe is precisely on the other foot: it is Socialism that subordinates all other considerations to man's material wellbeing. It is Conservatism that puts material things in their proper place – that has a structured view of the human being and of human society, in which economics plays only a subsidiary role.

The root difference between the Conservatives and the Liberals of today is that Conservatives take account of the *whole* man, while the Liberals tend to look only at the material side of man's nature. The Conservative believes that man is, in part, an economic, an animal creature; but that he is also a spiritual creature with spiritual needs and spiritual desires. What is more, these needs and desires reflect the *superior* side of man's nature, and thus take precedence over his economic wants. Conservatism therefore looks upon the enhancement of man's spiritual nature as the primary concern of political philosophy. Liberals, on the other hand – in the name of a concern for 'human beings' – regard the satisfaction of economic wants as the dominant mission of society. They are, moreover, in a hurry. So that their characteristic approach is to harness the society's political and economic forces into a collective effort to *compel* 'progress'. In this approach, I believe they fight against Nature.

Surely the first obligation of a political thinker is to understand the nature of man. The Conservative does not claim special powers of perception on this point, but he does claim a familiarity with the accumulated wisdom and experience of history, and he is not too proud to learn from the great minds of the past.

The first thing he has learned about man is that each member of the species is a unique creature. Man's most sacred possession is his individual soul – which has an immortal side, but also a mortal one. The mortal side establishes his absolute differentness from every other human being. *Only a philosophy that takes into account the essential differences between men, and, accordingly, makes provision for developing the different potentialities of each man can claim to be in accord with Nature.* We have heard much in our time about 'the common man'. It is a concept that pays little attention to the history of a nation that grew great through the initiative and ambition of uncommon men. The Conservative knows that to regard man as part of an undifferentiated mass is to consign him to ultimate slavery.

Secondly, the Conservative has learned that the economic and spiritual aspects of man's nature are inextricably intertwined. He cannot be economically free, or even economically efficient, if he is enslaved politically; conversely, man's political freedom is illusory if he is dependent for his economic needs on the State.

The Conservative realizes, thirdly, that man's development, in both its spiritual and material aspects, is not something that can be directed by outside forces. Every man, for his individual good and for the good of his society, is responsible for his *own* development. The choices that govern his life are choices that *he* must make; they cannot be made by any other human being, or by a collectivity of human beings. If the Conservative is less anxious than his Liberal brethren to increase Social Security 'benefits', it is because he is more anxious than his Liberal brethren that people be free throughout their lives to spend their earnings when and as they see fit.

So it is that Conservatism, throughout history, has regarded man neither as a potential pawn of other men, nor as a part of a general collectivity in which the sacredness and the separate identity of individual human beings are ignored. Throughout history, true Conservatism has been at war equally with autocrats and with 'democratic' Jacobins. The true Conservative was sympathetic with the plight of the hapless peasant under the tyranny of the French monarchy. And he was equally revolted at the attempt to solve that problem by a mob tyranny that paraded under the banner of egalitarianism. The conscience of the Conservative is pricked by *anyone* who would debase the dignity of the individual human being. Today, therefore, he is at odds with dictators who rule by terror, and equally with those gentler collectivists who ask our permission to play God with the human race.

With this view of the nature of man, it is understandable that the Conservative looks upon politics as the art of achieving the maximum amount of freedom for individuals that is consistent with the maintenance of the social order. The Conservative is the first to understand that the practice of freedom requires the establishment of order: it is impossible for one man to be free if another is able to deny him the exercise of his freedom. But the Conservative also recognizes that the political power on which order is based is a self-aggrandizing force; that its appetite grows with eating. He knows that the utmost vigilance and care are required to keep political power within its proper bounds.

In our day, order is pretty well taken care of. The delicate balance that ideally exists between freedom and order has long since tipped against freedom practically everywhere on earth. In some countries, freedom is altogether down and order holds absolute sway. In our country the trend is less far advanced, but it is well along and gathering momentum every day. Thus, for the American Conservative, there is no difficulty in identifying the day's over-riding political challenge: it is *to preserve and extend freedom.* As he surveys the various attitudes and institutions and laws that currently prevail in America, many questions will occur to him, but the Conservative's first concern will always be: *Are we maximizing freedom?*

3 *Progressives*

3.1 LAW AND MORALITY

From Oliver Wendell Holmes, an address on 'The Path of the Law'
printed in the Harvard Law Review, *Vol. 10, 25 March 1897.*

During the period treated in these readings the United States has
been fortunate in its capacity to produce outstanding jurists. The
names of Oliver Wendell Holmes Jr, Louis Brandeis, Roscoe
Pound and Felix Frankfurter are a sufficient testimony to this
fact. These men could be termed the guardians of the liberal
tradition in American jurisprudence during the present century.
Between them they contributed massively to the survival of that
tradition.

Oliver Wendell Holmes Jr was perhaps the most famous
Supreme Court Justice in the history of the court, with the possible
exception of John Marshall who served on the court for thirty-four
years (1801–35). Holmes's approach to the law was deeply historical and humane. In his book *The Common Law* (1881) Holmes
asserted 'the life of the law has not been logic: it has been experience. . . . The law embodies the story of a nation's development
through many centuries, and it cannot be dealt with as if it
contained only the axioms and corollaries of a book of mathematics.'

Some years later Holmes returned to this theme in an address he
gave on 'The Path of the Law'. Holmes wished to draw a distinction between law and morality in the section of his address given
here.

When we study law we are not studying a mystery but a well-known profession. We are studying what we shall want in order to appear before judges, or to advise people in such a way as to keep them out of court. The reason why it is a profession, why people will pay lawyers to argue for them or to advise them, is that in societies like ours the command of the public force is entrusted to the judges in certain cases, and the whole power of the state will be put forth, if necessary, to carry out their judgments and decrees. People want to know under what circumstances and how far they will run the risk of coming against what is so much stronger than themselves, and hence it becomes a business to find out when this danger is to be feared. The object of our study, then, is prediction, the prediction of the incidence of the public force through the instrumentality of the courts.

The means of the study are a body of reports, of treatises, and of statutes, in this country and in England, extending back for six hundred years, and now increasing annually by hundreds. In these sibylline leaves are gathered the scattered prophecies of the past upon the cases in which the axe will fall. These are what properly have been called the oracles of the law. Far the most important and pretty nearly the whole meaning of every new effort of legal thought is to make these prophecies more precise, and to generalize them into a thoroughly connected system. The process is one, from a lawyer's statement of a case, eliminating as it does all the dramatic elements with which his client's story has clothed it, and retaining only the facts of legal import, up to the final analyses and abstract universals of theoretic jurisprudence. . . .

The first thing for a business-like understanding of the matter is to understand its limits, and therefore I think it desirable at once to point out and dispel a confusion between morality and law, which sometimes rises to the height of conscious theory, and more often and indeed constantly is making trouble in detail without reaching the point of consciousness. You can see very plainly that a bad man has as much reason as a good one for wishing to avoid an encounter with the public force, and therefore you can see the practical importance of the distinction between morality and law. A man who cares nothing for an ethical rule which is believed and practised by his neighbours is likely nevertheless to care a good deal to avoid being made to pay money, and will want to keep out of jail if he can.

I take it for granted that no hearer of mine will misinterpret what I have to say as the language of cynicism. The law is the witness and external deposit of our moral life. Its history is the history of the moral development of the race. The practice of it, in spite of popular jests, tends to make good citizens and good men. When I emphasize the difference between law and morals I do so with reference to a single end, that of learning and understanding the law. For that purpose you must definitely master its specific marks, and it is for that I ask you for the moment to imagine yourselves indifferent to other and greater things.

I do not say that there is not a wider point of view from which the distinction between law and morals becomes of secondary or no importance, as all mathematical distinctions vanish in presence of the infinite. But I do say that that distinction is of the first importance for the object which we are here to consider – a right study and mastery of the law as a business with well understood limits, a body of dogma enclosed within definite lines. I have just shown the practical reason for saying so. If you want to know the law and nothing else, you must look at it as a bad man, who cares only for the material consequences which such knowledge enables him to predict, not as a good one, who finds his reasons for conduct, whether inside the law or outside of it, in the vaguer sanctions of conscience. The theoretical importance of the distinction is no less, if you would reason on your subject aright. The law is full of phraseology drawn from morals, and by the mere force of language continually invites us to pass from one domain to the other without perceiving it, as we are sure to do unless we have the boundary constantly before our minds. The law talks about rights, and duties, and malice, and intent, and negligence, and so forth, and nothing is easier, or, I may say, more common in legal reasoning, than to take these words in their moral sense, at some stage of the argument, and so to drop into fallacy. For instance, when we speak of the rights of man in a moral sense, we mean to mark the limits of interference with individual freedom which we think are prescribed by conscience, or by our ideal, however reached. Yet it is certain that many laws have been enforced in the past, and it is likely that some are enforced now, which are condemned by the most enlightened opinion of the time, or which at all events pass the limit of interference as many consciences would draw it. Manifestly, therefore, nothing but confusion of thought can result from assuming that the rights of man in a moral sense are equally rights in the sense of the Constitution and the law. No doubt simple and extreme cases can be put of imaginable laws which the statute-making power would not dare to enact, even in the absence of written constitutional prohibitions, because the community would rise in rebellion and fight; and this gives some plausibility to the proposition that the law, if not a part of morality, is limited by it. But this limit of power is not co-extensive with any system of morals. . . .

So much for the limits of the law. The next thing which I wish to consider is what are the forces which determine its content and its growth. You may assume, with Hobbes and Bentham and Austin, that all law emanates from the sovereign, even when the first human being to enunciate it are the judges, or you may think that law is the voice of the Zeitgeist, or what you like. It is all one to my present purpose. Even if every decision required the sanction of an emperor with despotic power and a whimsical turn of mind, we should be interested none the less, still with a view to prediction, in discovering some order, some rational explanation, and some principle of growth for the rules which he laid down. In every system there are such explanations and principles to be found. It is with regard to them that a second fallacy comes in, which I think it important to expose.

The fallacy to which I refer is the notion that the only force at work in the development of the law is logic. In the broadest sense, indeed, that notion would be true. The postulate on which we think about the universe is that there is a fixed quantitative relation between every phenomenon and its antecedents and consequents. If there is such a thing as a phenomenon without these fixed quantitative relations, it is a miracle. It is outside the law of cause and effect, and as such transcends our power of thought, or at least is something to or from which we cannot reason. The condition of our thinking about the universe is that it is capable of being thought about rationally, or, in other words, that every part of it is effect and cause in the same sense in which those parts are with which we are most familiar. So in the broadest sense it is true that the law is a logical development, like everything else. The danger of which I speak is not the admission that the principles of governing other phenomena also govern the law, but the notion that a given system, ours, for instance, can be worked out like mathematics from some general axioms of conduct. This is the natural error of the schools, but it is not confined to them. I once heard a very eminent judge say that he never let a decision go until he was absolutely sure that it was right. So judicial dissent often is blamed, as if it meant simply that one side or the other were not doing their sums right, and if they would take more trouble, agreement inevitably would come.

This mode of thinking is entirely natural. The training of lawyers is a training in logic. The processes of analogy, discrimination, and deduction are those in which they are most at home. The language of judicial decision is mainly the language of logic. And the logical method and form flatter that longing for certainty and for repose which is in every human mind. But certainty generally is illusion, and repose is not the destiny of man. Behind the logical form lies a judgement as to the relative worth and importance of competing legislative grounds, often an inarticulate and unconscious judgement, it is true, and yet the very root and nerve of the whole proceeding. You can give any conclusion a logical form. You always can imply a condition in a contract. But why do you imply it? It is because of some belief as to the practice of the community or of a class, or because of some opinion as to policy, or, in short, because of some attitude of yours upon a matter not capable of exact quantitative measurement, and therefore not capable of founding exact logical conclusions. Such matters really are battle grounds where the means do not exist for determinations that shall be good for all time, and where the decision can do no more than embody the preference of a given body in a given time and place. We do not realize how large a part of our law is open to reconsideration upon a slight change in the habit of the public mind. No concrete proposition is self evident, no matter how ready we may be to accept it.

3.2 FREEDOM OF SPEECH

Speech by Judge Brandeis in the case of Whitney v. California, *274 US 357, at 374–77, 1927.*

Louis Brandeis (1856–1941) was another great liberal Justice of the US Supreme Court. During the First World War, and following the Russian Revolution, the court was often called upon to decide cases of treason, sedition, or plots to subvert the government. The test in such cases was usually taken to be the opinion delivered by Holmes, which declared that the government had a right to punish, or to restrict ordinary freedoms, if the evidence in the case confirmed that there was a 'clear and present danger' to the institutions of government in the United States.

In 1927 the Supreme Court tried a case sent on appeal from the Californian courts, where an elderly social worker, Anita Whitney, had been sentenced for attending a meeting of the Communist Labor Party. Justice Brandeis delivered the following opinion in the case:

This Court has not yet fixed the standard by which to determine when a danger shall be deemed clear; how remote the danger may be and yet be deemed present; and what degree of evil shall be deemed sufficiently substantial to justify resort to abridgment of free speech and assembly as the means of protection. To reach sound conclusions on these matters, we must bear in mind why a state is, ordinarily, denied the power to prohibit dissemination of social, economic, and political doctrine which a vast majority of its citizens believes to be false and fraught with evil consequences.

Those who won our independence believed that the final end of the state was to make men free to develop their faculties; and that in its government the deliberative forces should prevail over the arbitrary. They valued liberty both as an end and as a means. They believed liberty to be the secret of happiness, and courage to be the secret of liberty. They believed that freedom to think as you will and to speak as you think are means indispensable to the discovery and spread of political truth; that without free speech and assembly discussion would be futile; that with them, discussion affords ordinarily adequate protection against the dissemination of noxious doctrine; that the greatest menace to freedom is an inert people; that public discussion is a political duty; and that this should be a fundamental principle of the American government. They recognized the risks to which all human institutions are subject. But they knew that order cannot be secured merely through fear of punishment for its infraction; that it is hazardous to discourage thought, hope, and imagination; that fear breeds repression; that repression breeds hate; that hate menaces stable government; that the path of safety lies in the opportunity to discuss freely supposed grievances and proposed remedies; and that the fitting remedy for evil counsels is good ones. Believing in the power of reason as applied through public discussion, they eschewed silence coerced by law – the argument of force in its worst form. Recognizing the occasional tyrannies of governing majorities, they amended the Constitution so that free speech and assembly should be guaranteed.

Fear of serious injury cannot alone justify suppression of free speech and assembly. Men feared witches and burnt women. It is the function of speech to free men from the bondage of irrational fears. To justify suppression of free speech there must be reasonable ground to fear that serious evil will result if free speech is practiced. There must be reasonable ground to believe that the danger apprehended is imminent. There must be reasonable ground to believe that the evil to be prevented is a serious one. Every denunciation of existing law tends in some measure to increase the probability that there will be violation of it. Condonation of a breach enhances the probability. Expressions of approval add to the probability. Propagation of the criminal state of mind by teaching syndicalism increases it. Advocacy of law-breaking heightens it still further. But even advocacy of violation, however reprehensible morally, is not a justification for denying free speech where the advocacy falls short of incitement and there is nothing to indicate that the advocacy would be immediately acted on. The wide difference between advocacy and incitement, between preparation and attempt, between assembling and conspiracy, must be borne in mind. In order to support a finding of clear and present danger it must be shown either that immediate serious violence was to be expected or was advocated, or that the past conduct furnished reason to believe that such advocacy was then contemplated.

Those who won our independence by revolution were not cowards. They did not fear political change. They did not exalt order at the cost of liberty. To courageous, self-reliant men, with confidence in the power of free and fearless reasoning applied through the processes of popular government, no danger flowing from speech can be deemed clear and present, unless the incidence of the evil apprehended is so imminent that it may befall before there is opportunity for full discussion. If there be time to expose through discussion the falsehood and fallacies, to avert the evil by the processes of education, the remedy to be applied is more speech, not enforced silence. Only an emergency can justify repression. Such must be the rule if authority is to be reconciled with freedom. Such, in my opinion, is the command of the Constitution. It is therefore always open to Americans to challenge a law abridging free speech and assembly by showing that there was no emergency justifying it.

3.3. DEMOCRACY IN FORM AND ESSENCE

From John Dewey, 'Democracy and Educational Administration',
School and Society, *XLV, 3 April 1937, pp. 457-9.*

John Dewey's pragmatism induced a healthy scepticism on the differences between the outward and visible forms of democracy, and their inner spirit or essence. In an article written in 1937 Dewey pointed out that a society might have all the forms and institutions of democracy, yet be profoundly undemocratic. The following extract gives the essence of his argument.

Universal suffrage, recurring elections, responsibility of those who are in political power to the voters, and the other factors of democratic government are means that have been found expedient for realizing democracy as the truly human way of living. They are not a final end and a final value. They are to be judged on the basis of their contribution to an end. It is a form of idolatry to erect means into the end which they serve. Democratic political forms are simply the best means that human wit has devised up to a special time in history. But they rest upon the idea that no man or limited set of men is wise enough or good enough to rule others without their consent; the positive meaning of this statement is that all those who are affected by social institutions must have a share in producing and managing them. The two facts that each one is influenced in what he does and enjoys and in what he becomes by the institutions under which he lives, and that therefore he shall have, in a democracy, a voice in shaping them, are the passive and active sides of the same fact.

The development of political democracy came about through substitution of the method of mutual consultation and voluntary agreement for the method of subordination of the many to the few enforced from above. Social arrangements which involve fixed subordination are maintained by coercion. The coercion need not be physical. There have existed, for short periods, benevolent despotisms. But coercion of some sort there has been; perhaps economic, certainly psychological and moral. The very fact of exclusion from participation is a subtle form of suppression. It gives individuals no opportunity to reflect and decide upon what is good for them. Others who are supposed to be wiser and who in any case have more power decide the question for them and also decide the methods and means by which subjects may arrive at the enjoyment of what is good for them. This form of coercion and suppression is more subtle and more effective than are overt intimidation and restraint. When it is habitual and embodied in social institutions, it seems the normal and natural state of affairs. The mass usually become unaware that they have a claim to a development of their own powers. Their experience is so restricted that they are not conscious of restriction. It is part of the democratic conception that they as individuals are not the only sufferers, but that the whole social body is deprived of the potential resources that should be at its service. The individuals of the submerged mass may not be very wise. But there is one thing they are wiser about than anybody else can be, and that is where the shoe pinches, the troubles they suffer from.

The foundation of democracy is faith in the capacities of human nature; faith in human intelligence and in the power of pooled and co-operative experience. It is not belief that these things are complete but that if given a show they will grow and be able to generate progressively the knowledge and wisdom needed to guide collective action. Every autocratic and authoritarian scheme of social action rests on a belief that the needed intelligence is confined to a superior few, who because of inherent natural gifts are endowed with the ability and the right to control the conduct of others; laying down principles and rules and directing the ways in which they are carried out. It would be foolish to deny that much can be said for this point of view. It is that which controlled human relations in social groups for much the greater part of human history. The democratic faith has emerged very, very recently in the history of mankind. Even where democracies now exist, men's minds and feelings are still permeated with ideas about leadership imposed from above, ideas that developed in the long early history of mankind. After democratic political institutions were nominally established, beliefs and ways of looking at life and of acting that originated when men and women were externally controlled and subjected to arbitrary power, persisted in the family, the church, business and the school, and experience shows that as long as they persist there, political democracy is not secure.

Belief in equality is an element of the democratic credo. It is not however, belief in equality of natural endowments. Those who proclaimed the idea of equality did not suppose they were enunciating a psychological doctrine, but a legal and political one. All individuals are entitled to equality of treatment by law and in its administration. Each one is affected equally in quality if not in quantity by the institutions under which he lives and has an equal right to express his judgement, although the weight of his judgement may not be equal in amount when it enters into the pooled result to that of others. In short, each one is equally an individual and entitled to equal opportunity of development of his own capacities, be they large or small in range. Moreover, each has needs of his own, as significant to him as those of others are to them.

3.4 FOUR FREEDOMS

From Franklin D. Roosevelt, 'Four Freedoms' message to Congress, Congressional Record, 77 Congress, 1 Session. LXXXVII, Part 1, pp. 45–7.

In their annual messages to Congress, or State of the Union addresses, American Presidents seldom make major contributions to the literature of democracy. Occasionally, however, there are exceptions. In January 1941, when Europe was engulfed by war, President Franklin D. Roosevelt delivered his now famous 'Four Freedoms' message to Congress. It reminded the Congress – and the American people – that the advance of totalitarianism in Europe demanded a special vigilance from Americans if their own democracy was to survive.

The Annual Message to the Congress 6 January 1941.
I address you, the Members of the Seventy-seventh Congress, at a moment unprecedented in the history of the Union. I use the word 'unprecedented', because at no previous time has

American security been as seriously threatened from without as it is today.

Since the permanent formation of our Government under the Constitution, in 1789, most of the periods of crisis in our history have related to our domestic affairs. Fortunately, only one of these – the four-year War Between the States – ever threatened our national unity. Today, thank God, one hundred and thirty million Americans, in forty-eight States, have forgotten points of the compass in our national unity.

It is true that prior to 1914 the United States often had been disturbed by events in other Continents. We had even engaged in two wars with European nations and in a number of undeclared wars in the West Indies, in the Mediterranean and in the Pacific for the maintenance of American rights and for the principles of peaceful commerce. But in no case had a serious threat been raised against our national safety or our continued independence. . . .

Every realist knows that the democratic way of life is at this moment being directly assailed in every part of the world – assailed either by arms, or by secret spreading of poisonous propaganda by those who seek to destroy unity and promote discord in nations that are still at peace.

During sixteen long months this assault has blotted out the whole pattern of democratic life in an appalling number of independent nations, great and small. The assailants are still on the march, threatening other nations, great and small.

Therefore, as your President, performing my constitutional duty to 'give to the Congress information of the state of the Union', I find it, unhappily, necessary to report that the future and the safety of our country and of our democracy are overwhelmingly involved in events far beyond our borders. . . .

Just as our national policy in internal affairs has been based upon a decent respect for the rights and the dignity of all our fellow men within our gates, so our national policy in foreign affairs has been based on a decent respect for the rights and dignity of all nations, large and small. And the justice of morality must and will win in the end.

Our national policy is this:

First, by an impressive expression of the public will and without regard to partisanship, we are committed to all-inclusive national defence.

Second, by an impressive expression of the public will and without regard to partisanship, we are committed to full support of all those resolute peoples, everywhere, who are resisting aggression and are thereby keeping war away from our Hemisphere. By this support, we express our determination that the democratic cause shall prevail; and we strengthen the defence and the security of our own nation.

Third, by an impressive expression of the public will and without regard to partisanship, we are committed to the proposition that principles of morality and considerations for our own security will never permit us to acquiesce in a peace dictated by aggressors and sponsored by appeasers. We know that enduring peace cannot be bought at the cost of other people's freedom. . . .

Certainly this is no time for any of us to stop thinking about the social and economic problems which are the root cause of the social revolution which is today a supreme factor in the world.

For there is nothing mysterious about the foundations of a healthy and strong democracy. The basic things expected by our people of their political and economic systems are simple. They are:

Equality of opportunity for youth and for others.

Jobs for those who can work.

Security for those who need it.

The ending of special privilege for the few.

The preservation of civil liberties for all.

The enjoyment of the fruits of scientific progress in a wider and constantly rising standard of living.

These are the simple, basic things that must never be lost sight of in the turmoil and unbelievable complexity of our modern world. The inner and abiding strength of our economic and political systems is dependent upon the degree to which they fulfil these expectations. . . .

In the future days, which we seek to make secure, we look forward to a world founded upon four essential human freedoms.

The first is freedom of speech and expression – everywhere in the world.

The second is freedom of every person to worship God in his own way – everywhere in the world.

The third is freedom from want – which, translated into world terms, means economic understandings which will secure to every nation a healthy peacetime life for its inhabitants – everywhere in the world.

The fourth is freedom from fear – which, translated into world terms, means a world-wide reduction of armaments to such a point and in such a thorough fashion that no nation will be in a position to commit an act of physical aggression against any neighbour – anywhere in the world.

That is no vision of a distant millennium. It is a definite basis for a kind of world attainable in our own time and generation. That kind of world is the very antithesis of the so-called new order of tyranny which the dictators seek to create with the crash of a bomb.

To that new order we oppose the greater conception – the moral order. A good society is able to face schemes of world domination and foreign revolutions alike without fear.

Since the beginning of our American history, we have been engaged in change – in a perpetual peaceful revolution – a revolution which goes on steadily, quietly adjusting itself to changing conditions – without the concentration camp or the quick-lime in the ditch. The world order which we seek is the co-operation of free countries, working together in a friendly, civilized society.

3.5 THE PRESS AND PROPAGANDA

From Carl Becker, lectures given at the University of Virginia published under the title Modern Democracy, *1941 (1950 edition), pp. 56–61.*

A free Press is commonly taken to be one of the central safeguards of a democratic tradition. Nevertheless the Press also represents a concentration of power and resources which no ordinary citizen can match. In a course of lectures at the University of Virginia in 1940 the American historian Carl Becker (1873–1945) drew attention to this problem.

In any society there is bound to be a close connection between economic and political power. In any society those who possess economic power, like other people, are disposed to identify their economic interests with the general good, and to promote their interests through the mechanism of politics and propaganda. But in modern industrial societies, based upon democratic political control and the principle of free economic enterprise, the beneficiaries of private property in the means of production are in a peculiarly advantageous position for moulding opinion and shaping legislation. Their advantage arises less from the fact that they can and do spend money freely for those purposes, than from the fact that political procedure and the instruments of propaganda are so integrated with the industrial system that legislation and opinion more or less automatically respond to the pressure of the system of free enterprise from which their economic power is derived.

In democratic societies political power is mediated through political parties organized primarily for the purpose of obtaining control of the government by winning elections. To win elections a political party must of course formulate a programme of legislation that will appeal to the voters. But elections are not won on the merits of a programme alone. The winning of an election is a practical business enterprise, which calls for a capital investment in the form of a campaign fund, and for an intricate organization of employees – a political machine managed by professional politicians whose business it is to deliver the vote. Contributions to the campaign fund may be made from interested or disinterested motives; but the largest contributions will commonly be made by wealthy men or corporations expecting in return that the party will not, at the very least, be altogether indifferent to the kind of legislation they desire.

The professional politician, whose business it is to deliver the vote, is concerned primarily with the vote of those whose loyalty to the party is determined less by the merits of the party programme than by the disposition of the party to confer tangible benefits upon them. The function of the highest species of politician is to handle the patronage, to distribute appointive offices to those who can best serve the party. The function of the lowest species of politician – the *déclassé* ward heeler – is to do what respectable statesmen know must be done but are prevented by the mores from doing themselves, namely, to see to it that the poor and dispossessed are provided with a minimum of subsistence, and not too much hampered in their private enterprises, even sometimes if they happen to be on the wrong side of the fence, by the majesty of the law. In delivering the vote, the ward heeler is the henchman of the political boss, the political boss has the necessary contacts with the party leaders who hold elective or appointive offices, and the political leaders have the necessary personal and social contacts with the businessmen who contribute so generously to the campaign fund. In every community, large or small, there is this unavowed, undercover integration of economic and political power; and apart from some unanticipated ethical disturbance in the climate of opinion, legislation, always defended by statesmen in terms of the common good, is always insensibly influenced by the pressure of the predominant industrial interest.

In moulding opinion, no less than in shaping legislation, those who possess economic power have a great advantage over the general run of citizens. This is not to say that freedom of speech and the Press does not exist in democratic societies. One has only to compare nondemocratic with democratic societies to realize that, in a very real and important sense, it does exist. In democratic societies any man may freely express his opinion without first looking furtively over his shoulder to see if a government spy is in the offing; any man may publish a book or a newspaper without first submitting it to an official censor. This is the fundamentally important privilege; and no cataloguing of incidental violations of civil liberties, serious and deplorable as they are, can obscure the fact that through the Press and the radio detailed information about events, and the most diverse opinions, are with little let or hindrance daily and hourly presented to the people.

Nevertheless, the average individual, although free to express his ideas, plays a distinctly minor role in the moulding of opinion: his role is not to initiate, but passively to receive information and ideas presented to him by others. The propaganda of social or political opinion, to be effective under modern conditions, must be organized; and its promoters will have an indifferent success unless they resort to mass production and distribution of their wares. The chief instruments of propaganda – the Press and broadcasting stations – are not readily available to the average individual for conveying his ideas: they can be effectively used only by the government, political parties and party leaders, prominent organizations, wealthy men and business corporations, associations organized for specific purposes, and the writers of books which publishing houses find it worth while to publish.

Even more important is the fact that the instruments of propaganda are themselves business corporations organized and financed for profit, and as such subject to those influences that condition and are conditioned by the system of free economic enterprise. Newspapers are free to print all the news that's fit to print; but they cannot consistently propagate ideas that will alienate the business interests whose paid advertisements enable them to distribute profits to the stockholders. Broadcasting corporations are free from government censorship, or reasonably so, reasonably free to broadcast what they will; but in the last analysis they will not broadcast that which seriously offends the prevailing mores, or the business enterprises which, in this country at least, sponsor and finance their programmes of entertainment. In democratic societies free and impartial discussion, from which the truth is supposed to emerge, is permitted and does occur. But the thinking of the average man is largely shaped by a wealth of factual information and the conflicting opinions which the selective process of competitive business enterprise presents to him for consideration: information, the truth of which he cannot verify; ideas, formulated by persons he does not know, and too often inspired by private economic interests that are never avowed.

Such, in broad outline, are the circumstances that may serve to explain the profound discord between democracy as an ideal and as a reality. In terms of the ideal there should have emerged from the liberal-democratic revolution a relatively simple society of free, equal, and prosperous citizens, fraternally co-operating to effect, by rational discussion and mutual concession, the common good. In fact there emerged an extremely complex society in which highly intricate and impersonal economic forces, stronger than goodwill or deliberate intention or rational direction, brought about an increasing concentration of wealth and power in the hands of the fortunate few, and thereby nullified, for the majority of the people, many of those essential liberties which provide both the theoretical justification and the necessary conditions for the practical success of democratic institutions.

3.6. PRAGMATIC LIBERALISM

From Alan P. Grimes, 'The Pragmatic Course of Liberalism', Western Political Quarterly, IX, no. 3, September 1956, pp. 633–40.

Liberalism has always eluded specific definition. This is one of its strengths but also, on occasion, one of its weaknesses, especially when liberal democracy is under attack. In the 1930s and also in the 1950s, liberalism in the United States was often under attack from the conservative Right. In both decades men came forward to defend liberalism. In the following extract an American scholar offers a definition and a defence, and links liberalism with another strand of American thought, pragmatism.

Liberal, and liberalism, have always presented problems in definition. Must we then despair of definition? Is a liberal nothing more than any man who calls himself one? Or is called one?

It seems to me that in spite of the obvious confusions associated with liberal and liberalism, we can at least attempt a definition which may be useful for classifying concepts and identifying ideas. There is certainly more to liberalism than the label. It represents a system of ideas that aims at the realization of the pluralistic society, favouring diversity in politics, economics, religion, and our cultural life. It is opposed to uniformity; it is opposed to conformity. It is, in the broadest sense of the word, anti-monopolistic; for it favours the widest possible degree of self-determination. It denotes an attitude towards human problems as well as goals for human endeavour. It seeks in its simplest sense to advance the freedom of man. It is essentially anti-authoritarian, and represents the claims of those who are out of power and thus lacking in authority; but who, had they the power, would not impose authoritarian solutions on others. It seeks to increase the individuality of man by increasing his area of choice and decision. It is essentially humanitarian in its appeal and therefore endorses toleration and is motivated by a sense of compassion for mankind. Finally it is flexible in the method of its realization and, while a doctrine, is itself not doctrinaire. These are, I believe, the basic components of liberalism. Let me explain them further.

1. If liberalism seeks to advance the freedom of man it would

seem to be implicit that the freedom of man, rather than his restraint, is a desirable end in itself. A truly liberal society would thus be a society of free men. The free man is thus the end product of the free society. Now, of course, the general issue of freedom always resolves itself into a specific question of whose freedom to do what. The diversity of our natures – of our temperaments, desires, and aversions – together with the organizational necessities of our social life, make impossible equal freedom to all men. Thus the question of 'whose freedom' is perhaps the most crucial issue in politics. The interdependence of modern society gives all 'freedoms' consequences. The group nature of society, however, places men in often conflicting camps, in competition for freedom as they are for power. The issue of freedom is in fact directly related to the issue of power in society so that the question 'whose freedom?' also involves the question 'whose power?' Freedom, to be realized, must be translated into power while power is the expression of those in authority exercising their freedom. I should qualify this to note that power is, of course, reciprocal and not the possession solely of those in command of institutions; those who are governed control in some manner those who do the governing. Indeed the vitality of this interaction is the measure of a democracy. But the preponderance of power, and freedom, is with those who make and enforce decisions with social consequences.

When the liberal talks about free men in a free society he is usually referring to that vast majority of men who do not directly make enforceable decisions with social consequences. These are the people whose freedoms the liberal wishes to extend, those people whose sphere of meaningful choices is at the time restricted. For all the inherent conflicts in society liberalism does not suppose with Hobbes that by maximizing the areas of private judgement society would eventuate in a war of all against all. It rather supposes with Locke no socially destructive conflict between private choices and majority rule; that the majority is best able to determine the social conditions of the public good and that men capable of this judgement will doubtless respect the human dignity of the minority.

To extend the freedom of some to make socially consequential decisions often curtails the freedom of others to make opposing decisions on the same subject. But we must always ask whose freedom was curtailed and whose extended, and what was the conventional status in authority of the respective groups, and how great was their number of supporters. Does this measure at issue promote the freedom of the many or the few? To work in the direction of a free society we must therefore maximize the freedoms of the many. Implicit therefore in liberalism is the concept of human worth, of human dignity, of man as the end and social institutions as the means. Social institutions have thus no greater dignity than man; indeed, to the contrary, they exist only to achieve the dignity of man by implementing his individuality, by helping him fulfil himself. The reverence for the institutions of society, which in part characterizes the conservative, is thus opposed to liberalism.

2. Liberalism, as has been indicated, is anti-authoritarian and arises as a protest of those out of power against the uses of power to which those in authority are subjecting them. Thus liberalism arises as a protest against traditional forms of authority wherever found. Because those in possession of power seldom believe that they are acting in an authoritarian fashion, this decision must be made by those subject to authority. Liberalism is thus by and large the creed of the dispossessed, the dissenter, of those who are subject to the decisions which others make. Because we live in a web of social relationships involving innumerable institutions, chains of command arising through prestige or power, man is continually brought under the control of authority possessed by others. The effort to remain free involves, as Jefferson said, 'eternal vigilance'. There is no final distribution of power which guarantees liberty for those not possessing authority. Using the analogy of Woodrow Wilson, we must be like the Red Queen constantly on the run in order even to maintain our present position. The freedoms of the past have a way of making possible the servitudes of the present. As social institutions change they present new problems in authority and restraint, and the zealous liberal finds that his struggle must take on new forms and new foes in order to preserve the liberties that now exist. Liberalism thus looks to those lacking in power in society for its test of the adequacies of present freedoms. And here again we may distinguish liberalism from conservatism, for the latter takes its cue from those traditionally in authority.

3. Liberalism seeks to increase the individuality of man by increasing his area of choice. This is, of course, closely allied with its anti-authoritarian impulse. It seeks to increase the individual's

opportunity for making meaningful decisions. It seeks, in other words, a continuous revolution in decision-making in the direction of those individuals who will be most subject to the consequences of the decision. The area of choice can never be constant or static, but moves with social flux, responding to the felt necessities of the times. Today's most vital choices may not appear very significant tomorrow. The question of meaningfulness must then be determined by those who feel the consequences of past decisions or fear the consequences of future ones. Thus liberalism usually follows the path of protest. Implicit, of course, is the assumption of equality; positing man as an end in himself carries with it the belief that to each man choices are important. Each man must decide where restraints are most oppressive, where freedom is most desired. The logic of free choice for all men thus rests upon the assumption of the equality of all men, otherwise we should have to accept the *élitist* argument in favour of free choice for only the few. Individuality, freedom of choice, and equality are thus mutually dependent concepts. Again, we may distinguish the liberal from the conservative, for at heart, if not overtly, the conservative rejects the belief in equality and the legitimacy of freedom of choice for all men. For the conservative inevitably argues in favour of freedom of choice restricted to the aristocracy, the *élite*, or those who claim to possess superior talents or ability.

4. Another core concept of liberalism is humanitarianism. It seeks to support the weak and curb the strong. It seeks to redirect the flow of society's benefits – to prevent them from becoming the monopoly of the few – into the hands of the many. The privileges of the past thus through liberalism become the necessities of the present. In education, health, employment, and housing we think less of privilege and more of necessity as the fruits of our co-operative living are distributed more widely. Without a sense of compassion for one's fellow man, a sense of social obligation, a sense of tolerance and goodwill that cuts through all the artificial distinctions that separate individuals, men would act like so many cats in a bag. The benefits of man's social experience would then fall to the predatory, the strong, and the cunning. It is the humanitarianism in liberalism which rejects the notion that benefits should accrue only to those who can take the most and which constantly pushes against social institutions to see that benefits get the widest distribution. Humanitarianism wages a constant warfare against

conservatism. Conservatism is full of little mottos about not killing geese that lay golden eggs and endless other reasons why a wider distribution of the benefits of social experience is not possible in the present. The practice of humanitarianism inevitably displaces the existing power relationships; the *status quo* of superiors and subordinates is always disturbed a little as new groups gain the privileges of other groups. Liberalism pushes the frontier of privilege forward with the distant goal constantly in view that all men as men are privileged and entitled to all the necessities and some of the luxuries of civilized living. Conservatives love charity, as rewarding the giver as well as the receiver, but draw the line at a commitment to a social obligation that disturbs the existing power relationships. Liberals prefer obligation to charity as more in keeping with a belief in the dignity of all men.

5. Finally, liberalism is not a static creed or dogma, for dogmatism provides its own restraints. It is rather a tentative attitude towards social problems which stresses the role of reason and human ingenuity. Were it to settle for the conclusions of yesterday then it would be succumbing to the authoritarian restraint of past precept. In its efforts to free mankind liberalism seeks to free the mind as well as clothe the body. As social institutions change, new formulas for liberation must be devised based upon the felt necessities of the present. Liberalism indeed ceases to be liberal when it employs shibboleth in place of searching inquiry, when it becomes committed to yesterday's formulas as final answers. Herein, I believe, lies the sin of many 'liberals' of the past. By equating classical economics with liberalism, Manchester liberals so abused the term that for nearly fifty years Americans had to resort to the word 'progressive' to describe the attitude of liberals. So opprobrious did the term liberalism become, with its Manchester connotation, that it is difficult to realize that at one time it represented a genuinely liberal doctrine. Modern liberalism did not reach its final triumph with the policies of the New Deal or Fair Deal and a liberalism dependent upon such formulas might well go the way of Manchester liberalism, which was committed to free trade and civil service reform, for example, and judged all men by these tenets. Thus liberalism must continually look ahead. It must look to new ways of doing things, to new tentative and temporary expedients to perennial problems, to new ideas and new institutions. In a word it must be pragmatic. It must seek practical

answers to evident problems, but answers which work constantly in the direction of those without power, of those who lack the benefits, of those in other words who need the most help in order to fulfil the requirements of their individuality. Liberalism thus looks ahead, with a flexible approach, seeking to make the future better for more people; as conservatism looks back, aiming mainly to preserve the attainments of the past.

Now drawing together these five components of liberalism, we may define the term as follows: Liberalism denotes an attitude which seeks to make possible those social conditions in which the individuality of all men may best be realized. Because as a general rule those who possess authority enjoy a large measure of freedom, liberals, impelled by humanitarianism, seek to advance the freedom of those without authority, of those without special benefits. Liberalism is then the doctrine of the social and economic underdog. It is usually on the side of those who are neglected by the conventions of society, and thus it must eternally plead the unconventional cause.

With this approach to liberalism, I think we may fairly note its pragmatic course in modern times. And liberalism, as a social concept, like democracy which it informs and gives value to, is essentially a modern conception. Liberalism, perpetually seeking to free mankind from the authorities that restrain, establishes the goals which democracy implements. The methods of liberalism change as situations change but the goal of liberation remains constant. Thus liberalism follows a pragmatic course to realize constant ends. Without the constant ends there would be no continuity to liberalism and the term would possess no meaning beyond that of a temporary and convenient party label; yet without the pragmatic means liberalism would indicate nothing beyond vague aspirations, incapable of fulfilment.

3.7 FREEDOM IN THE AMERICAN CONTEXT

From Max Lerner, America as a Civilization, *London edition, 1958, pp. 452–5.*

The American historian and columnist Max Lerner devoted ten years to the prodigious task of explaining 'the pattern and inner meaning of contemporary American civilization'. He completed his task in the mid 1950s, when his book *America as a Civilization* appeared. Not every student of American democracy will care to tackle the one thousand pages Max Lerner needed in order to render account, but many passages contain valuable, original insights on American problems. The following passage occurs in a discussion of civil liberties in America.

The most elusive word in the political vocabulary, 'freedom' is also one of the most important in the American consciousness. It is the first image the American invokes when he counts the blessings of his state. The inheritor of the English and French revolutions, as well as of his own, he has gazed so long into the pool of freedom that he has fallen half in love with his own reflection in it. He may be at the base of the income pyramid or a segregated Negro in the South, yet whatever his place in the social system, he sets store by freedom: it gives him a yardstick to measure his deprivation and a hope that he can remedy it. The historical record shows that the denials of freedom are part of the scar tissue of American culture and not its principle of growth and being.

In the triad of American 'liberal capitalist democracy', the 'liberal' component has generally meant the freedom to make your own decisions in your political and personal life. There are many constraints that the American does not regard as the denial of freedom. The conditions of his job, the rules of his union, the rigours of business fluctuations, the tyrannies of the community, and the prejudices of his fellow men may in fact represent harsh constraints on him. Yet he does not consider them violations of his freedom because they come as the fabric of his everyday life, and not as encroachment by anyone in authority. He is prepared to accept the informal but not the formal constraints, those from within the culture but not those from political authority.

To be cramped by someone who has power or superior position in a graded official hierarchy – that is counted the real denial of freedom. For example, the Great Depression of the 1930s wiped out billions in property values and income, reduced many to pauperism, saddled others with burdens it took a lifetime to discharge: yet it was not held to have diminished American freedom. The real threat was held to be the structure of bureaucracy built to cope with the periodic economic breakdowns. The spirit of this thinking shows up in the story of the Negro, living in squalor and precariousness, who was asked what he had gained by exchanging the security of slavery for poverty in freedom, and who answered, 'There's something about the *looseness* of this here freedom that I like.'

The obvious defect of this conception is its negativism. It stresses freedom *from* the powers and principalities of organized government, but not freedom *for* the creative phases of living. It derives from the whole freedom constellation of the eighteenth century, which saw a simple and natural plan of self-regulating human life, complete with an economic and political theory, a psychology and a metaphysics, and which asked only that the government keep its hands off and leave it alone. It underscored *let live* but forgot that in the jungle of the industrial culture *let live* without *help live* can be morally empty.

Yet there are few civilizations in history in which freedom has flourished as it has in America. What explains it?

There have been three principal explanations – the environmental, the political, the economic. The environmentalists say that the isolation of America, cut off by oceans for centuries from the wars and embroilments of Europe and Asia, kept it from standing armies and internal crises, and therefore free. They say also that the continuing availability of frontier land gave an outlet to energies that might otherwise have clashed in civil conflicts. The economic explanation holds that the core of American freedom is the free-enterprise economy, on the theory that free markets make free men, that political and social freedoms could not have been preserved without freedom of investment and the job. The political explanation stresses the separation of powers, the limited state, and the *laissez-faire* tradition.

The environmental theories, with their core of truth, fail to note that geography is only part of a larger social environment, that the span of distance America had from the European centres was less important than the spaciousness of American institutions and their distance from European feudalism. Similarly, the economic approach must be seen as part of the economic expansionism of American life. During one phase of American history *laissez faire* played an important and releasing role; but later experience showed that a mixed economy was a better base for freedom, since one of the great threats to it is economic breakdown.

Finally there is the political argument from the separation of powers. But there are other forms of it more crucial than the traditional splitting of the three political areas of power: the separation of economic from political power, the separation of church from state power, the separation of military from civilian power, and the separation of majority passions from the power of the law. This seems the more productive approach.

American freedom has been largely interstitial, located in the crevices between necessary power systems. It is protected by the fact that the men who run the economy do not always run the country – and also the other way around. It is also protected by the fact that the men of religion, who shape and organize the supernatural beliefs of Americans, cannot use the power of the government to make their creed exclusive – and also the other way around, in the fact that the government cannot interfere with freedom of worship. Further, it is protected by the fact that those who can send men to death in war are themselves held to account by civilian authority – and again (the other way around) in the fact that the political leaders cannot make themselves military heroes and go off on adventures of glory. It is strengthened by the fact that there is an independent judiciary which need not, although it sometimes does, respond to temporary waves of popular hatred against particular groups – and (the other way around) by the tradition of judicial nonparticipation in the tensions of political life.

Thus freedom may be seen partly as a function of the way power is distributed, separated, and diffused in a society. Americans tend to think of the government as the prime enemy of freedom, and see the history of freedom in America as the story of a Manichaean struggle between the angels of (individualist) light and the hosts of (governmental) darkness. But governmental power is only one form of social power. Wherever power is concentrated, whether in a government bureaucracy, a corporate combine, a big trade-union, a military staff, a powerful opinion empire, or a church organization disciplined to action, those who care about freedom must find ways of isolating that power, keeping it from combining with other power clusters, and holding it to account and responsibility.

But this effort to hold power accountable, which may sometimes involve attempts to break it up in its concentrated form, may itself endanger freedom by rousing latent social hostilities. With its lusty energies American life has always had a considerable violence potential which has flared into actual violence when a challenge has been offered to the continuance of some power structure. For concentrated power, whatever its form, is never so dangerous as when it feels itself in danger. A number of the movements chipping away at the civil-liberties tradition have come from power groups that felt their status to be in jeopardy. This was true of the Federalists who passed the Alien and Sedition Acts; of the White Supremacy movements in the post-war South, using night riders to terrorize and disfranchise Negroes; of the Oriental Exclusion Acts, supported both by the landowners and the trade-unionists of the West Coast; of the vigilantist violence used against labour organizers in communities where the police are tied in with the holders of economic power, and where even the churches sanction the fusion.

The history of a people is, from one angle, the story of the see-sawing acquisition and relinquishment of power by a number of competing and intermeshed groups. But to relinquish power is never pleasant. Sometimes it may lead to an almost paranoid fear of encirclement. Franklin Roosevelt expressed a double-edged truth when he listed 'freedom from fear' as one of the Four Freedoms. It is a truth because freedom from fear, rightly understood, can assure all the other freedoms. It is double-edged because the effort to achieve freedom from fear of the threats and challenges of foreign powers, and of subversion within, involves a military posture for the entire nation which itself breeds further fears and therefore dangers to freedom. One of the great difficulties is to distinguish between the fears which have a basis in reality and those which are anxieties and hallucinations.

3.8 THE DEMOCRATIC IDEA

From The Power of the Democratic Idea, *published by the Rockefeller Fund in 1960, pp. 400 ff.*

In recent years there has been a trend in the United States for gathering together scholars and specialists in order to discuss a single topic, or group of topics, in depth. The idea which underlies this trend is clearly in itself a democratic one: the assumption that truth is more likely to be discovered in certain areas of inquiry by means of joint discussion, rather than by the individual.

Between 1956 and 1960 the Rockefeller Fund of New York invited more than a hundred leading citizens of the United States to discuss the future prospects and problems of the American people. The participants included scholars, churchmen, labour leaders, industrialists, and members of Congress. One panel devoted itself to the topic 'The Power of the Democratic Idea'.

A distinctive conviction marks a democratic society. One part of this conviction is that all human arrangements are fallible. A second part is that men can improve the societies they inhabit if they are given the facts and are free to compare things as they are with their vision of things as they ought to be. It is a defining characteristic of a democratic society, accordingly, that nothing in its political or social life is immune to criticism and that it establishes and protects institutions whose purpose it is to subject the existing order of things to steady examination.

This process of self-examination has certain special features. It is conducted in the open. All members of the community are presumed to be free to engage in it, and all are held to be entitled to true information about the state of their society. Moreover, in a democratic society such public criticism has immediate and practical objectives. Men who are imbued with the democratic attitude are not likely to be content with the promise that the realization of their ideals must be put off to an indefinite future. They will want to see these ideals make a difference here and now.

A commitment to democracy, in short, is a commitment to an 'open society'. Democracy accepts its own fallibility. But it provides a method by which its mistakes can be corrected. It recognizes that men can be power-hungry and prone to self-delusion, that they can prefer old errors to new truths, that they can act without caring about what they are doing to others. And it believes that these human tendencies can only be held in check if they are exposed to the open air and subjected to other men's continuing judgement. This is the way, in the democratic view, that the goodness and rationality of men can have a chance to grow.

This belief in a process of criticism that is open to all brings us to another fundamental principle of a democratic outlook. The man with democratic feelings and convictions looks upon all men as members of the same moral community and as initially endowed with the same fundamental rights and obligations. He does not determine his obligations to others by considering their status in society or their racial or religious backgrounds. The respect and concern that a democratically-minded person shows for other men are shown for them as individuals; this respect and concern do not depend on their membership in any group.

Ideas that have kindled the struggle for democracy in the modern world – the rights of man, the dignity of the individual – have expressed this attitude. In this sense, the history of democracy records the growth in scope of man's sense of moral concern. Moreover, this democratic moral sense generally implies something not only about the goals that men should seek but the spirit in which they should seek them. A man of democratic temper will pursue human welfare, but he will not do so in a context of rigid ranks and hierarchies. For he seeks more than the improvement of men's material condition, he seeks their development as independent individuals and their entrance as full participants into the enterprises of their community. To believe in democracy is to wish to help individuals by giving them the tools to help themselves.

This sense that all men have an initially equal right to membership in the same moral community suggests another element in the democratic image of the good society. This is the acceptance of the simple fact that human beings are different. It is one thing to believe that all men have a right to be treated in accordance with the same fundamental rules. It is quite another thing to believe that there is any single style of life that is good for everybody. The democratic view is that the burden of proof rests on those who argue that the individual is not the best judge of the way to run his own life. To care about democracy is to care about human beings, not *en masse*, but one by one. It is to adopt the working hypothesis that the individual, if given the right conditions, does not need a master or a tutor to take care of him. The devoted believer in democracy will act on this hypothesis until he is proved wrong. And he will act on it again when the next individual comes along. For he believes that the exercise of individual judgement is itself an ultimate good of life.

A considered democratic outlook, therefore, will place a special premium on the value of privacy. It will hold that there are aspects of the individual's life that no government may touch and that no public pressure may be allowed to invade. In the absence of very strong considerations to the contrary, these include the individual's right to bring up his children as he desires, to go where he wishes, to associate with those he chooses, and to live by his own religion and philosophy, staking his destiny on the rightness of his choice.

There is, therefore, an extraordinary degree of human discipline involved in allegiance to a democratic ethic. It asks men to exercise their own judgements and to choose their own ultimate beliefs. But it asks them to care just as much about the liberties of others and the right of others to think differently. That such a discipline has actually been developed, and that it thrives at all, is a remarkable achievement. It is testimony to democracy's faith in the power of human intelligence and goodwill. But the very difficulty of this discipline indicates that the citizens of a democracy can never take the continued success of their social system for granted. There is always the temptation to relax such a discipline or to resent it. The survival of this discipline calls for constant vigilance.

Obviously a society that accepts the moral ideals that have been described can never say that its work is done. Nor can such a society have a neat and symmetrical design. It will be a mobile society without fixed class barriers, offering opportunities to individual talents and providing an arena within which diverse individuals can struggle for the achievement of their own purposes. Inevitably, furthermore, it will be a society in which groups clash and contend with one another and in which the determination and implementation of public policy must depend on something other than unanimous agreement.

We come at this point to a distinguishing feature of democracy as a political system. Democratic political arrangements rest on the recognition that shared purposes and co-operative endeavour are only one side of any complex society and that disagreement and conflict of interests are also persisting characteristics of any such social order. The working principle of a democracy is to deal with such conflicts by bringing them out in the open and providing a legal and social framework for them. It is this principle that gives a distinctive meaning to the classic political ideal of democracy – the ideal of government by the consent of the governed – as it is understood in the United States and other democracies, and that sets off the theory and practice of these democracies from totalitarian forms of government that use and abuse democratic language.

In the American tradition, 'the consent of the governed' has meant a number of things. It has meant, to begin with, that public policies should be subject to broad public discussion, that political leaders must be chosen in free elections where there is honest competition for votes, and that no one is punished or restrained, legally or extralegally, when he works for the political cause of his choice and remains short of violence and insurrection. But government by consent has also meant some things that are perhaps less obvious. For public discussion, free and honest elections, and the rights to freedom of speech and association are essential to achieving government by consent; but the history of democracy in the last century is marked by the growing recognition that they are not sufficient.

In addition to the legal guarantees that are implied by the ideal of government by consent, certain broad social conditions are also implied. Individuals with grievances, men and women with ideas and visions, are the sources of any society's power to improve itself. Modern democracy is an effort to provide such individuals not only with the freedom to struggle for what they think right but with some of the practical tools of struggle. Government by consent means that such individuals must eventually be able to find groups that will work with them and must be able to make their voices heard in these groups. It means that all important groups in the community should have a chance to try to influence the decisions that are made. And it means that social and economic power should be widely diffused in the community at large, so that no group is insulated from competition and criticism. The maintenance of such conditions is the steady business of a democratic society.

What such a society seeks is responsible government. Moreover, it seeks this ideal in a special way. Judged from its working procedures, a democracy does not define 'responsible government' as government by men who are benevolent, intelligent, and unselfishly interested in the general welfare. Naturally, a democracy seeks such men, and it will prosper if it finds them. But in aiming at responsible government, a democracy has its eye mainly on institutions, not persons. No matter how able its leaders, or how morally responsible they are as individuals, it reposes only a careful and limited confidence in them.

From the democratic point of view, a government is a responsible government only when those who make the decisions on which other men's destinies depend can be held effectively accountable for the results of their decisions. This means that they can be asked questions, that they have to give answers which satisfy those who ask them, and that they can be deprived of their power if they fail to do so. It means, moreover, that the decision-makers in a society are visible and that it is possible to fix responsibility for a policy on definite individuals or groups. Finally, it means that those who ask the questions must know how to ask the right ones and must have sufficient information and good sense to judge the answers they receive intelligently. To list these criteria of responsible government is to remind ourselves not only of what democracy has achieved but also of how much still remains to be accomplished and of new and urgent problems that have emerged in the present generation.

Thus, the ideal of government by consent involves more than free elections and constitutional government. It calls for the existence of instruments of communication that men can use to get in touch with one another when they wish to join together in a common cause. It demands that these instruments of communication be generally available to the community rather than monopolistically controlled. It requires the existence of independent groups that can give expression to the diverse interests that are bound to prevail in any sophisticated modern society and that can do so openly, legally and without fear of persecution. It requires that these groups be democratically controlled. Most of all, if government by consent is to work over the long pull, it needs the support of a population in which the average level of education is high. A people that dedicates itself to free government cares about its schools as it will care about little else. Government by consent does not exist once and for all, and a people cannot passively enjoy it. They must steadily create it.

4 *Dissenters*

4.1 PROPERTY AND THE LEISURE CLASS

Thorstein Veblen (1857–1929) was in some ways the American Karl Marx. Born of Norwegian parents who emigrated to America in 1847, Veblen's many attacks on capitalist institutions made him a very controversial figure throughout his adult life. He received a Ph.D. from Yale University in 1884, and set himself the task of tracing the connections between property, the capitalist ethic, and the social and economic conditions of industrial America. His reasoning tended to be evolutionary and deterministic, and very much in line with the European Marxists of his day. These traits show in the two extracts which follow.

4.1.1 'The Beginnings of Ownership.' *From Thorstein Veblen, 'The Beginnings of Ownership', The American Journal of Sociology, vol. IV, November 1898.*

In the accepted economic theories the ground of ownership is commonly conceived to be the productive labour of the owner. This is taken, without reflection or question, to be the legitimate basis of property; he who has produced a useful thing should possess and enjoy it. On this head the socialists and the economists of the classical line – the two extremes of economic speculation – are substantially at one. The point is not in controversy, or at least it has not been until recently; it has been accepted as an axiomatic premise. With the socialists it has served as the ground of their demand that the labourer should receive the full product of his labour. To classical economists the axiom has, perhaps, been as much trouble as it has been worth. It has given them no end of bother to explain how the capitalist is the 'producer' of the goods that pass into his possession, and how it is true that the labourer gets what he produces. Sporadic instances of ownership quite dissociated from creative industry are recognized and taken account of as departures from the normal; they are due to disturbing causes. The main position is scarcely questioned, that in the normal case wealth is distributed in proportion to – and in some cogent sense because of – the recipient's contribution to the product.

Not only is the productive labour of the owner the definitive ground of his ownership today, but the derivation of the institution of property is similarly traced to the productive labour of that putative savage hunter who produced two deer or one beaver or twelve fish. The conjectural history of the origin of property, so far as it has been written by the economists, has been constructed out of conjecture proceeding on the preconceptions of Natural Rights and a coercive Order of Nature. To anyone who approaches the question of ownership with only an incidental interest in its solution (as is true of the classical, pre-evolutionary economists), and fortified with the preconceptions of natural rights, all this seems plain. It sufficiently accounts for the institution, both in point of logical derivation and in point of historical development. The 'natural' owner is the person who has 'produced' an article, or who, by a constructively equivalent expenditure of productive force, has found and appropriated an object. It is conceived that such a person becomes the owner of the article by virtue of the immediate logical inclusion of the idea of ownership under the idea of creative industry.

This natural-rights theory of property makes the creative effort of an isolated, self-sufficing individual the basis of the ownership vested in him. In so doing it overlooks the fact that there is no isolated, self-sufficing individual. All production is, in fact, a production in and by the help of the community, and all wealth is such only in society. Within the human period of the race development, it is safe to say, no individual has fallen into industrial isolation, so as to produce any one useful article by his own independent effort alone. Even where there is no mechanical co-operation, men are always guided by the experience of others. The only possible exceptions to this rule are those instances of lost or cast-off children nourished by wild beasts, of which half-authenticated accounts have gained currency from time to time. But the anomalous, half-hypothetical life of these waifs can scarcely have affected social development to the extent of originating the institution of ownership.

Production takes place only in society – only through the co-operation of an industrial community. This industrial community may be large or small; its limits are commonly somewhat vaguely defined; but it always comprises a group large enough to contain and transmit the traditions, tools, technical knowledge, and usages without which there can be no industrial organization and no economic relation of individuals to one another or to their environment. The isolated individual is not a productive agent. What he can do at best is to live from season to season, as the non-gregarious animals do. There can be no production without technical knowledge; hence no accumulation and no wealth to be owned, in severalty or otherwise. And there is no technical knowledge apart from an industrial community. Since there is no individual production and no individual productivity, the natural-rights preconception that ownership rests on the individually productive labour of the owner reduces itself to absurdity, even under the logic of its own assumptions. . . .

Ownership is not a simple and instinctive notion that is naïvely included under the notion of productive effort on the one hand, nor under that of habitual use on the other. It is not something given to begin with, as an item of the isolated individual's mental furniture; something which has to be unlearned in part when men come to co-operate in production and make working arrangements and mutual renunciations under the stress of associated life – after the manner imputed by the social-contract theory. It is a conventional fact and has to be learned; it is a cultural fact which has grown into an institution in the past through a long course of habituation, and which is transmitted from generation to generation as all cultural facts are.

4.1.2 'Conspicuous Consumption and the Leisure Class.'
From Thorstein Veblen, The Theory of the Leisure Class, *1899,*
Chapter IV.

... As wealth accumulates, the leisure class develops further in function and structure, and there arises a differentiation within the class. There is a more or less elaborate system of rank and grades. This differentiation is furthered by the inheritance of wealth and the consequent inheritance of gentility. With the inheritance of gentility goes the inheritance of obligatory leisure; and gentility of a sufficient potency to entail a life of leisure may be inherited without the complement of wealth required to maintain a dignified leisure. Gentle blood may be transmitted without goods enough to afford a reputably free consumption at one's ease. Hence results a class of impecunious gentlemen of leisure, incidentally referred to already. These half-caste gentlemen of leisure fall into a system of hierarchical gradations. Those who stand near the higher and the highest grades of the wealthy leisure class, in point of birth, or in point of wealth, or both, outrank the remoter-born and the pecuniarily weaker. These lower grades, especially the impecunious, or marginal, gentlemen of leisure, affiliate themselves by a system of dependence or fealty to the great ones; by so doing they gain an increment of repute, or of the means with which to lead a life of leisure, from their patron. They become his courtiers or retainers, servants; and being fed and countenanced by their patron they are indices of his rank and vicarious consumers of his superfluous wealth. Many of these affiliated gentlemen of leisure are at the same time lesser men of substance in their own right; so that some of them are scarcely at all, others only partially, to be rated as vicarious consumers. So many of them, however, as make up the retainers and hangers-on of the patron may be classed as vicarious consumers without qualification. Many of these again, and also many of the other aristocracy of less degree, have in turn attached to their persons a more or less comprehensive group of vicarious consumers in the persons of their wives and children, their servants, retainers, etc. ...

The leisure class stands at the head of the social structure in point of reputability; and its manner of life and its standards of worth therefore afford the norm of reputability for the community. The observance of these standards, in some degree of approximation, becomes incumbent upon all classes lower in the scale. In modern civilized communities the lines of demarcation between social classes have grown vague and transient, and wherever this happens the norm of reputability imposed by the upper class extends its coercive influence with but slight hindrance down through the social structure to the lowest strata. The result is that the members of each stratum accept as their ideal of decency the scheme of life in vogue in the next higher stratum, and bend their energies to live up to that ideal. On pain of forfeiting their good name and their self-respect in case of failure, they must conform to the accepted code, at least in appearance.

The basis on which good repute in any highly organized industrial community ultimately rests is pecuniary strength; and the means of showing pecuniary strength, and so of gaining or retaining a good name, are leisure and a conspicuous consumption of goods. Accordingly, both of these methods are in vogue as far down the scale as it remains possible; and in the lower strata in which the two methods are employed, both offices are in great part delegated to the wife and children of the household. Lower still, where any degree of leisure, even ostensible, has become impracticable for the wife, the conspicuous consumption of goods remains and is carried on by the wife and children. The man of the household also can do something in this direction, and, indeed, he commonly does; but with a still lower descent into the levels of indigence – along the margin of the slums – the man, and presently also the children, virtually cease to consume valuable goods for appearances, and the woman remains virtually the sole exponent of the household's pecuniary decency. No class of society, not even the most abjectly poor, foregoes all customary conspicuous consumption. The last items of this category of consumption are not given up except under stress of the direst necessity. Very much of squalor and discomfort will be endured before the last trinket or the last pretence of pecuniary decency is put away. There is no class and no country that has yielded so abjectly before the pressure of physical want as to deny themselves all gratification of this higher or spiritual need. . . .

For the great body of the people in any modern community, the proximate ground of expenditure in excess of what is required for physical comfort is not a conscious effort to excel in the expensive-ness of their visible consumption, so much as it is a desire to live up to the conventional standard of decency in the amount and grade of goods consumed. This desire is not guided by a rigidly invariable standard, which must be lived up to, and beyond which there is no incentive to go. The standard is flexible; and especially it is indefinitely extensible, if only time is allowed for habituation to any increase in pecuniary ability and for acquiring facility in the new and larger scale of expenditure that follows such an increase. It is much more difficult to recede from a scale of expenditure once adopted than it is to extend the accustomed scale in response to an accession of wealth. Many items of customary expenditure prove on analysis to be almost purely wasteful, and they are there-fore honorific only, but after they have once been incorporated into the scale of decent consumption, and so have become an integral part of one's scheme of life, it is quite as hard to give up these as it is to give up many items that conduce directly to one's physical comfort, or even that may be necessary to life and health. That is to say, the conspicuously wasteful honorific expenditure that con-fers spiritual well-being may become more indispensable than much of that expenditure which ministers to the 'lower' wants of physical well-being or sustenance only. It is notoriously just as difficult to recede from a 'high' standard of living as it is to lower a standard which is already relatively low; although in the former case the difficulty is a moral one, while in the latter it may involve a material deduction from the physical comforts of life.

4.2 THE ANARCHIST CASE

From Emma Goldman, essay on Anarchism in Anarchism and Other Essays, *1911, pp. 58–62.*

The United States, like Europe, has had its share of anarchists. One of the most intelligent and sincere was Emma Goldman (1869–1940). All governments, she argued, place artificial barriers between people, thus destroying the natural and harmonious relations which would exist but for these barriers. A nostalgic romanticism lurks in her book *Anarchism and Other Essays* (1911), but Emma Goldman claimed respectable support for the views she put forward, as the following extract from her essays shows.

Anarchism is the only philosophy which brings to man the consciousness of himself; which maintains that God, the State, and society are non-existent, that their promises are null and void, since they can be fulfilled only through man's subordination. Anarchism is therefore the teacher of the unity of life; not merely in nature, but in man. There is no conflict between the individual and the social instincts any more than there is between the heart and the lungs: the one the receptacle of a precious life essence, the other the repository of the element that keeps the essence pure and strong. The individual is the heart of society, conserving the essence of social life; society is the lungs which are distributing the element to keep the life essence – that is, the individual – pure and strong.

'The one thing of value in the world,' said Emerson, 'is the active soul; this every man contains within him. The soul active sees absolute truth and utters truth and creates.' In other words, the individual instinct is the thing of value in the world. It is the true soul that sees and creates the truth alive, out of which is to come a still greater truth, the re-born social soul.

Anarchism is the great liberator of man from the phantoms that have held him captive; it is the arbiter and pacifier of the two forces for individual and social harmony. To accomplish that unity, Anarchism has declared war on the pernicious influences which have so far prevented the harmonious blending of individual and social instincts, the individual and society.

Religion, the dominion of the human mind; Property, the dominion of human needs; and Government, the dominion of human conduct, represent the stronghold of man's enslavement and all the horrors it entails. Religion! How it dominates man's mind, how it humiliates and degrades his soul. God is everything, man is nothing, says religion. But out of that nothing God has created a kingdom so despotic, so tyrannical, so cruel, so terribly exacting that naught but gloom and tears and blood have ruled the world since gods began. Anarchism rouses man to rebellion against this black monster. Break your mental fetters, says Anarchism to man, for not until you think and judge for yourself will you get rid of the dominion of darkness, the greatest obstacle to all progress.

Property, the dominion of man's needs, the denial of the right to satisfy his needs. Time was when property claimed a divine right, when it came to man with the same refrain, even as religion, 'Sacrifice! Abnegate! Submit!' The spirit of Anarchism has lifted man from his prostrate position. He now stands erect, with his face toward the light. He has learned to see the insatiable, devouring, devastating nature of property, and he is preparing to strike the monster dead.

'Property is robbery,' said the great French Anarchist Proudhon. Yes, but without risk and danger to the robber. Monopolizing the accumulated efforts of man, property has robbed him of his birth-right, and has turned him loose a pauper and an outcast. Property has not even the time-worn excuse that man does not create enough to satisfy all needs. The A B C student of economics knows that the productivity of labour within the last few decades far exceeds normal demand. But what are normal demands to an abnormal institution? The only demand that property recognizes is its own gluttonous appetite for greater wealth, because wealth means power; the power to subdue, to crush, to exploit, the power to enslave, to degrade. America is particularly boastful of her great power, her enormous national wealth. Poor America, of what avail is all her wealth, if the individuals comprising the nation are wretchedly poor? If they live in squalor, in filth, in crime, with hope and joy gone, a homeless, soilless army of human prey?

It is generally conceded that unless the returns of any business venture exceed the cost, bankruptcy is inevitable. But those engaged in the business of producing wealth have not yet learned even this simple lesson. Every year the cost of production in human life is growing larger (50,000 killed, 100,000 wounded in America last year); the returns to the masses, who help to create wealth, are ever getting smaller. Yet America continues to be blind to the inevitable bankruptcy of our business of production. Nor is this the only crime of the latter. Still more fatal is the crime of turning the producer into a mere particle of a machine, with less will and decision than his master of steel and iron. Man is being robbed not merely of the products of his labour, but of the power of free initiative, of originality, and the interest in, or desire for, the things he is making.

Real wealth consists in things of utility and beauty, in things that help to create strong, beautiful bodies and surroundings inspiring to live in. But if man is doomed to wind cotton around a spool, or dig coal, or build roads for thirty years of his life, there can be no talk of wealth. What he gives to the world is only grey and hideous things, reflecting a dull and hideous existence – too weak to live, too cowardly to die. Strange to say, there are people who extol this deadening method of centralized production as the proudest achievement of our age. They fail utterly to realize that if we are to continue in machine subserviency, our slavery is more complete than was our bondage to the King. They do not want to know that centralization is not only the death-knell of liberty, but also of health and beauty, of art and science, all these being impossible in a clocklike, mechanical atmosphere.

Anarchism cannot but repudiate such a method of production: its goal is the freest possible expression of all the latent powers of the individual. Oscar Wilde defines a perfect personality as 'one who develops under perfect conditions, who is not wounded, maimed, or in danger'. A perfect personality, then, is only possible in a state of society where man is free to choose the mode of work, the conditions of work, and the freedom to work. One to whom the making of a table, the building of a house, or the tilling of the soil, is what the painting is to the artist and the discovery to the scientist – the result of inspiration, of intense longing, and deep interest in work as a creative force. That being the ideal of Anarchism, its economic arrangements must consist of voluntary productive and distributive associations, gradually developing into free communism, as the best means of producing with the least waste of human energy. Anarchism, however, also recognizes the right of the individual, or numbers of individuals, to arrange at all times for other forms of work, in harmony with their tastes and desires.

Such free display of human energy being possible only under complete individual and social freedom, Anarchism directs its forces against the third and greatest foe of all social equality; namely, the State, organized authority, or statutory law – the dominion of human conduct.

Just as religion has fettered the human mind, and as property, or the monopoly of things, has subdued and stifled man's needs, so has the State enslaved his spirit, dictating every phase of conduct. 'All government in essence,' says Emerson, 'is tyranny.' It matters not whether it is government by divine right or majority rule. In

133

every instance its aim is the absolute subordination of the individual.

4.3 PROFESSIONAL SCEPTIC

From H. L. Mencken, Notes on Democracy, *1926.*

H. L. Mencken (1880–1956) was often sceptical, and occasionally scornful of the claims of democracy as a form of government. He became widely known as a Baltimore editor and journalist during the 1920s for his astringent comments on American values and institutions. Yet Mencken was also a man of considerable culture and his best-known work, *The American Language* displayed scholarship and wide learning as well as humour and irony. The following extract forms the concluding passage of Mencken's *Notes on Democracy* where the author's irony and scepticism are distinctly apparent.

I have alluded somewhat vaguely to the merits of democracy. One of them is quite obvious: it is, perhaps, the most charming form of government ever devised by man. The reason is not far to seek. It is based upon propositions that are palpably not true – and what is not true, as everyone knows, is always immensely more fascinating and satisfying to the vast majority of men than what is true. Truth has a harshness that alarms them, and an air of finality that collides with their incurable romanticism. They turn, in all the great emergencies of life, to the ancient promises, transparently false but immensely comforting, and of all those ancient promises there is none more comforting than the one to the effect that the lowly shall inherit the earth. It is at the bottom of the dominant religious system of the modern world, and it is at the bottom of the dominant political system. The latter, which is democracy, gives it an even higher credit and authority than the former, which is Christianity. More, democracy gives it a certain appearance of objective and demonstrable truth. The mob man, functioning as citizen, gets a feeling that he is really important to the world – that he is genuinely running things. Out of his maudlin herding after rogues and mountebanks there comes to him a sense of vast and mysterious power – which is what makes archbishops, police sergeants, the grand goblins of the Ku Klux and other such magnificoes happy. And out of it there comes, too, a conviction that he is somehow wise, that his views are taken seriously by his betters – which is what makes United States Senators, fortune-tellers and Young Intellectuals happy. Finally, there comes out of it a glowing consciousness of a high duty triumphantly done – which is what makes hangmen and husbands happy.

All these forms of happiness, of course, are illusory. They don't last. The democrat, leaping into the air to flap his wings and praise God, is for ever coming down with a thump. The seeds of his disaster, as I have shown, lie in his own stupidity: he can never get rid of the naïve delusion – so beautifully Christian! – that happiness is something to be got by taking it away from the other fellow. But there are seeds, too, in the very nature of things: a promise, after all, is only a promise, even when it is supported by divine revelation, and the chances against its fulfilment may be put into a depressing mathematical formula. Here the irony that lies under all human aspiration shows itself: the quest for happiness, as always, brings only *un*happiness in the end. But saying that is merely saying that the true charm of democracy is not for the democrat but for the spectator. That spectator, it seems to me, is favoured with a show of the first cut and calibre. Try to imagine anything more heroically absurd! What grotesque false pretences! What a parade of obvious imbecilities! What a welter of fraud! But is fraud unamusing? Then I retire forthwith as a psychologist. The fraud of democracy, I contend, is more amusing than any other – more amusing even, and by miles, than the fraud of religion. Go into your praying-chamber and give sober thought to any of the more characteristic democratic inventions: say, Law Enforcement. Or to any of the typical democratic prophets: say, the late Archangel Bryan. If you don't come out paled and palsied by mirth then you will not laugh on the Last Day itself, when Presbyterians step out of the grave like chicks from the egg, and wings blossom from their scapulae, and they leap into interstellar space with roars of joy.

I have spoken hitherto of the possibility that democracy may be a self-limiting disease, like measles. It is, perhaps, something more: it is self-devouring. One cannot observe it objectively without being impressed by its curious distrust of itself – its apparently ineradicable tendency to abandon its whole philosophy at the first sign of strain. I need not point to what happens invariably in democratic states when the national safety is menaced. All the great tribunes of democracy, on such occasions, convert themselves, by a process as simple as taking a deep breath, into despots of an almost fabulous ferocity. Lincoln, Roosevelt and Wilson come instantly to mind: Jackson and Cleveland are in the background, waiting to be recalled. Nor is this process confined to times of alarm and terror: it is going on day in and day out. Democracy always seems bent upon killing the thing it theoretically loves. I have rehearsed some of its operations against liberty, the very cornerstone of its political metaphysic. It not only wars upon the thing itself; it even wars upon mere academic advocacy of it. I offer the spectacle of Americans jailed for reading the Bill of Rights as perhaps the most gaudily humorous ever witnessed in the modern world. Try to imagine monarchy jailing subjects for maintaining the divine right of Kings! Or Christianity damning a believer for arguing that Jesus Christ was the Son of God! This last, perhaps, has been done: anything is possible in that direction. But under democracy the remotest and most fantastic possibility is a commonplace of every day. All the axioms resolve themselves into thundering paradoxes, many amounting to downright contradictions in terms. The mob is competent to rule the rest of us – but it must be rigorously policed itself. There is a government, not of men, but of laws – but men are set upon benches to decide finally what the law is and may be. The highest function of the citizen is to serve the state – but the first assumption that meets him, when he essays to discharge it, is an assumption of his disingenuousness and dishonour. Is that assumption commonly sound? Then the farce only grows the more glorious.

I confess, for my part, that it greatly delights me. I enjoy democracy immensely. It is incomparably idiotic, and hence incomparably amusing. Does it exalt dunderheads, cowards, trimmers, frauds, cads? Then the pain of seeing them go up is balanced and obliterated by the joy of seeing them come down. Is it inordinately wasteful, extravagant, dishonest? Then so is every other form of government: all alike are enemies to laborious and virtuous men. Is rascality at the very heart of it? Well, we have borne that rascality since 1776, and continue to survive. In the long run, it may turn out that rascality is necessary to human government, and even to civilization itself – that civilization, at bottom, is nothing but a colossal swindle. I do not know: I report only that when the suckers are running well the spectacle is infinitely exhilarating. But I am, it may be, a somewhat malicious man: my sympathies, when it comes to suckers, tend to be coy. What I can't make out is how any man can believe in democracy who feels for and with them, and is pained when they are debauched and made a show of. How can any man be a democrat who is sincerely a democrat?

4.4 SOCIALISM IN OUR TIME

From Norman Thomas, After the New Deal, What?, *1936, Chapter VII.*

For more than forty years Norman Thomas (1884–1968) was an eloquent expositor of the socialist case. In six successive Presidential elections, from 1928 to 1948, the American Socialist Party put forward the candidacy of Norman Thomas, though he never achieved a wide following. President Franklin Roosevelt's New Deal undoubtedly affected the fortunes and the appeal of socialism to poor Americans, but Norman Thomas argued that the New Deal would not solve the fundamental contradictions of American society.

Socialism is first of all a reasoned conviction that plenty and peace, freedom and fellowship, lie within the grasp of men. It is the assertion that our failure to conquer poverty in the midst of potential abundance is due to an acceptance of a system which is based on relative scarcity, and upon the exploitation of the masses by an owning class. Socialism believes that men may be free by making power-driven machinery the slave of mankind. It believes in planned production for the use of all rather than an unplanned production for the profit of an owning class. It asserts that this type of production for use requires social ownership of land, natural resources and the principal means of production and distribution, including, of course, the entire system of money, banking and credit. In the name of social ownership of land and tools it does not propose to house men in public barracks or to take from a worker his favourite hammer, violin or typewriter, or anything else which he uses without exploiting others. Socialism does intend to end absentee landlordism, but it intends to make men more, not less, secure in the occupancy and use of homes in which they live.

Because men will be more secure against the loss of their homes and their jobs there will be more real liberty. The statement that socialism will take from men civil and religious liberty is born either of malice or complete misunderstanding of the subject of socialism.

American Socialism has expressly recognized a man's right to the religion of his choice. Many socialists would go farther and quote approvingly the statement I heard a young socialist make to a woman perturbed that if she accepted socialism she would lose her religion. 'Madam,' said he, 'one does not have to be a Christian to be a socialist, but I cannot understand how you can be a true Christian in these times and not be a socialist.'

Social ownership of the great means of production and distribution is necessary for planning. It is the only basis on which we can end the dominion of profit. Even under capitalism social ownership has had an encouraging degree of success. Witness for instance such a list of publicly owned enterprises as schools, roads, parks, the post office, the Panama Canal, city water and sewer systems, power plants, and the like. They are supplemented, too, by the success of consumers' co-operatives carried on for the benefit of the consumers who are members of them and not for the private profit of any group of individuals.

It takes custom derived from a long historic development to explain how anything as utterly absurd as the legal control of private enterprises by absentee stockholders could come into existence. These stockholders know nothing about the conduct of the steel mills, electric power systems, railroads or banks which legally they own. They are concerned only with the profit they get. Their enterprises would fail disastrously except for the hired brains and hands employed by boards of directors to run them, not for the use of all, but for the profit of these same absentee stockholders. There was some rhyme and reason to the old individualistic capitalism where the capitalist assumed definite responsibility. In this age when the engineer, the technician, the manager, are the key to productive enterprise there is no reason under the sun why they should not work for society rather than for absentee owners. Logically they could do a much better job because the fact is that the interest of the absentee owners is by no means identical with the interest of the consumers, still less with the interest of the workers. So far is it from being true that the profit system puts the most advanced science and the more advanced inventions automatically to work, that, on the contrary, a great many inventions are kept off the market by the monopolists or semi-monopolists who can control them in order to protect profit. There is no reason to doubt that the engineers who have given us the modern automobile could also have added to the skill of their performance engines which would use less gasoline, but that would not suit powerful financial interests. Progress in railroad travel was held back for years by the belief, probably the mistaken belief, of directors that profits would not be increased by further improvements. . . .

It will be almost the first business of a socialist society to get rid of the ugliness as well as the discomfort of the slums and shacks which now disgrace America. Even more surely, it will be the first business of socialism to see that every boy and girl born into the world shall receive food necessary for physical health, training to enable him to do the work for which he is best fitted, a chance when he comes to working age to do that work, and to do it under conditions which give him both security and leisure.

It is logically possible today to house all our people in comfort and beauty; to feed them amply; to help them through a socialized medical service to get well and stay well; to provide them economic security against the vicissitudes of life; and to substitute for the present alternation between long hours of monotonous, ill-rewarded toil and bitter unemployment a shorter working week and enriched leisure.

To establish and maintain all this Socialists do not depend upon an omnipotent and omniscient state. They regard the state as the principal instrument that must be used for the establishment of a new social order. It is the business of workers with hand and brain to gain control of government in order to accomplish this great change. Between the fascist conception of the totalitarian state as an end in itself, and the socialist conception of the state as something to be used to establish the co-operative commonwealth, there is the difference between darkness and light. A socialist does not believe that the state is the only form of social organization which should be allowed to exist. It has no divine right. Its powers will have to be vigorously asserted and effectively used in a transition period, but as the habit of co-operation and functional self-government grows the coercive state should wither away. It should become a true commonwealth.

4.5 THE APPEAL OF FASCISM

From Lawrence Dennis, 'Fascism for America', in The Annals of the American Academy of Political and Social Science, *180, 1935.*

The economic collapse of 1929 and the depression which followed brought a mood of deep pessimism and self-doubt to the American people. Some thoughtful Americans argued that unrestrained capitalism had produced the crash, but others held that democracy itself was at least partly to blame. To avoid any future repetition of the catastrophe, many radical solutions were proposed. Some turned to left wing doctrines and communism; others looked to the extreme right and embraced fascism. Lawrence Dennis was one who admired the efficiency and strong leadership of the fascist dictatorships which emerged in Europe in the 1930s. Although he was never an out-and-out fascist, Dennis was attracted to the promise of political stability fascism seemed to hold. In this, Dennis shared the views of commentators as disparate as Father Charles Coughlin, a Canadian born priest who turned to fascism as an antidote to communism, and Senator Huey Long, ex-Governor of Louisiana, whose political methods often smacked of totalitarianism.

The Mind of the Masses
Many of the conservatives believe or seem to believe that the American people are attached to a given system and ideology. This is a delusion peculiar to the lawyers and the instructed classes. Ninety per cent of the American people have no grasp whatever of the ideological content of the system. They have not read the Federalist papers, Rousseau, Montesquieu, Adam Smith, or Blackstone. If they are moved by words or symbols, like 'Constitution', 'liberty', 'democracy', 'representative government', and so forth, it is purely a result of early emotional conditioning and the association of a given feeling with a given word, without the occurrence

of any understanding process. All these words or symbols can be incanted by any demagogue committed to any enterprise. A fascist dictatorship can be set up by a demagogue in the name of all the catchwords of the present system, just as a Communist dictatorship was set up in Russia in October 1917 in the name of democracy and other catchwords of the liberals.

It is also a mistake to suppose that the American people are averse to government regimentation, or orderly organization and procedure. We are the most organized, standardized, regimented, and docile people in the world so far as the processes of mass direction and management are concerned. People who fall into this erroneous generalization about the American people fail to see that most of our government is now done by large corporations and cultural associations rather than by the state. The state can easily include the corporation and most of the cultural associations within its scheme of social control without having the masses of the people notice the difference. The $25,000-a-year vice-president of a big bank or a big university is as much the yes-man of the power hierarchy on which his job depends as any communist or fascist party official, and he has about the same liberty of basic dissent.

I am not showing a contempt but a high respect for the masses in advancing these heterodox generalizations about them. The people have too much sense to take symbols and verbalisms, like the 'Constitution' and 'liberty', as seriously as our educated liberals and lawyers do. Both Senator Long and Father Coughlin, in harping on the calamities of our present situation and in clamouring for changes, are in far closer harmony with the logic of mass needs than are our intellectual exponents of liberalism, or conservatism, as you may care to call it, who are invoking symbols and verbalisms not as instruments of action but as deterrents to revolutionary action. The people want public order and the elements of subsistence. Liberty with these, yes; liberty without them is nonsense.

Character of Coming Fascism
Revolutionary change is indicated. It is beginning. Its velocity and momentum will accelerate. The *élite* of the present order have their chance now to reform their thinking and lead the trend. Whether our coming fascism is more or less humane and decent will depend largely on the contributions our humane *élite* can make to it in time.

There need be no acute class struggle, if the *élite* of the present order in both parties will but recognize that a planned economy can best be planned in the interests of the dominant *élite*, if it is also planned to give the masses the maximum output of human satisfactions. The larger the total product, the larger the cut for ownership and management. The problem can be that of organizing for the maximum social income as a part of organization for class advantage. It can also be a class struggle between the 'ins' fighting to defend their liberties, and the 'outs' fighting to capture them. It will depend largely on the decision of the 'ins' during the next few months.

4.6 MERITOCRACY OR PLUTOCRACY?

From Ralph Adams Cram, The End of Democracy, *1937, Chapter 9, pp. 144–50.*

Ralph Adams Cram also felt the appeal of extreme right wing doctrines. He was attracted to *élite* theory and in his book *The End of Democracy* (1937) he deplored the levelling tendencies of democracy. In the following extract Cram argues for a restricted franchise.

When universal suffrage came in, democracy went out as a practicable proposition. This formed no part of the original programme of the makers of the Constitution; if they had foreseen it they would have framed a very different sort of document. It cannot be too often reasserted that with hardly an exception they feared 'the people' as a source of original action, did all they could to forestall any such activity on their part, and only under protest allowed them a small share in such action in the politic hope that this would help the necessary ratification. As a matter of fact, it was never a 'People's Constitution' as has been so frequently claimed in Fourth of July celebrations, at Presidential elections, and on other similar occasions. They, the people, were never very much interested, either in the project itself or in the ratification of a form of national government. They did not particularly want anything of the sort and they did not like what came out of Philadelphia, but this distaste was not strong enough to overcome their natural lethargy, so only about five per cent. of the white male population voted as to whether the Constitution should be accepted or rejected. As it was it only got by by the skin of its teeth and by some clever management on the part of its proponents. As has already been said, the whole thing, in conception, formulation and realization, was the work of a small group of enthusiastic young men of property and position, with wiser heads on their shoulders than their years would argue as rationally possible, though they were not wise enough to foresee the unimaginable – but inevitable.

They did expect that the new Republic would vastly expand and its population increase immeasurably; also that in the very process of nature, conditions would change. They could not, however, foresee the revolution that coal, iron, steam and electricity, used under a system of free competition, would effect when complemented by that consummate invention of the lawyers and politicians, the limited liability or joint-stock company, nor that racial solidarity would ultimately be dislodged through the immigration of millions of alien stocks, nor that two factors then unknown, aggressive humanitarianism and medical science, would ultimately ensure the 'survival of the unfittest' and that the very 'democratic' theory they so gravely feared and against which they so earnestly strove, would one day negative all their pious efforts and place all power in the hands of a propertyless, unfree proletariat, organized, directed and exploited by a caste of professional politicians deriving directly from this same class of mass men.

It is possible that under the racial, social, economic and industrial conditions that existed in the last years of the eighteenth century, a representative democracy could have functioned acceptably within the safeguards erected by the Constitution of 1787. One generation later a process began that developed by geometrical progression, that made this impossible. Had the old selective social system, with its materialization in a frame of government based on qualitative rather than quantitative standards of value, been able to maintain itself, the same might have been true. It is conceivable that an entirely new world, which had come into being by 1865, might have been administered on the lines of the old, at least so far as its major principles are concerned. Had the new-born industrial, commercial, financial organism been directed, curbed and controlled by able, scrupulous, high-minded and honourable men of 'light and leading' instead of by emancipated proletarians and self-seeking politicians, the incalculable potential inherent in the new forces might have been directed for good.

This was not to be, and the Nemesis of order and value lay in universal manhood suffrage.

It all works out like a proposition in Euclid, if you accept the premise that the majority of human beings in Europe and the Americas (some sociologists and biologists rate the proportion as high as sixty or seventy per cent) are possessed of the mentality of a fourteen-year-old child. There are optimistic humanitarians who are disposed to question this, but it seems to me that the fact is pretty well proved by the sort of leadership that is accepted, the motives displayed in social and political action, and the conduct revealed under the influence of mob psychology. Another irrefutable evidence is the sort of thing provided for popular consumption by the newspapers, pulp magazines, the radio and Hollywood. Sometimes, as in this post-war period, popular action as displayed in French politics, the Spanish Revolution, and in our own social turmoil, combined with an average Presidential campaign, the depressed observer is inclined to accept the higher percentage of mental incapacity noted above, or even to posit a theory of subnormality.

Now, with this basis to work on, we find a combination of depressive influences that play incessantly on the unfortunate class of tabloid personalities, not only working against their advancement in character and intelligence, but actually degrading it to lower depths. . . . There is a widespread idea that formal school education will, or ought to, correct these deleterious influences, but apart from the well-established axiom relating to the manufacture of silk purses, we confront the fact that, even were this educative system perfectly adapted to its necessary and beneficent purpose, it functions only some six hours a day for about half the days in the year, while the specified depressive agencies work all the time, and overtime. In all this there is no implied condemnation or scorn for the mass man, but rather a sympathetic pity for him in the way he has been betrayed, and this betrayal extends not only to the concrete forces that have been brought to bear on his defencelessness, but also to those who, through the operation of the misinterpreted doctrine of human equality, have placed on him a burden of civic responsibility he is, by nature, unfitted to bear. . . .

Just what the answer is is none too easy to say. Of course, as has been said before, the first necessity is to get rid of the Reconstruction dogma that [the vote] is a natural right appertaining to all men (and women) by virtue of their humanity. It should be considered a solemn duty and high privilege granted for cause; something like a college degree, though not given for the same reasons. This is a council of perfection and probably as impossible of achievement as it would be 'politically inexpedient'. There are two things, however, that might, perhaps, be done, which would help not only in action, but in establishing a right judgement as to the nature of the franchise itself. These are: first, the withdrawal of the voting privilege from those convicted of any crime or misdemeanour involving 'moral turpitude'; second, the ownership of property, real or functional, as a prerequisite to the exercise of the electoral franchise.

Under the first heading, *permanent* disfranchisement would only follow conviction for the serious offences where a fundamental moral obliquity was clearly evident. Below this grade of crimes would come those of lesser moment (though also socially pernicious) where deprivation would run from a year upwards. To specify two or three of varying degrees, there would be adulteration of foods, libel, cruelty to man or beast, swindling of any sort, fraud, malicious mischief, *et cetera*. So to penalize antisocial action might prove to be the most effective protection of society.

Under the second heading, the vote would follow property. The statement in this form requires definition. 'Property' does not mean money, goods, securities, shares in industrial or commercial ventures. There is no actual *reality* in any of these things; they are tokens of potential value, mostly certificates of indebtedness. . . . 'Property' is, as has already been said, the ownership in fee simple of land, tools of trade, or an individually owned business or individually prasticed profession, sufficient to guarantee decent living conditions for an household. A wage or salary is not property and the recipient of such is, strictly speaking, a proletarian. A proletarian is not a free man and only free men can safely participate in government.

4.7 MARX AND AMERICA

From Earl Browder, Marx and America (1958) Chapter I, 'Marx's Ambiguity Regarding America', pp. 9–13.

Earl Browder was born in Kansas in 1891 and began studying Marx in 1907. He became an active trade unionist in 1914 and was Secretary of the American Communist Party from 1930 to 1945, when he was expelled for 'revisionism'. Thereafter Browder devoted himself to a systematic re-examination of Marxism, with particular reference to American experience.

In the following section Browder argues that Marx drew false analogies from England in his discussion of American capitalism, but the author also cautions against a total rejection of Marx's theories.

It will lay a solid basis for a deeper examination of Marx's theoretical system and the ambiguous position of America in it, if we reconstruct the picture of American development *as Marx saw it*, for the period from the Revolution to 1867 when the first volume of *Capital* was published. The following condensed summary does not go beyond the boundaries of Marx's own recorded observations.

When the thirteen British colonies liberated themselves in the Revolutionary War of Independence and established the United States of America, this country already possessed an economy which, in its basic structure, was more advanced than that of Western Europe and in some ways even of England. Its agriculture was, more than any European land, predominantly one of commodity production for the world market. Its iron production and fabrication, and general manufactures, compared favourably with those of England. The Revolution wiped out the semi-feudal colonial governments, and with them the social-economic remnants of feudalism, such as titles of nobility, quitrents, entails, primogeniture, tithes, and clerical domination in government. The great landed estates were broken up and, together with immense public lands, were distributed as small farms. Even chattel slavery, which remained in the South as the unfinished business of the Revolution until the Civil War of 1861–5, was wiped out in the North by legal action by 1800. Slavery was expected to die a quiet death because of its growing unprofitability but, by an irony of history, the invention of the cotton gin, a great technological advance, injected new profits into the dying institution and thereby caused the Civil War.

In short, the distinctive achievement of America was the abolition of almost all the remnants of pre-capitalist political and economic institutions and practices. The one conspicuous exception was slavery until the Civil War, and its remnants which only after another century are now being cleaned up in the sharpest struggles of domestic politics. Despite this one important exception to the rule, the United States is the unique example of a great nation which, from its foundation, proceeded to sweep away antiquated institutions and folkways incompatible with the needs of modern society. Thus America has the 'purest' capitalism, that is, it has the smallest intermixture of precapitalist remnants. This sweeping character of the American Revolution was the chief factor in bestowing upon this country, in final outcome, the position of world economic supremacy, by wiping out those hindrances to economic progress from the past, which in Europe and England persisted into the late nineteenth century and even to the present day.

The central factor in America's exceptionally favourable situation as compared with England and Europe lay in the system of free land in contrast with the closed-land monopoly of the Old World. Marx perceived this more clearly than any other economist of his time, and analysed it more deeply. That he failed to perceive *all* the consequences in the shaping of capitalist economy simply means that Marx was not, as some fanatical followers imply, a superman or god from another world, but simply the greatest thinker of his time, a head taller than his contemporaries but essentially one of them. Marx could not see that the American free land system furnished a refutation to the dogmas of impoverishment and the subsistence wage, not simply as a temporary obstacle, but more fundamentally as opening the way for the emergence of contrary forces that gave another direction to world development.

Thus arose the contradiction within Marx's thought about America, its ambiguous character that points in two directions simultaneously. Marx was far too intelligent to fail to see, and too rigorously honest to fail to register, all the facts in the America of his time that went contrary to his dogma of impoverishment as the absolute law of capitalist accumulation. But he was too much the prisoner of this dogma to relinquish it. He saved the dogma, however, not by denying the facts as do his modern dogmatic disciples, but by judging these facts to be temporary hindrances to the operation of the underlying economic laws, as signs of the 'undeveloped' character of America in the capitalist sense, and as doomed to be obliterated in the further development of American capitalism along the predetermined pattern earlier displayed by England's rise.

Let us sum up this first bird's-eye survey of the contradictory position of America in the Marxist system of thought.

On the one hand, Marx, judging America by norms and theories drawn from the study of England and from the established classical British political economy, and assuming that capitalist development in other lands must follow the same pattern, says that America is 'undeveloped' and as yet without the necessary conditions for the accumulation of capital on the scale required by the existing stage of technology and, therefore, 'speaking economically, still only a colony of Europe'. This is Marx the dogmatist.

On the other hand Marx, accepting facts as sacred and precious in their own right, freely and fully registers those facts which contradict his dogmas, namely: that the American economy was already superior to the English in his time, and would soon surpass it in every way; that nevertheless the American people were not being impoverished, but that they were well-to-do, independent, enterprising, and comparatively cultured; that American production, under a wage level two and more times that of England, was successfully competing with products in the world market and even in England itself. This is Marx the scientific analyst.

If in the final outcome the dogmas are to be overthrown in the minds of men, this will be done most expeditiously and completely if we enlist the help of Marx the scientific analyst.

A century of struggles and controversies has raised high obstacles to the understanding of Marx's thought. Perhaps the greatest of these has been the agreement, between enemies and adherents of Marx, that his thought is an organic whole that must be either accepted or rejected in its entirety. If that were true, it would be the first such case in the history of the human mind. But of course it is not true, and as a matter of fact, in real life nobody, literally nobody, actually follows such a course. Those who protest most loudly that they reject Marx *in toto* have, even if they do not know it, silently adopted into their thought and views of the world a great part of Marx's contribution to the general body of thought, because Marx changed the intellectual climate of the whole human race. And the dogmatic Marxists, who abstractly oppose the change of even a comma in Marx's writings, are in fact by their 'interpretations' among the most drastic revisionists of Marxism. Everyone is a revisionist even if he disagrees upon what is to be revised. In our modern world with its capitalism that Marx would not have been able to recognize if he had seen it – even as he would find great difficulty in recognizing our current 'socialism' – no one finds it really possible to accept or reject Marxism 'as a whole', no matter how loudly he protests that he does so.

It has become historically expedient, however, even if we are hesitant to use the strong word 'necessary', to make a more serious effort to understand Marx, forgetting about the false issue as to whether he is to be 'accepted' or 'rejected' as though one were dealing with a religious system. For everyone the serious question is a detailed separation of the wheat from the chaff, the science from the dogma.

Those who prefer to deal with chaff and dogma, whether to extol or denounce, may cling to that side of Marx as is their right in any free society. Those who prefer wheat and science will gain much profit from such critical study, even though the intellectual labour involved may be painful.

4.8 KARL MARX AND THE AMERICAN ACADEMY

From Herbert Aptheker, 'Marx and American Scholarship' in The Era of McCarthyism, *1955 (this ed. 1962) pp. 212–17.*

Herbert Aptheker has been a scholarly – if strident – expositor of Marxist ideas for more than three decades. Born in New York in 1915, he wrote his Ph.D. dissertation at Columbia University on the subject *American Negro Slave Revolts* (published in 1943). His scholarship was firmly established in his *Documentary History of the Negro People* (1951), and he has written no less than ten books on the history of the Negro.

During the McCarthy era of the early 1950s, Herbert Aptheker was one of few American academics prepared to risk his career by taking a public stand against anti-communist 'witch-hunting' led by Senator Joseph McCarthy. By December 1954, McCarthy had shot his bolt and was condemned – though not officially 'censured' by his colleagues in the United States Senate. Herbert Aptheker felt that McCarthyism had been partly sustained, if not encouraged, by the silence of his academic colleagues – a silence which extended to a pointed neglect of Marxist thought and ideas during the McCarthy era. In July 1954 Aptheker wrote an essay, 'Marx and American Scholarship' in which he contrasted the treatment of Marx by an earlier generation of American scholars with the conspicuous neglect by Aptheker's contemporaries. The following is a portion of that essay. The quotations from the scholars mentioned are of course self-evidently out of context, and some will feel it desirable to read *in extenso* the works referred to in order to avoid misrepresentation.

It is a fact, and everyone knows it, that the ideas most assaulted today are those of Marx. These are the ones *verboten* in American universities ... [which] have always been dominated by ecclesiastical and, more recently, financial hierarchies, and these have been particularly interested in distorting or censoring unorthodox and dissenting views. ... Nevertheless, it is also a fact that the greatest figures of the past in American academic history have resisted this assault upon reason and have, specifically, upheld the right to study Marx's ideas.

Indeed, these greatest intellectual figures – and this is a part of their greatness – not only upheld the right to study Marx, but insisted upon the necessity to study him if one was to have some grasp of reality. They acknowledged in Marx one of the outstanding geniuses in world history and therefore knew that any 'university' which barred Marx could only be a place of miseducation; that any 'teacher' who ignored or caricatured his ideas could only be a fraud; and that any student who was kept from those ideas was being cheated in his efforts to get at the truth. And they held to this notwithstanding vituperation and persecution.

It will not be amiss today to bring forward something of this most noble tradition in American academic history, and we propose to do it through the writings of the greatest giants in that history. I think that no one preparing a list of the dozen most eminent American university figures in the social sciences could fail to include these six names: Charles A. Beard (1874–1948); John R. Commons (1862–1945); James Harvey Robinson (1863–1936); E. R. A. Seligman (1861–1939); Albion W. Small (1854–1926); and Thorstein Veblen (1857–1929).

Each of these men was so distinguished that only the barest biographical data is necessary. Beard and Veblen were, respectively, the foremost historian and economist in American academic circles. Albion W. Small, a president of Colby College, was the founder of the first Department of Sociology (at the University of Chicago) and the founder and editor for many years, of the *American Journal of Sociology*. James Harvey Robinson, one of Beard's teachers, with whom Beard collaborated in early writing, was a Professor of History at Columbia University for almost thirty years, a founder of the New School for Social Research, and a one-time President of the American Historical Association. John R. Commons served for nearly thirty years as Professor of Economics at the University of Wisconsin and pioneered in the study of the American labour movement. Finally, E. R. A. Seligman was a Professor of Economics at Columbia University for forty-five years, editor of the *Political Science Quarterly*, Editor-in-Chief of the *Encyclopedia of Social Sciences*, and a President of the American Economic Association.

All these great scholars repeatedly referred in their lectures and writings to the ideas of Karl Marx, and – as befitted their stature – did not fail to mention explicitly the name of the man whose ideas they were considering or using. They were not themselves Marxists, but always they dealt with Marx respectfully and with a sense of responsibility. They did not use Marxism as an epithet; rather they treated it as one of the great seminal systems of world thought.

Since references to and discussions of Marxism recur in their work, it is not possible within the limits of an essay to offer a rounded presentation of their estimates of Marxism. But it is possible to offer representative excerpts which will be sufficient to establish my point. It is, perhaps, unnecessary to remark that many of the formulations in these excerpts are, I think, faulty. But that is irrelevant to our present purpose, namely, to indicate the respect and admiration which these leading American scholars had for Marx's ideas.

Thus, in one of James Harvey Robinson's books (*History,* Columbia University Press, 1908) we find this passage:

It was a philosopher, economist and reformer, not a professional student of history, who suggested a wholly new and wonderful series of questions which the historian might properly ask about the past, and moreover furnished him with a scientific explanation of many matters hitherto ill-understood. I mean Karl Marx.

John R. Commons, in an article devoted to a critique of 'Marx Today' – and written out of Professor Commons's conviction, typical in that period, that 'Ford had vanquished Marx' – nevertheless remarked: 'Karl Marx, the founder of materialistic socialism, is recognized by economists as one of the three or four greatest minds who have contributed to the progress of economic science' (*Atlantic Monthly*, November 1925).

Similarly, Thorstein Veblen, in a series of articles entitled, 'The Socialist Economics of Karl Marx and his Followers', felt it necessary to tell the academicians reading the *Quarterly Journal of Economics*, that Marx was to be studied with great care and attention, that he was 'neither ignorant, imbecile or disingenuous' and that: 'There is no system of economic theory more logical than that of Marx' (issues of August 1906 and February 1907). Joseph Dorfman, in his definitive biography of Veblen (Viking Press, 1935), cites Veblen's remark that Marx was 'coming to be more widely appreciated as he becomes better understood'. To his students, Veblen would often say, Professor Dorfman records, 'Read Marx. Uncover the roots of the problem.'

Professor Seligman, in a book devoted to an exposition (not very successful, I believe) of Marx's historical materialism, referred to Marx 'as one of those great pioneers who, even if they are not able themselves to reach the goal, nevertheless blaze out a new and promising path in the wilderness of human thought and progress'. Of Marx's philosophy of history, Professor Seligman declared:

Whether or not we are prepared to accept it as an adequate explanation of human progress in general, we must all recognize the beneficent influence that it has exerted in stimulating the thoughts of scholars and in broadening the concepts and the ideals of history and economics alike. If for no other reason, it will deserve well of future investigators and will occupy an honored place in the record of mental development and scientific progress.' (*The Economic Interpretation of History*, Columbia University Press, 1902.)

Albion W. Small published a long essay, 'Socialism in the Light of Social Science' in the *American Journal of Sociology*, in May, 1912. His theme was stated in one italicized sentence: '*Socialism has been the most wholesome ferment in modern society*.' Of Marx himself, this outstanding American sociologist wrote:

Marx was one of the few really great thinkers in the history of social science. His repute thus far has been that of every challenger of tradition. All the conventional, the world over, from the multitude of intellectual nonentities to thinkers whose failure to acknowledge in him more than a peer has seriously impeached their candor, have implicitly conspired to smother his influence by all the means known to obscurantism. From outlawry to averted glances, every device of repression and misrepresentation has been employed against him. . . .

He is worthy of the most respectful treatment which thinkers can pay to another thinker whose argument has never been successfully answered. . . .

I confidently predict that in the ultimate judgment of history, Marx will have a place in social science analogous with that of Galileo in physical science. . . .

Charles A. Beard, expressing annoyance at being baited as a 'Marxian' by a stuffed-shirt ignoramus who knew as little of Marx's philosophy as he did of Beard's, went on to write: 'Yet I freely pay tribute to the amazing range of Marx's scholarship and the penetrating character of his thought.' Summing up Marx's prodigious attainment in history, philosophy, economics and linguistics, Beard concluded:

However much one may dislike Marx's personal views, one cannot deny to him wide and deep knowledge – and a fearless and sacrificial life. He not only interpreted history, as everyone does who writes any history, but he helped to make history. Possibly he may have known something. At least the contemporary student, trying to look coldly and impartially on thought and thinkers in the field of historiography, may learn a little bit at least, from Karl Marx. (*American Historical Review*, October 1935.)

I have not, of course, called to the witness-stand six leading figures in the history of American scholarship in order to vindicate Marx or his philosophy. In the first place they were not partisans of that philosophy and in the second place the vindication is being written in life.

But I have brought forward the testimony of these six giants as tending to show the stultifying effect of the present all but complete prohibition of the study of Marx's thought which afflicts our educational system. I have brought it forward, too, in order to vindicate the right of schools and scholars to teach the Marxist world-outlook and the right, indeed, the duty, of the youth and of men and women to study that outlook.

4.9 THE NEW SCEPTICISM

From Daniel Bell, The End of Ideology; On the Exhaustion of Political Ideas in the Fifties, *revised ed. 1962, pp. 402–4, 406–7.*

At the end of the 1950s many American intellectuals concluded that political ideas were exhausted and that political theorizing had reached a dead end. Neither democratic politics on the western, parliamentary model, nor totalitarian models seemed to hold any promise of human fulfilment. A good example of this mood was provided by Daniel Bell in his collection of essays *The End of Ideology; On the Exhaustion of Political Ideas in the Fifties* (1960). The following extracts are from the concluding essay in the book.

Few serious minds believe any longer that one can set down 'blue-prints' and through 'social engineering' bring about a new utopia of social harmony. At the same time, the older 'counter-beliefs' have lost their intellectual force as well. Few 'classic' liberals insist that the State should play no role in the economy, and few serious conservatives, at least in England and on the Continent, believe that the Welfare State is 'the road to serfdom'. In the Western world, therefore, there is today a rough consensus among intellectuals on political issues: the acceptance of a Welfare State; the desirability of decentralized power; a system of mixed economy and of political pluralism. In that sense, too, the ideological age has ended.

And yet, the extraordinary fact is that while the old nineteenth-century ideologies and intellectual debates have become exhausted, the rising states of Asia and Africa are fashioning new ideologies

with a different appeal for their own people. These are the ideologies of industrialization, modernization, Pan-Arabism, colour,
and nationalism. In the distinctive difference between the two
kinds of ideologies lies the great political and social problems of the
second half of the twentieth century. The ideologies of the nineteenth century were universalistic, humanistic, and fashioned by
intellectuals. The mass ideologies of Asia and Africa are parochial,
instrumental, and created by political leaders. The driving forces
of the old ideologies were social equality and, in the largest sense,
freedom. The impulsions of the new ideologies are economic
development and national power.

And in this appeal, Russia and China have become models. The
fascination these countries exert is no longer the old idea of the free
society, but the new one of economic growth. And if this involves
the wholesale coercion of the population and the rise of new *élites*
to drive the people, the new repressions are justified on the ground
that without such coercions economic advance cannot take place
rapidly enough. And even for some of the liberals of the West,
'economic development' has become a new ideology that washes
away the memory of old disillusionments.

It is hard to quarrel with an appeal for rapid economic growth
and modernization, and few can dispute the goal, as few could ever
dispute an appeal for equality and freedom. But in this powerful
surge – and its swiftness is amazing – any movement that instates
such goals risks the sacrifice of the present generation for a future
that may see only a new exploitation by a new *élite*. For the newly-
risen countries, the debate is not over the merits of communism –
the content of that doctrine has long been forgotten by friends and
foes alike. The question is an older one: whether new societies can
grow by building democratic institutions and allowing people to
make choices – and sacrifices – voluntarily, or whether the new
élites, heady with power, will impose totalitarian means to transform their countries. Certainly in these traditional and old colonial
societies where the masses are apathetic and easily manipulated,
the answer lies with the intellectual classes and their conceptions
of the future.

Thus one finds, at the end of the fifties, a disconcerting caesura.
In the West, among the intellectuals, the old passions are spent.
The new generation, with no meaningful memory of these old
debates, and no secure tradition to build upon, finds itself seeking

new purposes within a framework of political society that has injected, intellectually speaking, the old apocalyptic and chiliastic visions. In the search for a 'cause', there is a deep, desperate, almost pathetic anger. The theme runs through a remarkable book, *Convictions*, by a dozen of the sharpest young Left Wing intellectuals in Britain. They cannot define the content of the 'cause' they seek, but the yearning is clear. In the US too there is a restless search for a new intellectual radicalism. Richard Chase, in his thoughtful assessment of American society, *The Democratic Vista*, insists that the greatness of nineteenth-century America for the rest of the world consisted in its radical vision of man (such a vision as Whitman's), and calls for a new radical criticism today. But the problem is that the old politico-economic radicalism (preoccupied with such matters as the socialization of industry) has lost its meaning, while the stultifying aspects of contemporary culture (e.g., television) cannot be redressed in political terms. At the same time, American culture has almost completely accepted the *avant-garde*, particularly in art, and the older academic styles have been driven out completely. The irony, further, for those who seek 'causes' is that the workers, whose grievances were once the driving energy for social change, are more satisfied with the society than the intellectuals. The workers have not achieved utopia, but their expectations were less than those of the intellectuals, and the gains correspondingly larger.

The young intellectual is unhappy because the 'middle way' is for the middle-aged, not for him; it is without passion and is deadening. Ideology, which by its nature is an all-or-none affair, and temperamentally the thing he wants, is intellectually devitalized, and few issues can be formulated any more, intellectually, in ideological terms. The emotional energies – and needs – exist, and the question of how one mobilizes these energies is a difficult one. Politics offers little excitement. Some of the younger intellectuals have found an outlet in science or university pursuits, but often at the expense of narrowing their talent into mere technique; others have sought self-expression in the arts, but in the wasteland the lack of content has meant, too, the lack of the necessary tension that creates new forms and styles.

Whether the intellectuals in the West can find passions outside of politics is moot. Unfortunately, social reform does not have any unifying appeal, nor does it give a younger generation the outlet for

'self-expression' and 'self-definition' that it wants. The trajectory
of enthusiasm has curved East, where, in the new ecstasies for
economic utopia, the 'future' is all that counts.

And yet, if the intellectual history of the past hundred years has
any meaning – and lesson – it is to reassert Jefferson's wisdom
(aimed at removing the dead hand of the past, but which can serve
as a warning against the heavy hand of the future as well), that 'the
present belongs to the living'. This is the wisdom that revolu-
tionists, old and new, who are sensitive to the fate of their fellow
men, rediscover in every generation. 'I will never believe,' says a
protagonist in a poignant dialogue written by the gallant Polish
philosopher Leszek Kolakowski, 'that the moral and intellectual
life of mankind follows the law of economics, that is by saving
today we can have more tomorrow; that we should use lives now
so that truth will triumph or that we should profit by crime to pave
the way for nobility.'

And these words, written during the Polish 'thaw', when the
intellectuals had asserted, from their experience with the 'future',
the claims of humanism, echo the protest of the Russian writer
Alexander Herzen, who, in a dialogue a hundred years ago,
reproached an earlier revolutionist who would sacrifice the present
mankind for a promised tomorrow: 'Do you truly wish to condemn
all human beings alive today to the sad role of caryatids . . . supporting a floor for others some day to dance on? . . . This alone
should serve as a warning to people: an end that is infinitely remote
is not an end, but, if you like, a trap; an end must be nearer – it
ought to be, at the very least, the labourer's wage or pleasure in the
work done. Each age, each generation, each life has its own
fullness. . . .'

4.10 PEOPLE WITHOUT A COUNTRY

From I. F. Stone, In A Time of Torment (1968), *pp. 153-62.*

I. F. Stone has been a vigorous critic of successive United States
governments for many years. Since 1953 he has edited and published *I. F. Stone's Weekly*, a radical newssheet of limited circula-
tion (c. 38,000) which is nevertheless widely respected for the
courage and sincerity of its editor. Stone has republished many of

his editorials in book form and the following is taken from the most recently published collection. The editorial itself appeared on 18 August 1966, and deals with a recently published symposium on *The Negro American*.

Some truths are too terrible to be uttered. They lead nowhere but to despair. They subvert hope, the ultimate pillar of the social order. We prefer to cast about for assuaging myths. One such truth which goes back to Heraclitus, the founder of the dialectic, is that conflict is the essence of life, that 'war' – in his own dark phrase – is 'the father of all things'. It is not a maxim on which to found a society for eternal peace. Another such truth casts its shadow over the civil rights movement. All kinds of insights, concepts, and hypotheses are trotted out and tested in the 750 pages of the huge symposium, *The Negro American*, except the one which seems to me the most fundamental of all. The confusion, frustration, and despair of the civil rights movement become comprehensible if one looks at the American Negro (a less hopeful but more accarate description) simply as a people without a county.

The Negro is the second oldest imported stock in our country. Only the white Anglo-Saxon Protestant predates him, and that only by a few years. The distinguished Negro historian, John Hope Franklin, in his contribution to this symposium, reminds us that the first Negro indentured servants were brought here in 1619. That was a year before the Pilgrims landed at Plymouth Rock. After three-and-a-half centuries of living in America, the Negro is still a race apart. Ours is the world's oldest and most successful experiment in *apartheid*. The South Carolina code of 1712 set up special laws for Negroes to 'restrain the disorders, rapines and inhumanity to which they are naturally prone and inclined'. This is still the white stereotype of the Negro. In 1964 it was heart-breakingly possible for the White Citizens Council to place in newspaper advertising a declaration of Negro inequality made one hundred years earlier at Peoria by Lincoln, his reluctant Emanci-pator. 'In a fundamental sense,' Philip M. Hauser writes in this same symposium, 'the Negro really did not enter white American society until the First World War.' And even after the First World War Negro soldiers returning from their segregated regiments were lynched, sometimes in their military uniforms, while the renascent Klan warned them to respect the rights of the white race 'in whose country they are permitted to reside'. Even now, in our enlightened time, Congress is queasy about passing a civil rights bill with an 'open housing' provision because most whites don't want to have Negroes as neighbours. After three-and-a-half-centuries in residence, the Negro still does not feel at home.

All these problems of open housing, educational standards, and different ways of life, would disappear, of course, if the American Negro, like other Negroes, had a territorial base in which he was the irrepressible majority instead of an unwanted minority. The American Negro may not yet be ready to compete on equal terms with the white man, but he is far more advanced than most of the darker peoples who have won their independence since the Second World War, and taken seats, in all their exotic splendour, in the United Nations. Neither in Africa nor in the Caribbean nor in Latin America is there any group of Negroes so prepared for self-government as our twenty million American Negroes. No other Negro group has so high a level of literacy, so wide an educated stratum, so large an *élite*, so much experience with politics, as the American Negro. But he alone of all these Negro or mulatto nations has no territory of his own.

Such cries as 'Freedom Now' or 'Black Power' reflect the repressed recognition of this bitter anomaly. As slogans or political programmes they may make little sense in a country where he is little more than a tenth of the population, and where he is fenced off by taboo as racially untouchable in marriage. What does 'Freedom Now' mean? Freedom from what? It really means freedom from the white man's presence, just as 'Black Power' really means the end of white man's power. If America's twenty million Negroes were concentrated in an African territory under white rule, or even concentrated in a Black Belt here, these cries clearly would make political sense. They would mean the end of white rule and the beginning of black rule. It might be less competent, and even more corrupt, but it would restore racial self-respect, as the end of white domination has done in Africa. This is the deep string these phrases pluck in black American hearts. This is what they cannot achieve in a white man's country and this is why you have leaders floundering around in despair, one day fighting segregation and the next day fighting integration. The basic emotion is hatred of 'Whitey' and this is why Black Nationalism of one variety or another strikes so deeply into the apathetic, disillusioned, and despairing black masses. Of the conventional leaders only Martin Luther King sways them, and he does so for reasons that have little to do with the creed he preaches. They see him as a Moses, but they have no Promised Land.

The Negro American is the most comprehensive survey of its kind since Myrdal's *An American Dilemma* was published twenty-two years ago. There is hardly one of its thirty essays which does not provide some fresh insight. But its viewpoints are limited to the establishment, as was to be expected from a work under the auspices of the American Academy of Arts and Sciences. Of the Negro leadership, only Whitney M. Young, Jr., of the National Urban League, appears in these pages; his organization might best be described as lily-black. His essay with John B. Turner is the least rewarding in the whole volume, though it does have one illuminating sentence, 'At least until now the Negro has not been so much trying to change the American system as attempting to become a part of it.' None of the newer organizations, CORE or SNCC or Mississippi Freedom Democratic Party, which seek to change the system as well as join it, are represented among the contributors; even the NAACP and Martin Luther King are absent. No Negro nationalist, no radical Marxist, or moderate socialist analysis is included, though there is a free enterprise approach in a vigorous essay by James Tobin which calls for changes in attitude and policy hardly less drastic. Tobin, Sterling Professor of Economics at Yale, sees the maintenance of full employment as 'the single most important step' the nation could take to help the Negro. He is for a guaranteed basic income in the form of 'a negative income tax' which would provide basic family allowances for the poor in a form which avoids the demeaning and degrading characteristics of the welfare system. He would revolutionize agricultural policy 'to give income support to people rather than price support to crops and to take people off the land rather than to take land out of cultivation'. He believes we are 'paying much too high a social price for avoiding creeping inflation and for protecting our gold stock and "the dollar"'. He sees the interests of 'the unemployed, the poor and the Negroes' under-represented in 'the comfortable consensus' behind policies which stress monetary stability more than full employment. He urges organizations of the poor and the Negro to study the relation between their plight and fiscal policy.

The nearest approach to a radical evaluation of the civil rights movement itself is Kenneth B. Clark's essay on it. His criticism of Martin Luther King's Gandhian philosophy anticipates the reaction against non-violence which has broken out in the civil rights movement since this symposium was written. 'In Hitler's Germany,' Dr Clark writes, 'the Jews suffered non-violently without stirring Nazi repentance; the early Christians who were eaten by lions seem to have stimulated not guilt but greed in the watching multitudes.' The non-violent oppressed cannot twinge the conscience of the oppressor unless he has one. In addition the whole approach becomes irrelevant where the Negro is up against not cruelty, as in the South, but an impersonal system masked by benign attitudes as in the North. 'What do you do,' Dr Clark asks, 'in a situation in which you have laws on your side, where whites smile and say to you that they are your friends, but where your white "friends" move to the suburbs . . . How can you demonstrate a philosophy of love in response to this? . . . One can be hailed justifiably as a Nobel Prize hero by the Mayor of New York, but this will not in itself change a single aspect of the total pattern of pathology which dominates the lives of the prisoners of the ghettoes of New York.'

The most striking gap in the area covered is the absence of any essay on the political leadership developed in the Negro community; perhaps no respectable writer could be found sufficiently intrepid to take on the phenomena of Adam Clayton Powell and William L. Dawson. We only have the sobering observation in an astringent essay by Oscar Handlin,

Nor is it to be expected that these people [i.e., the Negroes] will be more enlightened in the use of power than their predecessors. Politics is not the cure-all that some naïve observers consider it to be.

There is still an eighteenth-century naïveté under the surface of radical agitation about the Negro; he is unconsciously regarded by many leftists as the Noble Savage who will rejuvenate our politics, and give white radicalism a chance to re-enter with him the mainstream of American politics from which it has so long been shut off. In the so-called New Politics, these lost causes are to be the Black Man's Burden. We have found ourselves an American proletariat.

But ours is an age in which, in a manner late Victorian liberal and Marxist optimists had thought obsolete, the ancient divisive forces of nationalism and tribalism have demonstrated a furious vitality. It would be a mistake to dismiss their recurrence among American Negroes as a passing aberration. In an age of decolonization, it may be fruitful to regard the problem of the American Negro as a unique case of colonialism, an instance of internal imperialism, an underdeveloped people in our very midst. A clue is afforded by the demographic characteristics of the American Negro, which turn out to be like those of other under-developed peoples in our time. 'The Negro,' Hauser writes in the discussion of demographic factors he contributed to this volume,

like the inhabitant of the developing regions in Asia, Latin America, and Africa, in his exposure to the amenities of twentieth century living, is experiencing rapidly declining mortality while fertility rates either remain high or, as in urban areas, actually increase.

The high birth rate and the youthful age structure which mark the Negro community are characteristic of the under-developed world today. Unlike external colonies, however, the Negro community has not been a source of cheap raw materials; all it could offer was cheap labour, and the need for cheap labour has been declining on the farm, where most Negroes used to live and in the cities to which he has moved. The American Negro is condemned to live in Egypt, but it is an Egypt which has already built its Pyramids and no longer needs slaves. Mechanization on the farm and automation in industry have at last set him free, but now freedom turns out to be joblessness.

The most important Negro revolution of our time may be his transformation from a rural to an urban dweller; and to an increasing extent a dweller in idleness. In less than half a century the predominantly rural Negro has become more urban even than the white man. In 1960 the Negro was already 73 per cent urban as compared with 70 per cent for whites. At the same time, as Daniel P. Moynihan observes in his essay on 'Employment, Income and the Ordeal of the Negro Family,' the rate of Negro unemployment, 'from being rather less than that of whites, has steadily moved to the point where it is now regularly more than twice as great'. It is no wonder the Negro feels unwanted.

This is only true, however, of the Negro masses. The success of the civil rights movement has deepened the gap between the Negro *élite* and the Negro mass. 'Anyone with eyes to see,' Moynihan writes, 'can observe the emergence of a Negro middle class that is on the whole doing very well. This group has, if anything, a pre-ferred position in the job market. A nation catching up with cen-turies of discrimination has rather sharply raised the demand for a group on short supply. One would be hard put to describe a per-son with better job opportunities than a newly minted Negro Ph.D. .... At the same time there would also seem to be no ques-tion that opportunities for a large mass of Negro workers in the lower ranges of training and education have not been improving, that in many ways the circumstances of these workers relative to the white work force have grown worse.' The anarchist, Max Nomad, helped to popularize the theory that revolutions, national or social, are made by déclassé intellectuals seeking their place in the sun or, to switch metaphors, at the public trough. Our Negro Revolution, too, has so far primarily benefited the Negro *élite*. The masses have a long wait ahead for 'Black Power' but the trained minority is snapped up by government agencies and business firms anxious to acquire their own token Negroes.

A footnote to the Moynihan article points out that in 1964 'the number of corporation personnel representatives visiting the cam-pus of Lincoln University in Pennsylvania was twice that of the graduating class.' No one is more revolutionary than idle intellec-tuals; the Negroes are, in effect, being bought off.

As educational standards and technological requirements rise, it may become harder rather than easier for the Negro to join the ranks of the happy few. Rashi Fein in his essay, 'An Economic and Social Profile of the Negro American,' quotes from a 1962 Census Bureau report which said:

It thus appears that not only is the nonwhite population more poorly educated than the white population, but the net gain of nonwhites at higher levels of education, as calculated from the educational differences in the fathers' and sons' generations, has not been as great as for whites.

Fein's analysis shows that while the Negro like the white shows improvement in education, health, and welfare, white progress has been so much swifter than Negro that the differential between them is greater than a generation ago. Fein turns up some fascinat-ing statistics:

In 1940, for example, the absolute difference between the white and nonwhite infant mortality rate was 31 per 1,000 live births, while in

163

1962 the difference had declined to 19 per 1,000. Yet in 1949 nonwhite infant mortality was 70 per cent greater than that of whites and in 1962 it was 90 per cent greater.

The lag in rate of progress feeds Negro discontent.

Some of Fein's statistics starkly light up the background of that situation which gave us the 'Black Panther' party.

Even as late as 1952 [Fein writes] the chances were barely 50–50 that a Negro baby born in Mississippi was born in a hospital, but the chances were 99 to 100 for white Mississippi-born babies. And for Negro residents of Dallas County and Lowndes County, Alabama, the rates in 1962 were 27 and 9 per 100 (while rates for white residents were 99 and 96 respectively).

This disparity of nine Negro babies per hundred and ninety-six white babies per hundred born in hospitals in Lowndes County may help us to understand the context from which the cry of Black Power originated. The discrimination against the overwhelming black majority in counties like Lowndes is almost genocidal.

The picture which emerges from this symposium, however, has its more hopeful aspects. Lee Rainwater, in his essay on 'The Crucible of Identity', throws doubt on the view that slavery, by destroying the Negro family, has created characteristics which make it difficult for the Negro to shake off 'nigger-ness'. Rainwater points out that 'in the hundred years since Emancipation, Negroes in rural areas have been able to maintain full nuclear families almost as well as similarly situated whites'. The slum and the decline in the need for unskilled labour have more to do with the psychically crippling family conditions of the Negro than the heritage of slavery. Given half a chance, the Negro can respond as quickly as the white to the means for his own improvement. Adelaide Cromwell and Frederick S. Jaffe in their study of 'Negro Fertility and Family Size Preferences' show how responsive Negroes are to the birth control which is an essential step to the climb out of poverty. 'Privately organized Planned Parenthood centres in some 120 communities,' they write, 'are still the main birth-control clinics available to low-income families in the US; among the 282,000 patients served in their clinics in 1964, the largest single clinic group – 47 per cent – was Negro.' A wider availability of contraceptive knowledge for mothers and jobs for fathers would transform the Negro in a generation.

But there is no reason why this transformation must change the Negro merely into a darker version of the white man. The new emphasis on 'blackness' in the civil rights movement reflects a healthy instinct. The Negro has two basic needs. One is more jobs and the other is the restoration of self-respect. But how is self-respect to be restored if he rejects himself as Negro and aspires to be something else? Assimilation may come some day to the Negro, as it has to other ethnic groups in our American melting pot; the forces making for homogeneity may prove irresistible for him too. But on the way the Negro can only wipe out the self-contempt imposed upon him by three centuries of white supremacy by accepting and affirming and intensifying his negritude. A man must absorb, face, and not reject his past in order to stand fully erect, and that past includes the past of the people to which he belongs. To abandon part of one's self is by implication to accept that part's inferiority. The current revulsion against integration is made more understandable by Erik H. Erikson's essay on 'The Concept of Identity'.

Dr Erikson, who is lecturer on psychiatry at Harvard, shows us that the Negro is often asked to accept 'an unsure outer integration' at the cost of giving up that 'inner integration' in which he had learned to accept himself as a Negro. He quotes a young Negro woman student as exclaiming, 'What am I supposed to be integrated *out* of? I laugh like my grandmother – and I would rather die than not laugh like that.' Dr Erikson remarks: 'Desegregation, compensation, balance, reconciliation – do they all sometimes seem to save the Negro at the cost of an absorption which he is not sure will leave much of himself behind?'

This has implications for the Negro collectively as well as individually. Oscar Handlin's essay on 'The Goals of Integration' is not so far from the sharp new turn in the civil rights movement signalled by Stokely Carmichael.

It is the ultimate illogic of integration [Handlin writes] to deny the separateness of the Negro and therefore to inhibit him from creating the communal institutions which can help him cope with his problem . . . To confuse segregation, the function of which is to establish Negro inferiority, with the awareness of separate identity, the function of which is to generate the power for voluntary action, hopelessly confuses the struggle for equality.

Handlin restates calmly what the Negro radicals cry out in their anguish:

As long as common memories, experience and interests make the Negroes a group, they will find it advantageous to organize and act as such. And the society will better be able to accommodate them as equals on those terms than it could under the pretense that integration could wipe out the past.

This is the logic of 'black power', though devoid of those semantic, psychological, and mystical overtones that have spread it so swiftly through the Negro community, as if it were an incantation to the forgotten tribal gods long torn away from them.

The Negro requires and deserves the fullest measure of patience and understanding in his agony, for this is the agony of his rebirth. His racism, answering ours, is a necessary step towards our ultimate reconciliation. The riots – and they will become worse – have a logic of their own: Can we deny that only the fear of race war can force us finally to gird for Negro rehabilitation and reconstruction as we gird for war abroad, on a giant scale and with a generous hand? Of all I read in *The Negro American* what I liked best is a remark Robert Coles records from an unnamed Negro in Mississippi. 'Negroes don't have it so bad,' he said, 'they can recover mighty fast, if we only get a chance.' There lies the hope for him and for us and for what must become, in the fullest sense, our common country.

4.11 ACTION POLITICS

Resolution *passed by the SDS national council meeting in Austin, Texas, 20 March 1969.*

Of the many revolutionary groups emerging during the 1960s perhaps the most militant was *Students for a Democratic Society* (SDS). By 1969, one of the chief problems confronting SDS was its relationship with militant Negro groups such as the Black Panther Party. Many Negro leaders argue that black people should have nothing to do with whites, least of all the middle class whites who tend to emerge as leaders of the Student Left in America. At a meeting in Texas in March 1969 the SDS national council passed a resolution seeking an alliance with the Black Panther Party – now the strongest and best organized of the militant Negro organizations in the United States.

The phrasing of the resolution bears most of the characteristics of the revolutionary Left: passionate conviction; strong language and the use of epithet for opponents, real or imagined; a tendency to use portmanteau terms such as 'national chauvinism' and 'cultural nationalism'; and an urgent commitment to immediate action.

The Black Panther Party:
Towards the Liberation of the Colony

The sharpest struggles in the world today are those of the oppressed nations against imperialism and for national liberation. Within this country the sharpest struggle is that of the black colony for its liberation; it is a struggle which by its very nature is anti-imperialist and increasingly anti-capitalist. The demand for self-determination for the black colony – a demand which arises from the most oppressed elements within the black community – is anti-imperialist and anti-capitalist insofar as it challenges the power of the ruling class. Furthermore the black liberation movement consciously identifies with and expresses solidarity with the liberation struggles of other oppressed peoples.

Within the black liberation movement the vanguard force is the Black Panther party. Their development of an essentially correct programme for the black community and their ability to organize blacks around this programme have brought them to this leadership. An especially important part of the Panther programme is the Black People's Army – a military force to be used not only in the defence of the black community but also for its liberation. Given the military occupation of the black community, it is especially true that 'without a people's army the people have nothing'. A second important part of their programme is their efforts to organize black workers. They are increasingly moving into the factories and shops, e.g., Drum, Panther caucuses, Black Labour Federations, etc. It is important for us to understand that the black worker is not only a 'subject' in an oppressed colony fighting for its liberation but that he is also a member of the working class. Thus the black worker, as a result of this dual oppression, will play the vanguard role not only in the black liberation movement but also in uniting and

G

leading the whole working class in its fight against oppression and exploitation.

The fundamental reason for the success of the Black Panther party is that it has a correct analysis of American society. They see clearly the colonial status of blacks and the dual oppression from which they suffer: national oppression as a people and class exploitation as a super-exploited part of the working class. The demand for self-determination becomes the most basic demand of the oppressed colony. And nationalism becomes a necessary and effective means for organizing the black community and forging unity against the oppressor.

We must be very clear about the nature of nationalism. If the principal contradiction in the world today is that of the oppressed nations against imperialism, then support for these revolutionary national movements becomes the most important criterion for dividing revolutionaries from counter-revolutionaries (and revisionists). To say that 'in the name of nationalism, the bourgeoisie of all nations do their reactionary and dirty work' is to obscure the reality that in the name of national liberation the workers and peasants of all oppressed nations will struggle against and defeat imperialism. To say that 'all nationalism is reactionary' is objectively to ally with imperialism in opposition to the struggles of the oppressed nations.

Nationalism

But nationalism is not always revolutionary. There is a fundamental difference between revolutionary nationalism which is 'dependent upon a people's revolution' and reactionary nationalism in which the 'end goal is the oppression of the people'. What do the Panthers say about the reactionary, cultural or 'porkchop' variety of nationalism?

'We must destroy all cultural nationalism, because it is reactionary and has become a tool of Richard Milhous Nixon and all the US power structure which divides the poor and oppressed, and is used by the greasy-slick black bourgeoisie to exploit black people in the ghetto.'

George Mason Murray
Minister of Education, Black Panther Party

The Black Panther party is under no illusion that liberation for the black colony can be achieved while capitalism still exists. Their call for 'liberation in the colony, revolution in the mother country' clearly recognizes the dialectical relationship between liberation for the black colony and socialist revolution for the whole society.

'It's impossible for us to have control of the institutions in our community when a capitalistic system exists on the outside of it, when in fact the capitalistic system was the very system that enslaved us and is responsible for our continued oppression. So if we want to develop a socialistic system within the black community, we're saying it's also going to have to exist in the white community.'

Bobby Seale
Chairman, Black Panther Party

The correct and uncompromising leadership which the Black Panther party has brought to the black liberation movement has brought down the most vicious repression from the racist pig power structure. When the leading black revolutionary group is continually harassed, its leaders jailed, hounded out of the country and brutally assassinated, when Panther members daily face the provocations of the ruling class and its racist pigs, when their blood has been spilled and their list of revolutionary martyrs – Huey, Eldridge,[*] Bobby Hutton, Bunchy Carter, John Huggins – increases daily, then the time has come for SDS to give total and complete support to their defence efforts. To do less would be a mockery of the word 'revolutionary'. We must continually expose and attack the role of the pigs and the courts in oppressing the black community. We must publicize the inhuman, brutal and unjust nature of 'justice' in this society.

Fight White Supremacy
We see clearly the need to join with the Black Panther party and other revolutionary black groups in the fight against national chauvinism and white supremacy. The development of the Panthers as a disciplined and militant group fighting for black liberation has had a tremendous impact on the white radical movement. No longer can we refuse to deal with the chauvinism and white supremacy which exists both in the larger society and in our movement. Toleration of any vestige of white supremacy in the

[* Huey Newton and Eldridge Cleaver received short jail sentences on charges of provoking public disorder. In fact Eldridge Cleaver survived his 'martyrdom' to lecture at the University of California and publish a book, *Soul on Ice*.]

schools, shops and communities must be seen as nothing less than 'scabbing' on the black liberation movement and on possibilities for unity of the working class.

SDS *declares*: its support for the Black Panther party and their essentially correct programme for the liberation of the black colony; its commitment to defend the Black Panther party and the black colony against the vicious attacks of the racist pig power structure; its commitment to join with the Black Panther party and other black revolutionary groups in the fight against white national chauvinism and white supremacy; its total commitment to the fight for liberation in the colony and revolution in the mother country.

Implementation

Form Newton-Cleaver Defence Committees. The Black Panther party has requested that SDS join in setting up these committees. Huey P. Newton is 'the key political prisoner in this country at the present time'. The committees should first raise money for the defence of Newton, Cleaver and all other Panthers facing charges and second, educate the people about the real nature of 'justice' in this racist society.

The SDS national office should be mandated to print and distribute information about the history, development and programmes of the Black Panther party and other black revolutionary groups. Information about the repression directed against the black community should be kept up to date and distributed. Literature about the history of the black colony and its 400 years of unending struggle against oppression should be produced.

The national office should be mandated to print and distribute information about the organizing of black workers. This would include Panther organizing in the factories, Drum and other revolutionary black unions.

This resolution should stimulate SDS chapters and regions to develop and/or strengthen informal and formal relationships with the Panthers. We must keep in mind that the Black Panther party is not fighting black people's struggles only, but is in fact the vanguard in our common struggles against capitalism and imperialism.

This resolution should be seen as a formal repudiation of the resolution, 'Smash Racism: Build a Worker-Student Alliance', which was passed at the December national council. This previous resolution with its refusal to recognize the colonial oppression of blacks in this country, its statement that nationalism is 'the main ideological weapon of the ruling class' within the black liberation movement, and its inability to distinguish between revolutionary and reactionary nationalism, is at best non-revolutionary. SDS must not be on record as supporting any resolution which considers revolutionary nationalism – the main factor which ties all oppressed nations together in their fight against imperialism – as a 'weapon of the ruling class'. Anything less than complete repudiation of this previous resolution is a cop-out on the support and solidarity which we must give to the worldwide movement of oppressed peoples for national liberation.

5   *The Civil Rights Struggle*

5.1 NEGRO EMANCIPATION

From Booker T. Washington, Up From Slavery, *1901, this ed. 1963, pp. 11–15.*

Booker T. Washington (1856–1915) was the first national spokesman for the American Negro. His mother was a slave in the antebellum South, his father a white man. He studied at one of the Negro vocational schools set up during the Reconstruction period, then at a seminary before becoming a school teacher. Later he helped to found the Tuskegee Institute for Negro education at Tuskegee, Alabama.

In 1899 he wrote *The Future of the American Negro,* but his best known work is the autobiography *Up From Slavery* (1901). Today, advocates of Negro militancy would probably argue that Washington's book shows all the failings of the 'Uncle Tom' mentality which characterized the early, docile stage of the Negro Civil Rights movement. The following passage from Booker Washington's autobiography recalls the moment in his boyhood when Abraham Lincoln's Emancipation Proclamation was read – and the mixed reactions it brought to the former slaves.

I pity from the bottom of my heart any nation or body of people that is so unfortunate as to get entangled in the net of slavery. I have long since ceased to cherish any spirit of bitterness against the Southern white people on account of the enslavement of my race.

No one section of our country was wholly responsible for its introduction, and, besides, it was recognized and protected for years by
the General Government. Having once got its tentacles fastened on
to the economic and social life of the Republic, it was no easy
matter for the country to relieve itself of the institution. Then,
when we rid ourselves of prejudice, or racial feeling, and look facts
in the face, we must acknowledge that, notwithstanding the cruelty
and moral wrong of slavery, the ten million Negroes inhabiting this
country, who themselves or whose ancestors went through the
school of American slavery, are in a stronger and more hopeful
condition, materially, intellectually, morally, and religiously, than
is true of an equal number of black people in any other portion of
the globe. This is so to such an extent that Negroes in this country,
who themselves or whose forefathers went through the school of
slavery, are constantly returning to Africa as missionaries to en-
lighten those who remained in the fatherland. This I say, not to
justify slavery – on the other hand, I condemn it as an institution,
as we all know that in America it was established for selfish and
financial reasons, and not from a missionary motive – but to call
attention to a fact, and to show how Providence so often uses men
and institutions to accomplish a purpose. When persons ask me in
these days how, in the midst of what sometimes seem hopelessly
discouraging conditions, I can have such faith in the future of my
race in this country, I remind them of the wilderness through
which and out of which, a good Providence has already led us.

Ever since I have been old enough to think for myself, I have
entertained the idea that, notwithstanding the cruel wrongs
inflicted upon us, the black man got nearly as much out of slavery
as the white man did. The hurtful influences of the institution
were not by any means confined to the Negro. This was fully
illustrated by the life upon our own plantation. The whole machinery of slavery was so constructed as to cause labour, as a rule, to be
looked upon as a badge of degradation, of inferiority. Hence labour
was something that both races on the slave plantation sought to
escape. The slave system on our place, in a large measure, took the
spirit of self-reliance and self-help out of the white people. My old
master had many boys and girls, but not one, so far as I know, ever
mastered a single trade or special line of productive industry. The
girls were not taught to cook, sew or to take care of the house. All of
this was left to the slaves. The slaves, of course, had little personal

interest in the life of the plantation, and their ignorance prevented them from learning how to do things in the most improved and thorough manner. As a result of the system, fences were out of repair, gates were hanging half off the hinges, doors creaked, window-panes were out, plastering had fallen but was not replaced, weeds grew in the yard. As a rule, there was food for whites and blacks, but inside the house, and on the dining-room table, there was wanting that delicacy and refinement of touch and finish which can make a home the most convenient, comfortable, and attractive place in the world. Withal there was a waste of food and other materials which was sad. When freedom came, the slaves were almost as well fitted to begin life anew as the master, except in the matter of book-learning and ownership of property. The slave owner and his sons had mastered no special industry. They unconsciously had imbibed the feeling that manual labour was not the proper thing for them. On the other hand, the slaves, in many cases, had mastered some handicraft, and none were ashamed, and few unwilling, to labour.

Finally the war closed, and the day of freedom came. It was a momentous and eventful day to all upon our plantation. We had been expecting it. Freedom was in the air, and had been for months. Deserting soldiers returning to their homes were to be seen every day. Others who had been discharged, or whose regiments had been paroled, were constantly passing near our place. The 'grape-vine telegraph' was kept busy night and day. The news and mutterings of great events were swiftly carried from one plantation to another. In the fear of 'Yankee' invasions, the silverware and other valuables were taken from the 'big house', buried in the woods, and guarded by trusted slaves. Woe be to any one who would have attempted to disturb the buried treasure. The slaves would give the Yankee soldiers food, drink, clothing – anything but that which had been specifically entrusted to their care and honour. As the great day drew nearer, there was more singing in the slave quarters than usual. It was bolder, had more ring, and lasted later into the night. Most of the verses of the plantation songs had some reference to freedom. True, they had sung those same verses before, but they had been careful to explain that the 'freedom' in these songs referred to the next world, and had no connection with life in this world. Now they gradually threw off the mask; and were not afraid to let it be known that the 'freedom' in their songs meant freedom of the body in this world. The night before the eventful day, word was sent to the slave quarters to the effect that something unusual was going to take place at the 'big house' the next morning. There was little, if any, sleep that night. All was excitement and expectancy. Early the next morning word was sent to all the slaves, old and young, to gather at the house. In company with my mother, brother, and sister, and a large number of other slaves, I went to the master's house. All of our master's family were either standing or seated on the veranda of the house, where they could see what was to take place and hear what was said. There was a feeling of deep interest, or perhaps sadness, on their faces, but not bitterness. As I now recall the impression they made upon me, they did not at the moment seem to be sad because of the loss of property, but rather of parting with those whom they had reared and who were in many ways very close to them. The most distinct thing that I now recall in connection with the scene was that some man who seemed to be a stranger (a United States officer, I presume) made a little speech and then read a rather long paper – the Emancipation Proclamation, I think. After the reading we were told that we were all free, and could go when and where we pleased. My mother, who was standing by my side, leaned over and kissed her children, while tears of joy ran down her cheeks. She explained to us what it all meant, that this was the day for which she had been so long praying, but fearing that she would never live to see.

For some minutes there was great rejoicing, and thanksgiving, and wild scenes of ecstasy. But there was no feeling of bitterness. In fact, there was pity among the slaves for our former owners. The wild rejoicing on the part of the emancipated coloured people lasted but for a brief period, for I noticed that by the time they returned to their cabins there was a change in their feelings. The great responsibility of being free, of having charge of themselves, of having to think and plan for themselves and their children, seemed to take possession of them. It was very much like suddenly turning a youth of ten or twelve years out into the world to provide for himself. In a few hours the great questions with which the Anglo-Saxon race had been grappling for centuries had been thrown upon these people to be solved. These were the questions of a home, a living, the rearing of children, education, citizenship, and the establishment and support of churches. Was it any wonder that within a few hours the wild rejoicing ceased and a feeling of deep gloom seemed to pervade the slave quarters? To some it seemed that, now that they were in actual possession of it, freedom was a more serious thing than they had expected to find it. Some of the slaves were seventy or eighty years old; their best days were gone. They had no strength with which to earn a living in a strange place and among strange people, even if they had been sure where to find a new place of abode. To this class the problem seemed especially hard. Besides, deep down in their hearts there was a strange and peculiar attachment to 'old Marster' and 'old Missus', and to their children, which they found it hard to think of breaking off. With these they had spent in some cases nearly a half-century, and it was no light thing to think of parting. Gradually, one by one, stealthily at first, the older slaves began to wander from the slave quarters back to the 'big house' to have a whispered conversation with their former owners as to the future.

5.2 EQUAL RIGHTS FOR ALL

From Opinion delivered by Chief Justice Earl Warren in Brown v. Board of Education of Topeka, *347 US 483, 1954.*

The American Constitution provides that all US citizens must be given 'the equal protection of the laws'. As the Constitution is the supreme law of the land, every State in the Union is bound by its terms. But it is easier to read the Constitution than to give it practical effect in every part of the United States.

The United States Supreme Court, in a historic decision of 1896 (Plessy v. Ferguson) ruled that 'separate but equal' facilities for different racial groups could be maintained by State authorities under the terms of the Constitution. Half a century later it was abundantly clear that the 'separate but equal' doctrine was a figment, and that separation of the different ethnic or racial groups in the United States inevitably produced inequalities of different kinds. In another historic decision in 1954 the Supreme Court reversed the ruling in Plessy v. Ferguson. The 1954 decision involved *inter alia* separate educational facilities for Negro children in Topeka, Kansas. Chief Justice Earl Warren delivered the opinion of the Court as follows:

Chief Justice Warren. These cases come to us from the States of Kansas, South Carolina, Virginia, and Delaware. They are premised on different facts and different local conditions, but a common legal question justifies their consideration together in this consolidated opinion.

In each of the cases, minors of the Negro race, through their legal representatives, seek the aid of the courts in obtaining admission to the public schools of their community on a non-segregated basis. In each instance, they have been denied admission to schools attended by white children under laws requiring or permitting segregation according to race. This segregation was alleged to deprive the plaintiffs of the equal protection of the laws under the Fourteenth Amendment. In each of the cases other than the Delaware case, a three-judge federal district court denied relief to the plaintiffs on the so-called 'separate but equal' doctrine announced by this Court in Plessy v. Ferguson, 163 US 537. Under that doctrine, equality of treatment is accorded when the races are provided substantially equal facilities, even though these facilities be separate. In the Delaware case, the Supreme Court of Delaware adhered to that doctrine, but ordered that the plaintiffs be admitted to the white schools because of their superiority to the Negro schools.

The plaintiffs contend that segregated public schools are not 'equal' and cannot be made 'equal', and that hence they are deprived of the equal protection of the laws. Because of the obvious importance of the question presented, the Court took jurisdiction. Argument was heard in the 1952 Term, and re-argument was heard this Term on certain questions propounded by the Court.

Re-argument was largely devoted to the circumstances surrounding the adoption of the Fourteenth Amendment in 1868. It covered exhaustively consideration of the Amendment in Congress, ratification by the states, then existing practices in racial segregation, and the views of proponents and opponents of the Amendment. This discussion and our own investigation convince us that, although these sources cast some light, it is not enough to resolve the problem with which we are faced. At best, they are inconclusive. The most avid proponents of the post-War Amendments undoubtedly intended them to remove all legal distinctions among 'all persons born or naturalized in the United States'. Their opponents, just as certainly, were antagonistic to both the letter and the spirit of the

Amendments and wished them to have the most limited effect. What others in Congress and the state legislatures had in mind cannot be determined with any degree of certainty.

An additional reason for the inconclusive nature of the Amendment's history, with respect to segregated schools, is the status of public education at that time. In the South, the movement towards free common schools, supported by general taxation, had not yet taken hold. Education of white children was largely in the hands of private groups. Education of Negroes was almost non-existent, and practically all of the race were illiterate. In fact, any education of Negroes was forbidden by law in some states. Today, in contrast, many Negroes have achieved outstanding success in the arts and sciences as well as in the business and professional world. It is true that public education had already advanced further in the North, but the effect of the Amendment on Northern States was generally ignored in the congressional debates. Even in the North, the conditions of public education did not approximate those existing today. The curriculum was usually rudimentary; ungraded schools were common in rural areas; the school term was but three months a year in many states; and compulsory school attendance was virtually unknown. As a consequence, it is not surprising that there should be so little in the history of the Fourteenth Amendment relating to its intended effect on public education.

In the first cases in this Court construing the Fourteenth Amendment decided shortly after its adoption, the Court interpreted it as proscribing all state-imposed discriminations against the Negro race. The doctrine of 'separate but equal' did not make its appearance in this Court until 1896 in the case of Plessy v. Ferguson, supra, involving not education but transportation. American courts have since laboured with the doctrine for over half a century. . . .

In approaching this problem, we cannot turn the clock back to 1868 when the Amendment was adopted, or even to 1896 when Plessy v. Ferguson was written. We must consider public education in the light of its full development and its present place in American life throughout the Nation. Only in this way can it be determined if segregation in public schools deprives these plaintiffs of the equal protection of the laws.

Today, education is perhaps the most important function of state and local governments. Compulsory school attendance laws and the great expenditures for education both demonstrate our recognition of the importance of education to our democratic society. It is required in the performance of our most basic public responsibilities, even service in the armed forces. It is the very foundation of good citizenship. Today it is a principal instrument in awakening the child to cultural values, in preparing him for later professional training, and in helping him to adjust normally to his environment. In these days, it is doubtful that any child may reasonably be expected to succeed in life if he is denied the opportunity of an education. Such an opportunity, where the state has undertaken to provide it, is a right which must be made available to all on equal terms.

We come then to the question presented: Does segregation of children in public schools solely on the basis of race, even though the physical facilities and other 'tangible' factors may be equal, deprive the children of the minority group of equal educational opportunities? We believe that it does.

In Sweatt v. Painter, supra [339 US 629, 70 S.Ct. 850], in finding that a segregated law school for Negroes could not provide them equal educational opportunities, this Court relied in large part on 'those qualities which are incapable of objective measurement but which make for greatness in a law school'. In McLaurin v. Oklahoma State Regents, supra [339 US 637, 70 S.Ct. 853], the Court, in requiring that a Negro admitted to a white graduate school be treated like all other students, again resorted to intangible considerations: '. . . his ability to study, to engage in discussions and exchange views with other students, and, in general, to learn his profession.' Such considerations apply with added force to children in grade and high schools. To separate them from others of similar age and qualifications solely because of their race generates a feeling of inferiority as to their status in the community that may affect their hearts and minds in a way unlikely ever to be undone. The effect of this separation on their educational opportunities was well stated by a finding in the Kansas case by a court which nevertheless felt compelled to rule against the Negro plaintiffs:

'Segregation of white and colored children in public schools has a detrimental effect upon the colored children. The impact is greater when it has the sanction of the law; for the policy of separating the races is usually interpreted as denoting the inferiority of the Negro group. A sense of inferiority affects the motivation of a child to learn. Segregation with the sanction of law, therefore, has a tendency to retard the educational and mental development of Negro children and to deprive them of some of the benefits they would receive in a racially integrated school system.'

Whatever may have been the extent of psychological knowledge at the time of Plessy *v.* Ferguson, this finding is amply supported by modern authority. Any language in Plessy *v.* Ferguson contrary to this finding is rejected.

We conclude that in the field of public education the doctrine of 'separate but equal' has no place. Separate educational facilities are inherently unequal. Therefore, we hold that the plaintiffs and others similarly situated for whom the actions have been brought are, by reason of the segregation complained of, deprived of the equal protection of the laws guaranteed by the Fourteenth Amendment. This disposition makes unnecessary any discussion whether such segregation also violates the Due Process Clause of the Fourteenth Amendment.

Because these are class actions, because of the wide applicability of this decision, and because of the great variety of local conditions, the formulation of decrees in these cases presents problems of considerable complexity. On re-argument, the consideration of appropriate relief was necessarily subordinated to the primary question – the constitutionality of segregation in public education. We have now announced that such segregation is a denial of the equal protection of the laws.

5.3 CONGRESSIONAL BACKLASH

From Congressional Record, *84 Congress, 2 Session, CII, Part 4, cc. 4459–4460.*

The Supreme Court decision in Brown *v.* Topeka Board of Education (see previous document) aroused strong hostility among members of the US Congress representing southern states. On 12 March 1956, nineteen Senators and eighty-one Congressmen, drawn from eleven southern States, presented a 'Southern Manifesto' to the Congress. Its terms were as follows:

The unwarranted decision of the Supreme Court in the public

school cases is now bearing the fruit always produced when men substitute naked power for established law.

The Founding Fathers gave us a Constitution of checks and balances because they realized the inescapable lesson of history that no man or group of men can be safely entrusted with unlimited power. They framed this Constitution with its provisions for change by amendment in order to secure the fundamentals of government against the dangers of temporary popular passion or the personal predilections of public office-holders.

We regard the decision of the Supreme Court in the school cases as a clear abuse of judicial power. It climaxes a trend in the Federal Judiciary undertaking to legislate, in derogation of the authority of Congress, and to encroach upon the reserved rights of the States and the people.

The original Constitution does not mention education. Neither does the fourteenth amendment nor any other amendment. The debates preceding the submission of the fourteenth amendment clearly show that there was no intent that it should affect the system of education maintained by the States.

The very Congress which proposed the amendment subsequently provided for segregated schools in the District of Columbia.

When the amendment was adopted in 1868, there were thirty-seven States of the Union. Every one of the twenty-six States that had any substantial racial differences among its people, either approved the operation of segregated schools already in existence or subsequently established such schools by action of the same law-making body which considered the fourteenth amendment.

As admitted by the Supreme Court in the public school case (Brown v. Board of Education), the doctrine of separate but equal schools 'apparently originated in Roberts v. City of Boston (1849), upholding school segregation against attack as being violative of a State constitutional guarantee of equality'. This constitutional doctrine began in the North, not in the South, and it was followed not only in Massachusetts, but in Connecticut, New York, Illinois, Indiana, Michigan, Minnesota, New Jersey, Ohio, Pennsylvania and other northern States until they, exercising their rights as States through the constitutional processes of local self-government, changed their school systems.

In the case of Plessy v. Ferguson in 1896 the Supreme Court

expressly declared that under the fourteenth amendment no person was denied any of his rights if the States provided separate but equal public facilities. This decision has been followed in many other cases. It is notable that the Supreme Court, speaking through Chief Justice Taft, a former President of the United States, unanimously declared in 1927 in Lum v. Rice that the 'separate but equal' principle is 'within the discretion of the State in regulating its public schools and does not conflict with the fourteenth amendment'.

This interpretation, restated time and again, became a part of the life of the people of many of the States and confirmed their habits, customs, traditions, and way of life. It is founded on elemental humanity and commonsense, for parents should not be deprived by Government of the right to direct the lives and education of their own children.

Though there has been no constitutional amendment or act of Congress changing this established legal principle almost a century old, the Supreme Court of the United States, with no legal basis for such action, undertook to exercise their naked judicial power and substituted their personal political and social ideas for the established law of the land.

This unwarranted exercise of power by the Court, contrary to the Constitution, is creating chaos and confusion in the States principally affected. It is destroying the amicable relations between the white and Negro races that have been created through ninety years of patient effort by the good people of both races. It has planted hatred and suspicion where there has been heretofore friendship and understanding.

Without regard to the consent of the governed, outside agitators are threatening immediate and revolutionary changes in our public-school systems. If done, this is certain to destroy the system of public education in some of the States.

With the gravest concern for the explosive and dangerous condition created by this decision and inflamed by outside meddlers:

We reaffirm our reliance on the Constitution as the fundamental law of the land.

We decry the Supreme Court's encroachments on rights reserved to the States and to the people, contrary to established law, and to the Constitution.

We commend the motives of those States which have declared the intention to resist forced integration by any lawful means.

We appeal to the States and people who are not directly affected by these decisions to consider the constitutional principles involved against the time when they too, on issues vital to them, may be the victims of judicial encroachment.

Even though we constitute a minority in the present Congress, we have full faith that a majority of the American people believe in the dual system of government which has enabled us to achieve our greatness and will in time demand that the reserved rights of the States and of the people be made secure against judicial usurpation.

We pledge ourselves to use all lawful means to bring about a reversal of this decision which is contrary to the Constitution and to prevent the use of force in its implementation.

In this trying period, as we all seek to right this wrong, we appeal to our people not to be provoked by the agitators and troublemakers invading our States and to scrupulously refrain from disorder and lawless acts.

5.4 A PHILOSOPHY OF NONVIOLENCE

From Martin Luther King, Stride Toward Freedom, *1958, pp. 92–7.*

The Reverend Martin Luther King, Jr (1929–68), was the modern successor to Booker T. Washington as national spokesman for the American Negro. The Reverend King's great strength lay with the spoken, rather than the written word, and the printed page cannot capture the biblical fervour and rolling cadences of his speeches. But his writings do help to convey the humility and compassion of a fundamentally religious man. His assassination in 1968 must be counted as a tragedy for the whole American people and not merely for the American Negro.

In his fragment of autobiography, *Stride Toward Freedom,* Martin Luther King traced the intellectual paths which led him to his philosophy of non-violence. The following passage also shows King's reactions to his readings of Karl Marx.

During the Christmas holidays of 1949 I decided to spend my spare time reading Karl Marx to try to understand the appeal of communism for many people. For the first time I carefully scrutinized *Das Kapital* and *The Communist Manifesto*. I also read some interpretive works on the thinking of Marx and Lenin. In reading such Communist writings I drew certain conclusions that have remained with me as convictions to this day. First I rejected their materialistic interpretation of history. Communism, avowedly secularistic and materialistic, has no place for God. This I could never accept, for as a Christian I believe that there is a creative personal power in this universe who is the ground and essence of all reality – a power that cannot be explained in materialistic terms. History is ultimately guided by spirit, not matter. Second, I strongly disagreed with communism's ethical relativism. Since for the Communist there is no divine government, no absolute moral order, there are no fixed, immutable principles; consequently almost anything – force, violence, murder, lying – is a justifiable means to the 'millennial' end. This type of relativism was abhorrent to me. Constructive ends can never give absolute moral justification to destructive means, because in the final analysis the end is pre-existent in the means. Third, I opposed communism's political totalitarianism. In communism the individual ends up in subjection to the state. True, the Marxist would argue that the state is an 'interim' reality which is to be eliminated when the classless society emerges; but the state is the end while it lasts, and man only a means to that end. And if any man's so-called rights or liberties stand in the way of that end, they are simply swept aside. His liberties of expression, his freedom to vote, his freedom to listen to what news he likes or to choose his books are all restricted. Man becomes hardly more, in communism, than a depersonalized cog in the turning wheel of the state.

This deprecation of individual freedom was objectionable to me. I am convinced now, as I was then, that man is an end because he is a child of God. Man is not made for the state; the state is made for man. To deprive man of freedom is to relegate him to the status of a thing, rather than elevate him to the status of a person. Man must never be treated as a means to the end of the state, but always as an end within himself.

Yet, in spite of the fact that my response to communism was and is negative, and I considered it basically evil, there were points at which I found it challenging. The late Archbishop of Canterbury, William Temple, referred to communism as a Christian heresy.

By this he meant that communism had laid hold of certain truths which are essential parts of the Christian view of things, but that it had bound up with them concepts and practices which no Christian could ever accept or profess. Communism challenged the late Archbishop and it should challenge every Christian – as it challenged me – to a growing concern about social justice. With all of its false assumptions and evil methods, communism grew as a protest against the hardships of the underprivileged. Communism in theory emphasized a classless society, and a concern for social justice, though the world knows from sad experience that in practice it created new classes and a new lexicon of injustice. The Christian ought always to be challenged by any protest against unfair treatment of the poor, for Christianity is itself such a protest, nowhere expressed more eloquently than in Jesus' words: 'The Spirit of the Lord is upon me, because he hath anointed me to preach the gospel to the poor; he hath sent me to heal the broken-hearted, to preach deliverance to the captives, and recovering of sight to the blind, to set at liberty them that are bruised, to preach the acceptable year of the Lord.'

I also sought systematic answers to Marx's critique of modern bourgeois culture. He presented capitalism as essentially a struggle between the owners of the productive resources and the workers, whom Marx regarded as the real producers. Marx interpreted economic forces as the dialectical process by which society moved from feudalism through capitalism to socialism, with the primary mechanism of this historical movement being the struggle between economic classes whose interests were irreconcilable. Obviously this theory left out of account the numerous and significant complexities – political, economic, moral, religious, and psychological – which played a vital role in shaping the constellation of institutions and ideas known today as Western civilization. Moreover, it was dated in the sense that the capitalism Marx wrote about bore only a partial resemblance to the capitalism we know in this country today.

But in spite of the shortcomings of his analysis, Marx had raised some basic questions. I was deeply concerned from my early teen days about the gulf between superfluous wealth and abject poverty and my reading of Marx made me ever more conscious of this gulf. Although modern American capitalism had greatly reduced the gap through social reforms, there was still need for a better distribution of wealth. Moreover, Marx had revealed the danger of the profit motive as the sole basis of an economic system: capitalism is always in danger of inspiring men to be more concerned about making a living than making a life. We are prone to judge success by the index of our salaries or the size of our automobiles, rather than by the quality of our service and relationship to humanity – thus capitalism can lead to a practical materialism that is as pernicious as the materialism taught by communism.

In short, I read Marx as I read all of the influential historical thinkers – from a dialectical point of view, combining a partial yes and a partial no. In so far as Marx posited a metaphysical materialism, an ethical relativism, and a strangulating totalitarianism, I responded with an unambiguous 'no'; but in so far as he pointed to weaknesses of traditional capitalism, contributed to the growth of a definite self-consciousness in the masses, and challenged the social conscience of the Christian churches, I responded with a definite 'yes'.

My reading of Marx also convinced me that truth is found neither in Marxism nor in traditional capitalism. Each represents a partial truth. Historically capitalism failed to see the truth in collective enterprise and Marxism failed to see the truth in individual enterprise. Nineteenth-century capitalism failed to see that life is social and Marxism failed and still fails to see that life is individual and personal. The Kingdom of God is neither the thesis of individual enterprise nor the antithesis of collective enterprise, but a synthesis which reconciles the truths of both.

During my stay at Crozer, I was also exposed for the first time to the pacifist position in a lecture by Dr A. J. Muste. I was deeply moved by Dr Muste's talk, but far from convinced of the practicability of his position. Like most of the students of Crozer, I felt that while war could never be a positive or absolute good, it could serve as a negative good in the sense of preventing the spread and growth of an evil force. War, horrible as it is, might be preferable to surrender to a totalitarian system – Nazi, Fascist, or Communist.

During this period I had about despaired of the power of love in solving social problems. Perhaps my faith in love was temporarily shaken by the philosophy of Nietzsche. I had been reading parts of *The Genealogy of Morals* and the whole of *The Will to Power*. Nietzsche's glorification of power – in his theory all life expressed the will to power – was an outgrowth of his contempt for ordinary morals. He attacked the whole of the Hebraic-Christian morality – with its virtues of piety and humility, its otherworldliness and its attitude towards suffering – as the glorification of weakness, as making virtues out of necessity and impotence. He looked to the development of a superman who would surpass man as man surpassed the ape.

Then one Sunday afternoon I travelled to Philadelphia to hear a sermon by Dr Mordecai Johnson, president of Howard University. He was there to preach for the Fellowship House of Philadelphia. Dr Johnson had just returned from a trip to India, and, to my great interest, he spoke of the life and teachings of Mahatma Gandhi. His message was so profound and electrifying that I left the meeting and bought a half-dozen books on Gandhi's life and works.

Like most people, I had heard of Gandhi, but I had never studied him seriously. As I read I became deeply fascinated by his campaigns of non-violent resistance. I was particularly moved by the Salt March to the Sea and his numerous fasts. The whole concept of 'Satyagraha' (*Satya* is truth which equals love, and *agraha* is force; 'Satyagraha', therefore, means truth-force or love force) was profoundly significant to me. As I delved deeper into the philosophy of Gandhi my scepticism concerning the power of love gradually diminished, and I came to see for the first time its potency in the area of social reform. Prior to reading Gandhi, I had about concluded that the ethics of Jesus were only effective in individual relationship. The 'turn the other cheek' philosophy and the 'love your enemies' philosophy were only valid, I felt, when individuals were in conflict with other individuals; when racial groups and nations were in conflict a more realistic approach seemed necessary. But after reading Gandhi, I saw how utterly mistaken I was.

Gandhi was probably the first person in history to lift the love ethic of Jesus above mere interaction between individuals to a powerful and effective force on a large scale. Love for Gandhi was a potent instrument for social and collective transformation. It was in this Gandhian emphasis on love and non-violence that I discovered the method for social reform that I had been seeking for so many months. The intellectual and moral satisfaction that I failed to gain from the utilitarianism of Bentham and Mill, the revolutionary methods of Marx and Lenin, the social contract theory of Hobbes, the 'back to nature' optimism of Rousseau, and the superman philosophy of Nietzsche, I found in the non-violent resistance philosophy of Gandhi. I came to feel that this was the only morally and practically sound method open to oppressed people in their struggle for freedom.

5.5 THE MOVE TO NEGRO MILITANCY

From James Baldwin, The Fire Next Time, *1963, pp. 76–83.*

During the 1960s a mood of militancy grew among some of the younger leaders of the Negro Civil Rights movement. They felt, sincerely and passionately, that the freedoms promised by Abraham Lincoln more than a century earlier had not been realized and were too long in coming. Furthermore, they argued, those Negro leaders who counselled patience and non-violence were merely encouraging white Americans to ignore the plight of the Negro. Only militant action could rid white people of the deeply implanted prejudices instilled by centuries of exploitation of the Negro. Among the many Negro writers who contributed to the new mood of militancy was the novelist James Baldwin.

The Negroes of this country may never be able to rise to power, but they are very well placed indeed to precipitate chaos and ring down the curtain on the American dream.

This has everything to do, of course, with the nature of that dream and with the fact that we Americans, of whatever colour, do not dare examine it and are far from having made it a reality. There are too many things we do not wish to know about ourselves. People are not, for example, terribly anxious to be equal (equal, after all, to what and to whom?) but they love the idea of being superior. And this human truth has an especially grinding force here, where identity is almost impossible to achieve and people are perpetually attempting to find their feet on the shifting sands of status. (Consider the history of labour in a country in which, spiritually speaking, there are no workers, only candidates for the hand of the boss's daughter.) Furthermore, I have met only a very few people – and most of these were not Americans – who had any real desire to be free. Freedom is hard to bear. It can be objected that I am speaking of political freedom in spiritual terms, but the political institutions of any nation are always menaced and are ultimately controlled by the spiritual state of that nation. We are controlled here by our confusion, far more than we know, and the American dream has therefore become something much more closely resembling a nightmare, on the private, domestic, and international levels. Privately, we cannot stand our lives and dare not examine them; domestically, we take no responsibility for (and no pride in) what goes on in our country; and, internationally, for many millions of people, we are an unmitigated disaster. Whoever doubts this last statement has only to open his ears, his heart, his mind, to the testimony of – for example – any Cuban peasant or any Spanish poet, and ask himself what *he* would feel about us if *he* were the victim of our performance in pre-Castro Cuba or in Spain. We defend our curious role in Spain by referring to the Russian menace and the necessity of protecting the free world. It has not occurred to us that we have simply been mesmerized by Russia, and that the only real advantage Russia has in what we think of as a struggle between the East and the West is the moral history of the Western world. Russia's secret weapon is the bewilderment and despair and hunger of millions of people of whose existence we are scarcely aware. The Russian Communists are not in the least concerned about these people. But our ignorance and indecision have had the effect, if not of delivering them into Russian hands, of plunging them very deeply in the Russian shadow, for which effect – and it is hard to blame them – the most articulate among them, and the most oppressed as well, distrust us all the more. Our power and our fear of change help bind these people to their misery and bewilderment, and in so far as they find this state intolerable we are intolerably menaced. For if they find their state intolerable, but are too heavily oppressed to change it, they are simply pawns in the hands of larger powers, which, in such a context, are always unscrupulous, and when, eventually, they do change their situation – as in Cuba – we are menaced more than ever, by the vacuum that succeeds all violent upheavals. We should certainly know by now that it is one thing to overthrow a dictator or repel an invader and quite another thing really to achieve a revolution. Time and time and time again, the people discover that they have merely betrayed themselves into the hands of yet another Pharaoh, who, since he was necessary to put the broken country together, will not let them go. Perhaps, people being the conundrums that they are, and having so little desire to shoulder the burden of their lives, this is what will always happen. But at the bottom of my heart I do not believe this. I think that people can be better than that, and I know that people can be better than they are. We are capable of bearing a great burden, once we discover that the burden is reality and arrive where reality is. Anyway, the point here is that we are living in an age of revolution, whether we will or no, and that America is the only Western nation with both the power and, as I hope to suggest, the experience that may help to make these revolutions real and minimize the human damage. Any attempt we make to oppose these outbursts of energy is tantamount to signing our death warrant.

Behind what we think of as the Russian menace lies what we do not wish to face, and what white Americans do not face when they regard a Negro: reality – the fact that life is tragic. Life is tragic simply because the earth turns and the sun inexorably rises and sets, and one day, for each of us, the sun will go down for the last, last time. Perhaps the whole root of our trouble, the human trouble, is that we will sacrifice all the beauty of our lives, will imprison ourselves in totems, taboos, crosses, blood sacrifices, steeples, mosques, races, armies, flags, nations, in order to deny the fact of death, which is the only fact we have. It seems to me that one ought to rejoice in the *fact* of death – ought to decide, indeed, to *earn* one's death by confronting with passion the conundrum of life. One is responsible to life: It is the small beacon in that terrifying darkness from which we come and to which we shall return. One must negotiate this passage as nobly as possible for the sake of those who are coming after us. But white Americans do not believe in death, and this is why the darkness of my skin so intimidates them. And this is also why the presence of the Negro in this country can bring about its destruction. It is the responsibility of free men to trust and to celebrate what is constant – birth, struggle, and death are constant, and so is love, though we may not always think so – and to apprehend the nature of change, to be able and willing to change. I speak of change not on the surface but in the depths – change in the sense of renewal. But renewal becomes impossible if one supposes things to be constant that are not – safety, for example, or money, or power. One clings then to chimeras, by which one can only be betrayed, and the entire hope – the entire possibility – of freedom disappears. And by destruction I mean precisely the abdication by Americans of any effort really to be free. The Negro can precipitate this abdication because white Americans have never, in all their long history, been able to look on him as a man like themselves. This point need not be laboured; it is proved over and over again by the Negro's continuing position here, and his indescribable struggle to defeat the strategems that white Americans have used, and use, to deny him his humanity. America could have used in other ways the energy that both groups have expended in this conflict. America, of all the Western nations, has been best placed to prove the uselessness and the obsolescence of the concept of colour. But it has not dared to accept this opportunity, or even to conceive of it as an opportunity. White Americans have thought of it as their shame, and have envied the more civilized and elegant European nations that were untroubled by the presence of black men on their shores. This is because white Americans have supposed 'Europe' and 'civilization' to be synonyms – which they are not – and have been distrustful of other standards and other sources of vitality, especially those produced in America itself, and have attempted to behave in all matters as though what was best for Europe was also best for them. What it comes to is that if we, who can scarcely be considered a white nation, persist in thinking of ourselves as one, we condemn ourselves, with the truly white nations, to sterility and decay, whereas if we could accept ourselves *as we are*, we might bring new life to the Western achievements, and transform them. The price of this transformation is the unconditional freedom of the Negro; it is not too much to say that he, who has been so long rejected, must now be embraced, and at no matter what psychic or social risk. He is *the* key figure in his country, and the American future is precisely as bright or as dark as his. And the Negro recognizes this, in a negative way. Hence the question: Do I really *want* to be integrated into a burning house?

White Americans find it as difficult as white people elsewhere do to divest themselves of the notion that they are in possession of some intrinsic value that black people need, or want. And this assumption – which, for example, makes the solution to the Negro problem depend on the speed with which Negroes accept and adopt white standards – is revealed in all kinds of striking ways, from Bobby Kennedy's assurance that a Negro can become President in forty years to the unfortunate tone of warm congratulation with which so many liberals address their Negro equals. It is the Negro, of course, who is presumed to have become equal – an achievement that not only proves the comforting fact that perseverance has no colour but also overwhelmingly corroborates the white man's sense of his own value. Alas, this value can scarcely be corroborated in any other way; there is certainly little enough in the white man's public or private life that one should desire to imitate. White men, at the bottom of their hearts, know this. Therefore, a vast amount of the energy that goes into what we call the Negro problem is produced by the white man's profound desire not to be judged by those who are not white, not to be seen as he is, and at the same time a vast amount of the white anguish is rooted in the white man's equally profound need to be seen as he is, to be released from the tyranny of his mirror. All of us know, whether or not we are able to admit it, that mirrors can only lie, that death by drowning is all that awaits one there. It is for this reason that love is so desperately sought and so cunningly avoided. Love takes off the masks that we fear we cannot live without and know we cannot live within. I use the word 'love' here not merely in the personal sense but as a state of being, or a state of grace – not in the infantile American sense of being made happy but in the tough and universal sense of quest and daring and growth. And I submit, then, that the racial tensions that menace Americans today have little to do with real antipathy – on the contrary, indeed – and are involved only symbolically with colour. These tensions are rooted in the very same depths as those from which love springs, or murder. The white man's unadmitted – and apparently, to him, unspeakable – private fears and longings are projected on to the Negro. The only way he can be released from the Negro's tyrannical power over him is to consent, in effect, to become black himself, to become a part of that suffering and dancing country that he now watches wistfully from the heights of his lonely power and, armed with spiritual traveller's cheques, visits surreptitiously after dark. How can one respect, let alone adopt, the values of a people who do not, on any level whatever, live the way they say they do, or the way they say they should? I cannot accept the proposition that the four-hundred-year travail of the American Negro should result merely in his attainment of the present level of the American civilization. I am far from convinced that being released from the African witch doctor was worthwhile if I am now – in order to support the moral contradictions and the spiritual aridity of my life – expected to become dependent on the American psychiatrist. It is a bargain I refuse. The only thing white people have that black people need, or should want, is power – and no one holds power for ever. White people cannot, in the generality, be taken as models of how to live. Rather, the white man is himself in sore need of new standards, which will release him from his confusion and place him once again in fruitful communion with the depths of his own being. And I repeat: The price of the liberation of the white people is the liberation of the blacks – the total liberation, in the cities, in the towns, before the law, and in the mind. Why, for example – especially knowing the family as I do – I should *want* to marry your sister is a great mystery to me. But your sister and I have every right to marry if we wish to, and no one has the right to stop us. If she cannot raise me to her level, perhaps I can raise her to mine.

In short, we, the black and the white, deeply need each other here if we are really to become a nation – if we are really, that is, to achieve our identity, our maturity, as men and women. To create one nation has proved to be a hideously difficult task; there is certainly no need now to create two, one black and one white. But white men with far more political power than that possessed by the Nation of Islam movement have been advocating exactly this, in effect, for generations. If this sentiment is honoured when it falls from the lips of Senator Byrd, then there is no reason it should not be honored when it falls from the lips of Malcolm X. And any Congressional committee wishing to investigate the latter must also be willing to investigate the former. They are expressing exactly the same sentiments and represent exactly the same danger. There is absolutely no reason to suppose that white people are better equipped to frame the laws by which I am to be governed than I am. It is entirely unacceptable that I should have no voice in the political affairs of my own country, for I am not a ward of America; I am one of the first Americans to arrive on these shores.

5.6 FROM NON-VIOLENCE TO DIRECT ACTION

From Martin Luther King, 'Letter from Birmingham Jail' in Why We Can't Wait, *1964, pp. 80–3.*

Although Martin Luther King remained a Christian pacifist all his life, by 1963 he had come to accept a policy of direct action and civil disobedience for the Negro cause. No doubt he had become personally convinced of the need for this policy, but perhaps it also reflected his awareness that the more militant leaders of the Negro community were attracting greater support. In his book *Why We Can't Wait* (1964) – whose title catches the spirit of the author's new attitude – Martin Luther King showed why he had come to advocate a policy of direct action.

The Reverend King often found himself in jail, especially in the American South, as he led his followers in acts of civil disobedience. In April 1963, whilst in jail in Birmingham, Alabama, he noticed a press statement from some of his fellow-clergymen, of several denominations but mostly Anglo-Saxon by birth, calling his actions 'unwise and untimely'. Martin Luther King was moved to reply to them in his eloquent 'Letter from Birmingham Jail', from which the following extract is taken.

My dear fellow clergymen . . .

. . . Lamentably, it is an historical fact that privileged groups seldom give up their privileges voluntarily. Individuals may see the moral light and voluntarily give up their unjust posture; but, as Reinhold Niebuhr has reminded us, groups tend to be more immoral than individuals.

We know through painful experience that freedom is never voluntarily given by the oppressor; it must be demanded by the oppressed. Frankly, I have yet to engage in a direct-action campaign that was 'well timed' in the view of those who have not suffered unduly from the disease of segregation. For years now I have heard the word 'Wait!' It rings in the ear of every Negro with piercing familiarity. This 'Wait' has almost always meant 'Never'. We must come to see, with one of our distinguished jurists, that 'justice too long delayed is justice denied'.

We have waited for more than 340 years for our constitutional and God-given rights. The nations of Asia and Africa are moving with jetlike speed towards gaining political independence, but we still creep at horse-and-buggy pace towards gaining a cup of coffee at a lunch counter. Perhaps it is easy for those who have never felt the stinging darts of segregation to say, 'Wait'. But when you have seen vicious mobs lynch your mothers and fathers at will and drown your sisters and brothers at whim; when you have seen hate-filled policemen curse, kick and even kill your black brothers and sisters; when you see the vast majority of your twenty million Negro brothers smothering in an airtight cage of poverty in the midst of an affluent society; when you suddenly find your tongue twisted and your speech stammering as you seek to explain to your six-year-old daughter why she can't go to the public amusement park that has just been advertised on television, and see tears welling up in her eyes when she is told that Funtown is closed to coloured children, and see ominous clouds of inferiority beginning to form in her little mental sky, and see her beginning to distort her personality by developing an unconscious bitterness towards white people; when you have to concoct an answer for a five-year-old son who is asking: 'Daddy, why do white people treat coloured people so mean?'; when you take a cross-country drive and find it necessary to sleep night after night in the uncomfortable corners of your automobile because no motel will accept you; when you are humiliated day in and day out by nagging signs reading 'white' and 'coloured'; when your first name becomes 'nigger', your middle name becomes 'boy' (however old you are) and your last name becomes 'John', and your wife and mother are never given the respected title 'Mrs'; when you are harried by day and haunted by night by the fact that you are a Negro, living constantly at tiptoe stance, never quite knowing what to expect next, and are plagued with inner fears and outer resentments; when you are forever fighting a degenerating sense of 'nobodiness' – then you will understand why we find it difficult to wait. There comes a time when the cup of endurance runs over, and men are no longer willing to be plunged into the abyss of despair. I hope, sirs, you can understand our legitimate and unavoidable impatience.

You express a great deal of anxiety over our willingness to break laws. This is certainly a legitimate concern. Since we so diligently urge people to obey the Supreme Court's decision of 1954 outlawing segregation in the public schools, at first glance it may seem rather paradoxical for us consciously to break laws. One may well ask: 'How can you advocate breaking some laws and obeying others?' The answer lies in the fact that there are two types of laws: just and unjust. I would be the first to advocate obeying just laws. One has not only a legal but a moral responsibility to obey just laws. Conversely, one has a moral responsibility to disobey unjust laws. I would agree with St Augustine that 'an unjust law is no law at all'.

Now, what is the difference between the two? How does one determine whether a law is just or unjust? A just law is a man-made code that squares with the moral law or the law of God. An unjust law is a code that is out of harmony with the moral law. To put it in the terms of St Thomas Aquinas: An unjust law is a human law that is not rooted in eternal law and natural law. Any law that uplifts human personality is just. Any law that degrades human personality is unjust. All segregation statutes are unjust because segregation distorts the soul and damages the personality. It gives the segregator a false sense of superiority and the segregated a false sense of inferiority. Segregation, to use the terminology of the Jewish philosopher Martin Buber, substitutes an 'I–it' relationship for an 'I–thou' relationship and ends up relegating persons to the status of things. Hence segregation is not only politically, economically and sociologically unsound, it is morally wrong and sinful. Paul Tillich has said that sin is separation. Is not segregation an existential expression of man's tragic separation, his awful estrangement, his terrible sinfulness? Thus it is that I can urge men to obey the 1954 decision of the Supreme Court, for it is morally right; and I can urge them to disobey segregation ordinances, for they are morally wrong.

5.7 BLACK POWER

From Stokely Carmichael and Charles Hamilton, Black Power; the Politics of Liberation in America, *1967, this ed. 1969, London, pp. 44–8.*

During the mid-1960s, Negro militancy began to crystallize around the Black Power movement. The term means different things to different sections of the movement. For some it means Black Separatism; for others it means race war and the use of violence to achieve political and economic goals. To more moderate leaders it means pressing legitimate demands for equal opportunity and equality of treatment for the Negro in every walk of life. But all sections of the movement are agreed that a prime task is to give the American Negro a sense of pride in his colour, a sense of community, and thus of personal identity. In this sense, it is claimed, Black Power is an entirely healthy development, encouraging the Negro to escape from the defeatism and passivity instilled by centuries of exploitation by the white man.

Stokely Carmichael emerged in the 1960s as one of the most articulate spokesmen for the Black Power movement. The following extract is from the book he wrote with a Negro colleague, Charles V. Hamilton.

The adoption of the concept of Black Power is one of the most legitimate and healthy developments in American politics and race relations in our time. The concept of Black Power speaks to all the needs mentioned in this chapter. It is a call for black people in this country to unite, to recognize their heritage, to build a sense of community. It is a call for black people to begin to define their own goals, to lead their own organizations and to support those organizations. It is a call to reject the racist institutions and values of this society.

The concept of Black Power rests on a fundamental premise: *Before a group can enter the open society, it must first close ranks.* By this we mean that group solidarity is necessary before a group can operate effectively from a bargaining position of strength in a pluralistic society. Traditionally, each new ethnic group in this society has found the route to social and political viability through the organization of its own institutions with which to represent its needs within the larger society. Studies in voting behaviour specifically, and political behaviour generally, have made it clear that politically the American pot has not melted. Italians vote for Rubino over O'Brien; Irish for Murphy over Goldberg, etc. This phenomenon may seem distasteful to some, but it has been and remains today a central fact of the American political system. There are other examples of ways in which groups in the society have remembered their roots and used this effectively in the political arena. Theodore Sorensen describes the politics of foreign aid during the Kennedy Administration in his book *Kennedy*:

No powerful constituencies or interest groups backed foreign aid. The Marshall Plan at least had appealed to Americans who traced their roots to the Western European nations aided. But there were few voters who identified with India, Colombia or Tanganyika [p. 351].

The extent to which black Americans can and do 'trace their roots' to Africa, to that extent will they be able to be more effective on the political scene.

A white reporter set forth this point in other terms when he made the following observation about white Mississippi's manipulation of the anti-poverty programme:

The war on poverty has been predicated on the notion that there is such a thing as a community which can be defined geographically and mobilized for a collective effort to help the poor. This theory has no relationship to reality in the deep South. In every Mississippi county there are two communities. Despite all the pious platitudes of the moderates on both sides, these two communities habitually see their interests in terms of conflict rather than co-operation. Only when the Negro community can muster enough political, economic and professional strength to compete on somewhat equal terms, will Negroes believe in the possibility of true co-operation and whites accept its necessity. *En route* to integration, the Negro community needs to develop a greater independence – a chance to run its own affairs and not cave in whenever 'the man' barks – or so it seems to me, and to most of the knowledgeable people with whom I talked in Mississippi. To OEO,[*] this judgement may sound like black nationalism. . . .†

The point is obvious: black people must lead and run their own organizations. Only black people can convey the revolutionary idea – and it is a revolutionary idea – that black people are able to do things themselves. Only they can help create in the community an aroused and continuing black consciousness that will provide the basis for political strength. In the past, white allies have often

[* OEO: Office of Economic Opportunity. A Federal Government agency set up in 1964 to fight poverty and deprivation among neglected communities, especially the Black community, and backed by Federal funds Ed.].

† Christopher Jencks, 'Accommodating Whites: A New Look at Mississippi', *The New Republic* (April 16, 1966).

furthered white supremacy without the whites involved realizing it, or even wanting to do so. Black people must come together and do things for themselves. They must achieve self-identity and self-determination in order to have their daily needs met.

Black Power means, for example, that in Lowndes County, Alabama, a black sheriff can end police brutality. A black tax assessor and tax collector and county board of revenue can lay, collect, and channel tax monies for the building of better roads and schools serving black people. In such areas as Lowndes, where black people have a majority, they will attempt to use power to exercise control. This is what they seek: control. When black people lack a majority, Black Power means proper representation and sharing of control. It means the creation of power bases, of strength, from which black people can press to change local or nation-wide patterns of oppression – instead of from weakness.

It does not mean *merely* putting black faces into office. Black visibility is not Black Power. Most of the black politicians around the country are not examples of Black Power. The power must be that of a community, and emanate from there. The black politicians must start from there. The black politicians must stop being representatives of 'downtown' machines, whatever the cost might be in terms of lost patronage and holiday handouts.

Black Power recognizes – it must recognize – the ethnic basis of American politics as well as the power-oriented nature of American politics. Black Power therefore calls for black people to consolidate behind their own, so that they can bargain from a position of strength. But while we endorse the *procedure* of group solidarity and identity for the purpose of attaining certain goals in the body politic, this does not mean that black people should strive for the same kind of rewards (i.e., end results) obtained by the white society. The ultimate values and goals are not domination or exploitation of other groups, but rather an effective share in the total power of the society.

Nevertheless, some observers have labelled those who advocate Black Power as racists; they have said that the call for self-identification and self-determination is 'racism in reverse' or 'black supremacy'. This is a deliberate and absurd lie. There is no analogy – by any stretch of definition or imagination – between the advocates of Black Power and white racists. Racism is not merely exclusion on the basis of race but exclusion for the purpose of subjugating or maintaining subjugation. The goal of the racists is to keep black people on the bottom, arbitrarily and dictatorially, as they have done in this country for over three hundred years. The goal of black self-determination and black self-identity – Black Power – is full participation in the decision-making processes affecting the lives of black people, and recognition of the virtues in themselves as black people. The black people of this country have not lynched whites, bombed their churches, murdered their children and manipulated laws and institutions to maintain oppression. White racists have. Congressional laws, one after the other, have not been necessary to stop black people from oppressing others and denying others the full enjoyment of their rights. White racists have made such laws necessary. The goal of Black Power is positive and functional to a free and viable society. No white racists can make this claim.

6 *Towards a Science of Society*

6.1 DEFINING THE ROLE OF THE STATE

From Theodore Woolsey, Political Science: or, The State Theoreti- cally and Practically Considered, *2 vols, 1877, I, pp. 208–11.*

Theodore Woolsey (1801–89) played an important part in turning the study of politics from normative discourse towards greater 'scientism'. His academic career began with theological studies at Yale and Princeton, but after study abroad at Paris, Berlin, Leipzig and Bonn, he turned to history, law and politics. In a two volume work on political science Woolsey attempted an exhaustive analysis of the role of political institutions in contemporary society. The following extract is from this magnum opus.

SPHERE AND ENDS OF STATE

A question of extreme importance in the state is, what is the proper sphere within which state-action ought to move? Or the question may be put in a form different in terms but in substance the same, what are the ends which a state or nation ought to seek? Does it exist only to protect the rights of the individuals living within the territory – to defend their bodies and goods, as the expression is, or must it have a wider care of their welfare, reaching to all the interests of education, culture, morality and religion, to the assistance of the poor, to the encouragement of industry and of intercourse? Still further, does the office of the state require it to shield the individual from *impending* evil, or must its intervention begin, when the rights of the individual are invaded? With our view of the extent of the state's sphere, our view, also, of the duty to punish offenders of the law, must vary. If there were no duty but to protect the body and goods of individuals, it does not appear how there could be any criminal law, which contemplates the state or the people as the aggrieved party, because the reparation of the individual is not punishment but payment of due. Thus we have, on one construction of the state, a community watched over in all its interests, a *régime* going far beyond the demands of justice and of security, the perpetual presence of power which may meddle with the affairs of private persons even in the exercise of their acknowledged rights; or, on the contrary, a government where all forward movement must come from single persons or bodies, while the state itself will be as much out of sight as possible, and thereby fulfil its true office of only seconding and securing such as need its aid.

It is impossible for those who seek to carry out the narrowest view of the state's sphere to make a consistent explanation of what they themselves hold to be necessary. We might ask them why, on their theory, it is not enough to make rights real by opening the courts to the wronged, and helping them to right themselves by the servants of justice enforcing the judicial decision. Why prevent the occurrence of wrongs by any kind of force like that of a police? Or we might ask them whether any government has existed, any code of laws ever been framed, in which 'body and goods' alone were the subject-matter of legislation. It is a great thing to allow the individual to develop himself in the community, to cultivate his own individual powers in his own way; but it is of equal importance to mankind, to the progress and welfare of the world, that the interests of the whole body should be cared for. The problem as thus presented seems to combine two opposite tendencies – a care for the whole and a care for the individual. How to adjust and unite these so that the individual shall not be unduly controlled, nor the general welfare neglected, is a difficult problem, but it must be solved, somehow or other.

It may be of use at this stage of our subject to attempt to arrange the different particulars which make up the state's offices or duties, without counting those relating to external bodies or governments.

1. First we have the office of giving redress to the individual or family or association which has been wronged. Of this enough has

been said, and that this is an essential office of the state will not be disputed.

2. It is also properly an office of the state to secure the individual from injury beforehand, to *prevent* the invasion of rights. Otherwise we must say that all force, as far as the individual is concerned, is to be exerted in enabling him to obtain redress and that he ought on a right theory to have no protection until he is injured. But surely no one can maintain this proposition. The guarding against wrong is prevention of wrong; the sense of security is essential to all steady prosecution of the work of life; if the public force cannot keep off violence but only redress the injuries occasioned by it, what will protection be worth in cases innumerable. Prevention is better than cure. The same force that gives redress can save the necessity of seeking redress.

State action, in all other cases beside these two, does not provide for the just claims of a single individual family or small community, but for the wants or rights of the entire community. Whatever else a state does, may be said to aim at the good of the whole first, but its office as defender of justice aims originally at the good of the personal subject of rights. *In the other work of the state it may do too much or do too little and yet be a state*; in the work of protecting rights it is doing what no state has a right to neglect. *One state* may have no public system of education, another may have a complete one; both are states, if they maintain justice, but one is less perfect than the other, because it fails to make provision for the education of all. *Again, much of the work except the administration of justice maybe concurrently undertaken by individuals and by the community*, as will be the policy more or less in all free governments. A person can found colleges, support the poor, cherish the fine arts, and he may do this better than the state can. So that there may be in civilized societies a continual doubt whether on the whole true progress can best be secured by one or by the other of these two agents. But on the other hand the state is the monopolist of the administration of justice, and for individuals to invade this province would be to attempt the state's destruction. *Finally, the state's action in some of these departments may be very limited and dependent on circumstances*. There may be no poor to receive public charity, no sense of the value of the fine arts, and no need of public and connected ways of communication.

3. With these explanations we add *in the third place* that the

state's sphere of action may include a certain degree and kind of care of the *outward welfare of the community*, as of industry, roads, health.

4. It may embrace all cultivation of the spiritual nature by educating the religious nature, the moral sense, the taste, the intellect. It may enforce moral observances, may protect and even institute religious worship, and may provide for the wants of the needy and the distressed. In other words it may express in action the intellect, the aesthetic feeling, moral sense, religious feeling, and humanity of a community of men. *It may do all this,* I mean to say, without necessarily going out of its own proper province. Whether *it ought actually to provide for* as well as protect all these great interests is a point to be discussed in the future. They are named at present as the departments from which by no just theory the state can be excluded. . . .

In order to do its work, the state must have adequate means at its disposal for the purpose of protecting and securing all these interests. These means in general are *armed force* for preventing or redressing wrong from within or without; *taxation* on some just principle, and a *police power* for the purposes of general security. More important still is the state's power of *punishing public wrongs,* which is a different form of justice from that which consists in repairing private wrongs.

6.2 TOWARDS A SCIENCE OF SOCIETY

From William Graham Sumner, Collected Essays in Political and Social Science, *1885, pp. 77 ff.*

By the end of the nineteenth century politics and sociology were regarded as cognate disciplines in America. Clearly, a science of society could not ignore the political context, and the political theorist could not ignore social problems and possibilities. William Graham Sumner (1840–1910) was one who helped to marry politics and sociology.

Sociology is the science of life in society. It investigates the forces which come into action wherever a human society exists. It studies the structure and functions of the organs of human society, and its aim is to find out the laws* in subordination to which human society takes its various forms, and social institutions grow and change. Its practical utility consists in deriving the rules of right social living from the facts and laws which prevail by nature in the constitution and functions of society. It must, without doubt, come into collision with all other theories of right living which are founded on authority, tradition, arbitrary invention, or poetic imagination.

Sociology is perhaps the most complicated of all the sciences, yet there is no domain of human interest the details of which are treated ordinarily with greater facility. Various religions have various theories of social living, which they offer as authoritative and final. It has never, so far as I know, been asserted by anybody that a man of religious faith (in any religion) could not study sociology or recognize the existence of any such science; but it is incontestably plain that a man who accepts the dogmas about social living which are imposed by the authority of any religion must regard the subject of right social living as settled and closed, and he cannot enter on any investigation the first groundwork of which would be doubt of the authority which he recognizes as final. Hence social problems and social phenomena present no difficulty to him who has only to cite an authority or obey a prescription. . . .

Then again the *dilettanti* make light work of social questions. Everyone, by the fact of living in society, gathers some observations of social phenomena. The belief grows up, as it was expressed some time ago by a professor of mathematics, that everybody knows about the topics of sociology. Those topics have a broad and generous character. They lend themselves easily to generalizations. There are as yet no sharp tests formulated. Above all, and worst lack of all as yet, we have no competent criticism. Hence it is easy for the aspirant after culture to venture on this field without great danger of being brought to account, as he would be if he attempted geology, or physics, or biology. Even a scientific man of high

* It has been objected that no proof is offered that social laws exist in the order of nature. By what demonstration could any such proof be given *a priori*? If a man of scientific training finds his attention arrested, in some group of phenomena, by those sequences, relations, and recurrences which he has learned to note as signs of action of law, he seeks to discover the law. If it exists, he finds it. What other proof of its existence could there be?

attainments in some other science, in which he well understands what special care, skill, and training are required, will not hesitate to dogmatize about a topic of sociology. A group of half-educated men may be relied upon to attack a social question and to hammer it dead in a few minutes with a couple of commonplaces and a sweeping *a priori* assumption. Above all other topics, social topics lend themselves to the purposes of the diner-out.

Two facts, however, in regard to social phenomena need only be mentioned to be recognized as true. (1) Social phenomena always present themselves to us in very complex combinations, and (2) it is by no means easy to interpret the phenomena. The phenomena are often at three or four removes from their causes. Tradition, prejudice, fashion, habit, and other similar obstacles continually warp and deflect the social forces, and they constitute interferences whose magnitude is to be ascertained separately for each case. It is also impossible for us to set up a social experiment. To do that, we should need to dispose of the time and liberty of a certain number of men. It follows that sociology requires a special method, and that probably no science requires such peculiar skill and sagacity in the observer and interpreter of the phenomena which are to be studied. One peculiarity may be especially noted because it shows a very common error of students of social science. A sociologist needs to arrange his facts before he has obtained them; that is to say, he must make a previous classification so as to take up the facts in a certain order. If he does not do this he may be overwhelmed in the mass of his material so that he never can master it. How shall any-one know how to classify until the science itself has made some progress? . . .

It must be confessed that sociology is yet in a tentative and inchoate state. All that we can affirm with certainty is that social phenomena are subject to law, and that the natural laws of the social order are in their entire character like the laws of physics. We can draw in grand outline the field of sociology and foresee the shape that it will take and the relations it will bear to other sciences. We can also already find the standpoint which it will occupy, and, if a figure may be allowed, although we still look over a wide land-scape largely enveloped in mist, we can see where the mist lies, and define the general features of the landscape, subject to further corrections. To deride or condemn a science in this state would certainly be a most unscientific proceeding. We confess, however,

that so soon as we go beyond the broadest principles of the science
we have not yet succeeded in discovering social laws, so as to be
able to formulate them. A great amount of labour yet remains to
be done in the stages of preparation. There are, however, not more
than two or three other sciences which are making as rapid progress
as sociology, and there is no other which is as full of promise for
the welfare of man. That sociology has an immense department of
human interests to control is beyond dispute. Hitherto this
department has been included in moral science, and it has not only
been confused and entangled by dogmas no two of which are
consistent with each other, but also it has been without any growth,
so that at this moment our knowledge of social science is behind the
demands which existing social questions make upon us. . . . It is to
the science of society, which will derive true conceptions of society
from the facts and laws of the social order, studied without prejudice or bias of any sort, that we must look for the correct answer
to these questions. By this observation the field of sociology and
the work which it is to do for society are sufficiently defined.

6.3 PRAGMATISM DEFINED

From William James, Pragmatism, *1907, pp. 44 ff.*

Although William James (1842–1910) was not the founder of
pragmatism, his name and authority gave it respectability. When
the rules and tenets of pragmatism were absorbed into American
discourse, they deeply affected both the form and content of
political studies. Ideas and truths must be linked to purposes,
James argued, otherwise they are useless and sterile. It is not
difficult to see how this doctrine furthered the links between political science and sociology, especially in their ameliorative roles.

The pragmatic method is primarily a method of settling metaphysical disputes that otherwise might be interminable. Is the
world one or many? – fated or free? – material or spiritual? – here
are notions either of which may or may not hold good of the world;
and disputes over such notions are unending. The pragmatic
method in such cases is to try to interpret each notion by tracing
its respective practical consequences. What difference would it

practically make to anyone if this notion rather than that notion were true? If no practical difference whatever can be traced, then the alternatives mean practically the same thing, and all dispute is idle. Whenever a dispute is serious, we ought to be able to show some practical difference that must follow from one side or the other's being right.

A glance at the history of the idea will show you still better what pragmatism means. The term is derived from the same Greek word πργυα, meaning action, from which our words 'practice' and 'practical' come. It was first introduced into philosophy by Mr Charles Peirce in 1878. In an article 'How to Make Our Ideas Clear', in the *Popular Science Monthly* for January of that year Mr Peirce, after pointing out that our beliefs are really rules for action, said that, to develop a thought's meaning, we need only determine what conduct it is fitted to produce: that conduct is for us its sole significance. And the tangible fact at the root of all our thought-distinctions, however subtle, is that there is no one of them so fine as to consist in anything but a possible difference of practice. To attain perfect clearness in our thoughts of an object, then, we need only consider what conceivable effects of a practical kind the object may involve – what sensations we are to expect from it, and what reactions we must prepare. Our conception of these effects, whether immediate or remote, is then for us the whole of our conception of the object, so far as that conception has positive significance at all. . . .

It is astonishing to see how many philosophical disputes collapse into insignificance the moment you subject them to this simple test of tracing a concrete consequence. There can *be* no difference anywhere that doesn't *make* a difference elsewhere – no difference in abstract truth that doesn't express itself in a difference in concrete fact and in conduct consequent upon that fact, imposed on somebody, somehow, somewhere, and somewhen. The whole function of philosophy ought to be to find out what definite difference it will make to you and me, at definite instants of our life, if this world-formula or that world-formula be the true one.

There is absolutely nothing new in the pragmatic method. Socrates was an adept at it. Aristotle used it methodically. Locke, Berkeley, and Hume made momentous contributions to truth by its means. Shadworth Hodgson keeps insisting that realities are only what they are 'known as'. But these forerunners of pragmatism used it in fragments: they were preluders only. Not until in our time has it generalized itself, become conscious of a universal mission, pretended to a conquering destiny. I believe in that destiny, and I hope I may end by inspiring you with my belief.

Pragmatism represents a perfectly familiar attitude in philosophy, the empiricist attitude, but it represents it, as it seems to me, both in a more radical and in a less objectionable form than it has ever yet assumed. A pragmatist turns his back resolutely and once for all upon a lot of inveterate habits dear to professional philosophers. He turns away from abstraction and insufficiency, from verbal solutions, from bad *a priori* reasons, from fixed principles, closed systems, and pretended absolutes and origins. He turns towards concreteness and adequacy, towards facts, towards action and towards power. That means the empiricist temper regnant and the rationalist temper sincerely given up. It means the open air and possibilities of nature, as against dogma, artificiality, and the pretence of finality in truth.

At the same time it does not stand for any special results. It is a method only. But the general triumph of that method would mean an enormous change in what I called in my last lecture the 'temperament' of philosophy. Teachers of the ultrarationalistic type would be frozen out, much as the courtier type is frozen out in republics, as the ultra-montane type of priest is frozen out in Protestant lands. Science and metaphysics would come much nearer together, would in fact work absolutely hand in hand.

Metaphysics has usually followed a very primitive kind of quest. You know how men have always hankered after unlawful magic, and you know what a great part in magic *words* have always played. If you have his name, or the formula of incantation that binds him, you can control the spirit, genie, afrite, or whatever the power may be. Solomon knew the names of all the spirits, and having their names, he held them subject to his will. So the universe has always appeared to the natural mind as a kind of enigma, of which the key must be sought in the shape of some illuminating or power-bringing word or name. That word names the universe's *principle*, and to possess it is after a fashion to possess the universe itself. 'God', 'Matter', 'Reason', 'the Absolute', 'Energy', are so many solving names. You can rest when you have them. You are at the end of your metaphysical quest.

But if you follow the pragmatic method, you cannot look on any such word as closing your quest. You must bring out of each word its practical cash-value, set it at work within the stream of your experience. It appears less as a solution, then, than as a programme for more work, and more particularly as an indication of the ways in which existing realities may be *changed*.

Theories thus become instruments, not answers to enigmas, in which we can rest. We don't lie back upon them, we move forward, and, on occasion, make nature over again by their aid. Pragmatism unstiffens all our theories, limbers them up and sets each one at work. Being nothing essentially new, it harmonizes with many ancient philosophic tendencies. It agrees with nominalism for instance, in always appealing to particulars; with utilitarianism in emphasizing practical aspects; with positivism in its disdain for verbal solutions, useless questions and metaphysical abstractions.

All these, you see, are *anti-intellectualist* tendencies. Against rationalism as a pretension and a method pragmatism is fully armed and militant. But, at the outset, at least, it stands for no particular results. It has no dogmas, and no doctrines save its method. As the young Italian pragmatist Papini has well said, it lies in the midst of our theories, like a corridor in a hotel. Innumerable chambers open out of it. In one you may find a man writing an atheistic volume; in the next someone on his knees praying for faith and strength; in a third a chemist investigating a body's properties. In a fourth a system of idealistic metaphysics is being excogitated; in a fifth the impossibility of metaphysics is being shown. But they all own the corridor, and all must pass through it if they want a practicable way of getting into or out of their respective rooms.

No particular results then, so far, but only an attitude of orientation, is what the pragmatic method means. *The attitude of looking away from first things, principles, 'categories', supposed necessities; and of looking towards last things, fruits, consequences, facts.*

6.4 THE NEW POLITICAL SCIENCE

From Arthur Bentley, The Process of Government, *1908, Chapter 7, pp. 200 ff.*

During the first decade of the present century, Chicago University became the home of the new approach to political studies. The touchstone was 'scientific' investigation of observable facts. It imitated, as far as possible, the methods of natural science. Quantification gradually displaced qualitative discussion. Professor Arthur Bentley was one of the founding fathers of the new approach, and in his book *The Process of Government* (1908) he put forward some bold statements.

Group Activities

It is impossible to attain scientific treatment of material that will not submit itself to measurement in some form. Measure conquers chaos. Even in biology notable advances by the use of statistical methods are being made. And what is of most importance, the material the biologist handles is of a kind that is susceptible of measurement and quantitative comparison all the way through. The occasional recrudescence of vitalism in biology is not irreconcilable with this statement. It simply indicates that from time to time some investigator directs his attention to phases of life, ever lessening in extent, which, he holds, are not measurable by present processes, and which, it pleases him to feel, will remain unmeasurable.

In the political world, the dictum, 'the greatest good of the greatest number', stands for an effort to make measurements. Sometimes, of course, it is simply the rallying-cry of particular causes. If we take it, however, where it pretends to be a general rule of measurement, we shall find that it applies itself not to what actually happens in legislation, but merely to what a thinker in some particular atmosphere believes ought to be the law; and this, no matter what systematic content of 'goods' is pumped into it. I hope to make it clear later that even such a generalized social theory as this is nothing but a reflection, or an index, or a label, of some particular set of demands made by some particular section of society. It is not a measure of social facts which we can use for scientific purposes, and it would not be thus useful even if logically it could be regarded as a standard of measurement, which, of course, it cannot be without further specification.

Statistics of social facts as we ordinarily get them are, of course, measurements. But even after they have been elaborately interpreted by the most expert statisticians, they must still undergo much further interpretation by the people who use them with reference to their immediate purposes of use. As they stand on the printed page, they are commonly regarded as 'dead', and they receive much undeserved disparagement. But by this very token it is clear that they do not adequately state the social facts. People who are in close connection with all that rich life-activity indicated by the 'feelings' and the 'ideas' feel that the heart of the matter is lacking in them.

But, now, the idea and feeling elements, stated for themselves, are unmeasurable as they appear in studies of government. This is a fatal defect in them. Any pretence of measuring them, no matter with what elaborate algebra, will prove to be merely an attribution to them of powers inferred from their results. Usually they appear in social discussions with wholly fictitious values, in support of which not even a pretence of actual measurement is presented. The measurements of experimental psychology are not such measurements as we need. They are measurements of activity looked upon as within the physical individual. The social content is incidental to them and is not measured.

If a statement of social facts which lends itself better to measurement is offered, that characteristic entitles it to attention. Providing the statement does not otherwise distort the social facts, the capability of measurement will be decisive in its favour. The statement that takes us farthest along the road towards quantitative estimates will inevitably be the best statement.

In practical politics a large amount of rough measuring is done. There is measurement with the sword when one nation defeats another in war. South American revolutions, which answer to North American elections, also use the sword as their standard of measure. Under Walpole the different elements in politics sought equilibrium in great part by the agency of gold coin and gold-bearing offices. In an election at its best in the United States, the measurement goes by the counting of heads. In a legislative body, likewise, the counting of heads appears. A referendum vote is political measurement.

This measuring process appears in various degrees of differentiation. In a battle the social quantities, and the measuring of those quantities which is taking place on the spot, are fused together, so that one has to make an effort to consider them separately. But in a vote the federal House of Representatives differentiation appears. Here a much more complicated measuring process is carried through, which appears finally in a simplified form in the announcement of the vote for and against the project by the tellers. The student of political life has some hint of the measurements in the figures of the vote; but it is necessary for him to measure the measure, to go far back and examine the quantities that have been in play to produce the given results. The best of these practical political measures are indeed exceedingly crude. The practical politician himself is estimating quantities all the time; indeed his success is in direct proportion to his ability to make good estimates. He may show a preternatural skill. But his skill is of little or no direct use for the scientific student. The practical politician will never under any circumstances consent to make a plain statement of his estimates; indeed it is rare that he knows how to tell, even if he should wish to.

The quantities are present in every bit of political life. There is no political process that is not a balancing of quantity against quantity. There is not a law that is passed that is not the expression of force and force in tension. There is not a court decision or an executive act that is not the result of the same process. Under-standing any of these phenomena means measuring the elements that have gone into them.

If we can get our social life stated in terms of activity, and of nothing else, we have not indeed succeeded in measuring it, but we have at least reached a foundation upon which a coherent system of measurements can be built up. Our technique may be very poor at the start, and the amount of labour we must employ to get scanty results will be huge. But we shall cease to be blocked by the intervention of unmeasurable elements, which claim to be themselves the real causes of all that is happening, and which by their spook-like arbitrariness make impossible any progress towards dependable knowledge.

6.5 POLITICAL SCIENTISTS FOREGATHER

Arnold B. Hall, extracts from a report in The American Political Science Review, *vol. XIX, No. 1, 1925, pp. 104–10.*

In September 1924 American political scientists met at Chicago to discuss the state of the discipline. The pursuit of a science of politics now united many scholars of different persuasions and interests. The chairman was Arnold B. Hall, and as the following extracts from the chairman's remarks make plain, political science had now arrived in the American academy.

The following quotation from an economist is of great significance to the modern student of politics. 'There is danger that the natural sciences must always outstrip the social sciences. In the first place the natural sciences can use the experiment method, and the social sciences have hardly yet devised an adequate substitute. Then again in the natural sciences, the inventor and original thinker is rewarded and honoured, but in the social sciences the inventive mind is more or less ostracized and new ideas that touch upon the key problems of modern life, namely, the control of human and economic activities, are at once branded as radical and dangerous.' This apparent discrimination against the social sciences is entitled to careful consideration. Is it a necessary difficulty inherent in the very nature of the social disciplines? Or is it due, at least in part, to inadequate and inconclusive methods of social research?

Without attempting to speak for the other social sciences, the writer has but little doubt that much of the hostility encountered by the political pioneer is due to the unscientific character of his conclusions. The announcement of new discoveries by the scholar in material sciences is generally accompanied by a summary of material evidence, practical tests, precise measurements, or actual demonstrations, that afford strong and persuasive evidence of the reality of the discovery. The issue of the validity of the new theory is generally reduced to a question of fact, for the proof or disproof of which objective evidence is available.

Compare this procedure with that used in connection with the announcement of new suggestions, theories and ideas of political science. How many contributions to political thought or to governmental theory have been preceded by a patient, painstaking gathering of all the evidence and facts that might be material in determining the validity of the new discovery? How many even go through the form of striving to ground their theories on a basis of ascertainable facts? In view of the attendant circumstances it is not even passing strange that new political theories, which frequently encounter existing prejudice and deeply rooted convictions, should be received with either hostility or indifference. But the important question is, is this evil an inherent one?

It is true that this apparent antagonism to new political discoveries has been occasionally relied upon as a moral alibi for the lack of a more aggressive campaign of political research. But is this a fair attitude to assume? Is it not more in the nature of a challenge than an excuse? Does it not point the way to the necessity of placing political research upon a scientific basis of objective fact? Is there any reason to suppose that the truth about government will find a more hostile and belligerent opposition than the truth about biology, chemistry, or physics, when it is accompanied by a body of objective evidence, scientifically arranged?

The unfortunate element in the situation is the painful fact that the pressure of everyday political problems requires the application of new theories before there has been time for appropriate investigation and research. The author does not wish to imply a criticism upon those who, under the stress of modern political needs, have offered what tentative ideas they had, without waiting to check their accuracy through the slow-moving methods of scientific investigation. To have thus withheld one's contribution to the public problems of the hour would frequently have been in clear violation of patriotic duty. Professor Merriam has made a valuable suggestion in this connection. He distinguishes between political prudence and political science. The opinion of public men and of political scholars may be of great value in determining public questions upon which scientific studies are not available. But such opinions, valuable though they may be, cannot be the basis of political science, and it is the business of the latter so to extend and perfect its technique and increase its activities, that more and more of the field now pre-empted by political prudence will be occupied by a science of politics.

The need of placing political science upon a really scientific basis will be obvious to everyone. There is scarcely a phase of the subject that does not offer the most alluring and virgin opportunities. Moreover, these opportunities are of more than academic interest. The results of scientific investigation would be, in many instances, of incalculable value to the efficiency of our governments and to the tremendous interests that they serve.

6.6 SCIENCE AND SOCIETY

John Dewey, essay from Philosophy and Civilization, *1931.*

In America, as in Europe, philosophers have often enriched political discourse. John Dewey (1859–1952), perhaps the best known native-American philosopher, often touched on the problems of democracy and society in his writings. He was especially interested in the new sets of problems brought by applied science and technology. In his essay *Science and Society* Dewey tackled the central problem of whether we should welcome, or whether we should fear the continued advances of applied science in the twentieth century.

The significant outward forms of the civilization of the western world are the product of the machine and its technology. Indirectly they are the product of the scientific revolution which took place in the seventeenth century. In its effect upon men's external habits, dominant interests, the conditions under which they work and associate, whether in the family, the factory, the state, or internationally, science is by far the most potent social factor in the modern world. It operates, however, through its undesigned effects rather than as a transforming influence of men's thoughts and purposes. This contrast between outer and inner operation is the great contradiction in our lives. Habits of thought and desire remain in substance what they were before the rise of science, while the conditions under which they take effect have been radically altered by science.

When we look at the external social consequences of science, we find it impossible to apprehend the extent or gauge the rapidity of their occurrence. Alfred North Whitehead has recently called attention to the progressive shortening of the time-span of social change. That due to basic conditions seems to be of the order of half a million years; that due to lesser physical conditions, like alterations in climate, to be of the order of five thousand years. Until almost our own day the time-span of sporadic technological changes was of the order of five hundred years; according to him no great technological changes took place between say, A.D. 100 and A.D. 1400. With the introduction of steam-power, the fifty years from 1780 to 1830 were marked by more changes than are found in any previous thousand years. The advance of chemical techniques and in use of electricity and radio-energy in the last forty years makes even this last change seem slow and awkward.

Domestic life, political institutions, international relations and personal contacts are shifting with kaleidoscopic rapidity before our eyes. We cannot appreciate and weigh the changes; they occur too swiftly. We do not have time to take them in. No sooner do we begin to understand the meaning of one such change than another comes and displaces the former. Our minds are dulled by the sudden and repeated impacts. Externally, science through its applications is manufacturing the conditions of our institutions at such a speed that we are too bewildered to know what sort of civilization is in process of making.

Because of this confusion, we cannot even draw up a ledger account of social gains and losses due to the operation of science. But at least we know that the earlier optimism which thought that the advance of natural science was to dispel superstition, ignorance, and oppression, by placing reason on the throne, was unjustified. Some superstitions have given way, but the mechanical devices due to science have made it possible to spread new kinds of error and delusion among a larger multitude. The fact is that it is foolish to try to draw up a debit and credit account for science. To do so is to mythologize; it is to personify science and impute to it a will and an energy on its own account. In truth science is strictly impersonal; a method and a body of knowledge. It owes its operation and its consequences to the human beings who use it. It adapts itself passively to the purposes and desires which animate these human beings. It lends itself with equal impartiality to the kindly offices of medicine and hygiene and the destructive deeds of war. It elevates some through opening new horizons; it depresses others by making them slaves of machines operated for the pecuniary gain of owners.

The neutrality of science to the uses made of it renders it silly to talk about its bankruptcy, or to worship it as the usherer in of a new age. In the degree in which we realize this fact, we shall devote our attention to the human purposes and motives which control its application. Science is an instrument, a method, a body of technique. While it is an end for those inquirers who are engaged in its pursuit, in the large human sense it is a means, a tool. For what ends shall it be used? Shall it be used deliberately, systematically, for the promotion of social well-being, or shall it be employed primarily for private aggrandizement, leaving its larger social results to chance? Shall the scientific attitude be used to create new mental and moral attitudes, or shall it continue to be subordinated to service of desires, purposes and institutions which were formed before science came into existence? Can the attitudes which control the use of science be themselves so influenced by scientific technique that they will harmonize with its spirit?

The beginning of wisdom is, I repeat, the realization that science itself is an instrument which is indifferent to the external uses to which it is put. Steam and electricity remain natural forces when they operate through mechanisms; the only problem is the purposes for which men set the mechanisms to work. The essential technique of gunpowder is the same whether it be used to blast rocks from the quarry to build better human habitations, or to hurl death upon men at war with one another. The airplane binds men at a distance in closer bonds of intercourse and understanding, or it rains missiles of death upon hapless populations. We are forced to consider the relation of human ideas and ideals to the social consequences which are produced by science as an instrument.

The problem involved is the greatest which civilization has ever had to face. It is, without exaggeration, the most serious issue of contemporary life. Here is the instrumentality, the most powerful, for good and evil, the world has ever known. What are we going to do with it? Shall we leave our underlying aims unaffected by it, treating it merely as a means by which unco-operative individuals may advance their own fortunes? Shall we try to improve the hearts of men without regard to the new methods which science puts at our disposal? There are those, men in high position in church and state, who urge this course. They trust to a transforming influence of morals and religion which have not been affected by science to change human desire and purpose, so that they will employ science and machine technology for beneficent social ends. . . .

Science and machine technology are young from the standpoint of human history. Though vast in stature, they are infants in age. Three hundred years are but a moment in comparison with thousands of centuries man has lived on the earth. In view of the inertia of institutions and of the mental habits they breed, it is not surprising that the new technique of apparatus and calculation, which is the essence of science, has made so little impression on underlying human attitudes. The momentum of traditions and purposes that preceded its rise took possession of the new instrument and turned it to their ends. Moreover, science had to struggle for existence. It had powerful enemies in church and state. It needed friends and it welcomed alliance with the rising capitalism which it so effectively promoted. If it tended to foster secularism and to create predominantly material interests, it could still be argued that it was in essential harmony with traditional morals and religion. But there were lacking the conditions which are indispensable to the serious application of scientific method in reconstruction of fundamental beliefs and attitudes. In addition, the development of the new science was attended with so many internal difficulties that energy had to go to perfecting the instrument just as an instrument. Because of all these circumstances the fact that science was used in behalf of old interests is nothing to be wondered at.

The conditions have now changed, radically so. The claims of natural science in the physical field are undisputed. Indeed, its prestige is so great than an almost superstitious aura gathers about its name and work. Its progress is no longer dependent upon the adventurous inquiry of a few untrammelled souls. Not only are universities organized to promote scientific research and learning, but one may almost imagine the university laboratories abolished and still feel confident of the continued advance of science. The development of industry has compelled the inclusion of scientific inquiry within the processes of production and distribution. We find in the public prints as many demonstrations of the benefits of science from a business point of view as there are proofs of its harmony with religion. . . .

It is a common saying that our physical science has far outrun our social knowledge; that our physical skill has become exact and comprehensive while our humane arts are vague, opinionated, and narrow. The fundamental trouble, however, is not lack of sufficient information about social facts, but unwillingness to adopt the scientific attitude in what we do know. Men floundered in a morass of opinion about physical matters for thousands of years. It was when they began to use their ideas experimentally and to create a technique or direction of experimentation that physical science advanced with system and surety. No amount of mere fact-finding develops science nor the scientific attitude in either physics or social affairs. Facts merely amassed and piled up are dead; a burden which only adds to confusion. When ideas, hypotheses, begin to play upon facts, when they are methods for experimental use in action, then light dawns; then it becomes possible to discriminate significant from trivial facts, and relations take the place of isolated scraps. Just as soon as we begin to use the knowledge and skills we have to control social consequences in the interest of shared abundant and secured life, we shall cease to complain of the backwardness of social knowledge. We shall take the road which leads to the assured building up of social science just as men built up physical science when they actively used the techniques of tools and numbers in physical experimentation.

In spite, then, of all the record of the past, the great scientific revolution is still to come. It will ensue when men collectively and co-operatively organize their knowledge for application to achieve and make secure social values; when they systematically use scientific procedures for the control of human relationships and the direction of the social effects of our vast technological machinery. Great as have been the social changes of the last century, they are not to be compared with those which will emerge when our faith in scientific method is made manifest in social works. We are living in a period of depression.[*] The intellectual function of trouble is to lead men to think. The depression is a small price to pay if it induces us to think about the cause of the disorder, confusion, and insecurity which are the outstanding traits of our social life. If we do not go back to their cause, namely our half-way and accidental use of science, mankind will pass through depressions, for they are the graphic record of our unplanned social life. The story of the achievement of science in physical control is evidence of the possibility of control in social affairs. It is our human intelligence and human courage which are on trial; it is incredible that men who have brought the technique of physical discovery, invention, and use to such a pitch of perfection will abdicate in the face of the infinitely more important human problem.

[* Viz. the economic depression which began in 1929 and brought a national mood of deep pessimism and doubt. Thoughtful Americans were driven to question almost every belief and assumption in American politics and society. Ed.]

6.7 POLITICS: ART OR SCIENCE

From Alpheus T. Mason, 'Politics, Art or Science?, Southwestern Social Science Quarterly, *vol. 16, No. 3, 1935, pp. 1–10.*

Although by 1935 the study of politics was widely regarded as a social science in many parts of the United States, some American scholars had doubts about the claims of objective, 'value-free' analysis offered by the new orthodoxy. One scholar, Alpheus T. Mason, expressed his doubts in an article in which he concluded that 'politics is a science only in a very limited sense'.

If vagueness and doubt enshroud the subject matter of politics the reason is not that philosophers and statesmen have been more careless and lazy than scientists, but rather that political conclusions are so frequently predetermined by the particular facts examined. There is perhaps an even stronger reason, and one which needs special emphasis – the peculiar nature of politics itself.

However widely and carefully the material be gathered, it is doubtful whether politics can ever be a science as botany, chemistry, or mathematics are sciences. The point has been often emphasized and explained but never quite so well as by Edmund Burke. A statesman as well as a philosopher, with scarcely an equal in his understanding of the complexity and ever-shifting combination of political facts, Burke observed: 'The lines of politics are not like the lines of mathematics. They are broad and deep as well as long. They admit of exceptions; they demand modifications. No lines can be laid down for civil or political wisdom. They are a matter incapable of exact definition.'

Disraeli put words not unlike these in the mouth of the cynical old statesman in his novel, *Contarini Fleming*: 'Few ideas are correct ones, and what are correct no one can say; but with words we govern men.'

There are reasons other than the nature of the subject itself that may account for this unscientific quality. Few subjects have suffered so much from prejudice, partisanship, fear of change, the greed for power, and the habit of hasty inference and rash conclusion. Nearly every political thinker whose writings have stood the test of time wrote under the compelling and even heating influence of events of his own day. Rarely has political speculation been motivated by true scientific purpose. Thomas Hobbes wrote the *Leviathan* in 1651 in order to establish the claims of absolute government on grounds other than divine right; John Locke in 1690 produced the second treatise of civil government for the deliberate purpose of justifying the glorious revolution of 1688; in 1790 Edmund Burke wrote his *Reflections on the French Revolution* in an effort to stay the threat of revolutionary doctrine then gaining such headway because of the dramatic force with which Rousseau had voiced his doctrines of liberty, equality, and popular sovereignty. All these political thinkers, curiously enough, employ very much the same terminology – liberty, property, equality, sovereignty, rights, law – but seldom are these words intended to convey the same meanings.

What has been said doubtless raises in one's mind the question whether the materials of politics, the thoughts of men, their habits, customs, and institutions, are such as to be incapable of scientific treatment. Just because politics is not a science like mathematics or chemistry is no reason for concluding that no scientific deductions may be made from its study. There is in the phenomena of human society one constant, one element or factor which is practically always the same and therefore forms some scientific basis for politics. This is Human Nature itself. 'The tendencies of human nature,' James Bryce wrote in 1920, 'are the permanent basis of study which gives to the subject called political science whatever scientific quality it may possess.' Men have like passions and desires; they are stirred by like motives; they think along similar lines. Human nature is that basic and ever-present element in the endless flux of social and political phenomena which enables us to deduce certain general principles that hold good everywhere.

If this is true, it becomes pertinent to consider those traits of human nature on which certain rules of political action can be based. What qualities are there stout enough to bear the weight of general conclusions? The most fundamental one is the individual and collective instinct for dominion over others. The means by which men seek such dominion is force; force of mind; force of body; force of wealth or property. The primary trait of man, according to this theory, is the *will to power*, and this *will to power* is an innate human quality. Thus a non-political society is incompatible with what we know of ourselves. Since every individual whether acting singly or in groups shows the same tendencies or traits, there is bound to be a clash; conflict ensues between individuals and groups of individuals. This struggle for power constitutes the very essence of politics as we see it in history. The seventeenth-century political philosopher, Thomas Hobbes, had noted this underlying aspect of politics when he wrote: 'Happiness itself is a perpetual and ceaseless desire for power that ceaseth only in death.' Every person from childhood to death uses a force of mind with which to think, to know and to persuade; a force of body with which to act, to attract and constrain the bodies of others; finally, a force of wealth (money, lands, stocks, bonds, lucrative jobs) by means of which he may control others. There is considerable difference of opinion among writers as to which of these various forces is the most effective control over one's fellows.

John Stuart Mill placed great store on the power of opinion, belief, and persuasion. He stated this view very pointedly in his *Representative Government*: 'One person with a belief is a social power equal to ninety-nine who have only interest.' Mill cites compelling examples to show how far mere physical and economic power is from being the whole of social power. The history of all peoples records strong illustrations of this. It was not by any change in the distribution of material interests, not by physical force, but by the spread of moral and rational conviction that Negro slavery was destroyed. It was not battalions and armies that enabled the frail and shrunken Gandhi to win his way in India; it was belief in a principle which even Great Britain at last had to respect. That little 'saint in politics' by merely sitting quietly and holding doggedly to a belief, sometimes with no food save a bit of parched corn and goat's milk, succeeded in arousing political consciousness and finally in dominating 350 million people when others with greater physical, economic, and intellectual power had failed to move them.

Alexander Hamilton and many other wise men have believed that economic power alone is basic in politics. Power over a man's pocketbook, Hamilton wrote in *The Federalist*, amounts to control over his will. Madison, too, although at odds with Hamilton on many points, agreed that 'the most common and durable source of factions has been the various and unequal distribution of property'. Some of the greatest names in the literature of politics, Aristotle,

Machiavelli, Harrington, Burke, Marx, and others testify to the deep impress of economics on politics.

Physical force, violence, and resort to arms have in many periods of history been recognized as basic in politics. Some have gone so far as to contend that force, superior physical power, explains the origin of civil society itself.

Quite apart from the relative strength of these human factors in politics, it is undoubtedly true that every man and woman uses one and perhaps all of them to obtain dominion over others, to live more securely, to satisfy his or her desires – whether good or bad. The strip cartoons show that every day. And, interestingly enough, these tactics by which power is gained are in as common use among men who have won places in formal political government as among those seeking to oust them. There is no situation where a single one of these innate human qualities has been eliminated from the political struggle. The rule of a Mussolini, a Hitler, or a Roosevelt may appear well-established, but it is not difficult to find these men resorting to the power of wealth, the power of persuasion, as Mr Roosevelt's broadcasts,[*] the power of force, as the terrorist methods of Hitler and Stalin. And, of course, the underdog is hopefully using the same tactics to put himself on top. Politics, in short, is a struggle for power among men who do not respect power. It results from the effort of each human being or group to induce, persuade, or compel other human beings to do his will and, conversely, not to be himself induced, persuaded, or compelled into doing theirs. This struggle is always going on and can never be brought to any conclusion.

The political association known as the state is not the only grouping in which a few men control others. Government is not so exclusive and peculiar an institution as has been pictured. It is only one of a series of control systems such as the trade union, the church, the social, industrial, and economic groups. Each of these has its own internal machinery of control, constitution, bylaws, officers, and so on. There are any number of men, and women too, who are not on a borough council or in a legislative or judicial body, and yet they assume some form of group responsibility and thus exercise what really are functions of government so far as their own

[* President Franklin Roosevelt initiated the practice of addressing the American people by means of 'Fireside Chats' on the radio. Needless to say his Republican opponents were strongly opposed to the practice.]

particular group is concerned. They consult, deputize, administer, and enforce the rules of their organization. Sometimes such authority may be exercised arbitrarily. Just the other day a rival labour union criticized President William Green for his alleged dictatorship in the councils of labour. Churchmen, too, have been severely criticized for their arbitrary dominance in the affairs of their associations. Each of these groups, whether trade union, manufacturers' association, or church, seeks to make its influence felt; each tries to deflect the course of formal political government for the benefit of its own interests. Each is demonstrating that desire for power and dominion, which in Hobbes's words, 'ceaseth only with death'. The means employed are always the same: power of mind, persuasion and propaganda; power of body, physical force and violence as in racketeering; power of wealth, which may take the form of bribery or a fat contribution to the political campaign funds.

Political government does not always have dominion. Certain important groups deliberately avoid responsibility, do not try to elect their own political representatives. Our trade unionists, for example, have never formed a Labour party, but seek to gain their ends by 'rewarding friends and punishing enemies' within the established parties. It results that political government may be in actual subservience to a power stronger than itself; so that by acquiescing and deferring to this or that interest, certain outside or private persons achieve real authority.

No one has probed more deeply into the subtleties of politics than the sixteenth-century Florentine philosopher, Machiavelli. It was he who inspired Mussolini. But many other politicians have successfully followed his advice without being aware they were doing so. Machiavelli's advice to his imaginary prince is as frank as it is subtle. In telling the prince, once established, how best to maintain his power, Machiavelli warns him to take account of the conflict of classes out of which political power springs and to pit one against the other, leaning to the right or to the left as occasion demands. By this shifting of 'affection' or preference or favour, the prince is told he can cause the passions and ambitions of each class to nullify those of the other, and so keep himself secure in power. Machiavelli's specific advice was as follows: 'As cities are generally divided into guilds and classes, the prince should keep account of these bodies and occasionally be present at their assemblies, and should set an example of his affability and magnificence, preserving however always the majesty of his dignity.'

This advice was given holders of high political office nearly 300 years ago, but it is faithfully followed today by our own statesmen from the President down to the mayor of the smallest hamlet. . . .

I should not like to leave the impression that every individual in society has an insatiable will to power. Any country may be divided, generally speaking, into three groups: the dominant group, consisting of those who for the time being have gained power; the beaten or defeated group, those who are struggling for power; and the disinterested or passive masses who take little or no active part in politics.

The art of politics consists also in controlling, by whatever means will work, this indifferent or supine element in society. And in the exercise of this all important art, unfounded beliefs are quite as important as sound ones. F. D. Roosevelt's talk about the 'forgotten man' no less than Huey Long's[*] 'share-our-wealth' patter was designed and calculated to gain the attention and support of the masses. Politicians understand that it is 'with words we govern men'. Nor need the words they use be either sincere or intelligible. Politicians seem always to recall the observation of Machiavelli: 'It is unnecessary for a prince to have all the good qualities (fidelity, friendship, humanity, and religion) I have enumerated, but it is very necessary to appear to have them.' It is equally unnecessary that the words of politicians be understood; indeed their effectiveness may consist in no small measure in their vagueness. . . .

The conclusion is that politics is a science only in a very limited sense. In the political process there is no way of controlling conditions, a control so necessary for the establishment of scientific conclusions. Even if the conditions could be fixed, human beings, unlike atoms and electrons, cannot be expected to act and react in the same way. The appeal 'back to normalcy' was strikingly effective in 1920, but there can be no assurance that at any future time it will again achieve the result desired. No prediction can be made save that the struggle for power is unending. As to the form that

[* Huey Long (1893–1935): a colourful demagogue who was Governor, then Senator for the State of Louisiana. Long gathered popular support by promising welfare in his 'Share-the-Wealth' campaigns. He was assassinated in 1935.]

struggle will take, we can only say, with Bryce, that it will differ from the past.

Politics is art rather than science, an art which has never been codified or completely explained; nor can it really be learned by people lacking in what may be called the political sense, which presupposes native talent and highly intuitive technique. Any concrete political situation, however seemingly transparent, cannot be dealt with by reason alone; it can only be grasped by a process similar to artistic perception. How, in a given situation, to seize power to extend one's dominion; how to stage an election at the right moment, heat up a campaign to the proper point; how to confuse the ignorant by specious oratory, bold misstatements of fact, misleading nomenclature, emotional and moral appeals to indwelling prejudice; how to invoke the taboos of public morality and sectarian religion; how to establish political structure and party machinery; how, in a word, to make the most for one's own purposes out of all available human elements inherent in a given political situation – all this has never been hidden from the acute, the astute, and the daring. Such knowledge is gained by instinct and experience, for reason helps little or not at all.